# SOCIAL SERVICES
## in North Carolina

John L. Saxon

UNC
SCHOOL OF GOVERNMENT

THE UNIVERSITY
*of* NORTH CAROLINA
*at* CHAPEL HILL

The School of Government at the University of North Carolina at Chapel Hill works to improve the lives of North Carolinians by engaging in practical scholarship that helps public officials and citizens understand and strengthen state and local government. Established in 1931 as the Institute of Government, the School provides educational, advisory, and research services for state and local governments. The School of Government is also home to a nationally ranked graduate program in public administration and specialized centers focused on information technology, environmental finance, and civic education for youth.

As the largest university-based local government training, advisory, and research organization in the United States, the School of Government offers up to 200 classes, seminars, schools, and specialized conferences for more than 12,000 public officials each year. In addition, faculty members annually publish approximately fifty books, periodicals, and other reference works related to state and local government. Each day that the General Assembly is in session, the School produces the *Daily Bulletin*, which reports on the day's activities for members of the legislature and others who need to follow the course of legislation.

The Master of Public Administration Program is a full-time, two-year program that serves up to sixty students annually. It consistently ranks among the best public administration graduate programs in the country, particularly in city management. With courses ranging from public policy analysis to ethics and management, the program educates leaders for local, state, and federal governments and nonprofit organizations.

Operating support for the School of Government's programs and activities comes from many sources, including state appropriations, local government membership dues, private contributions, publication sales, course fees, and service contracts. Visit www.sog.unc.edu or call 919.966.5381 for more information on the School's courses, publications, programs, and services.

Michael R. Smith, DEAN
Thomas H. Thornburg, SENIOR ASSOCIATE DEAN
Frayda S. Bluestein, ASSOCIATE DEAN FOR PROGRAMS
Todd A. Nicolet, ASSOCIATE DEAN FOR INFORMATION TECHNOLOGY
Ann Cary Simpson, ASSOCIATE DEAN FOR DEVELOPMENT AND COMMUNICATIONS
Bradley G. Volk, ASSOCIATE DEAN FOR ADMINISTRATION

FACULTY

Gregory S. Allison
David N. Ammons
Ann M. Anderson
A. Fleming Bell, II
Maureen M. Berner
Mark F. Botts
Joan G. Brannon
Michael Crowell
Shea Riggsbee Denning
James C. Drennan
Richard D. Ducker
Robert L. Farb
Joseph S. Ferrell
Milton S. Heath Jr.
Norma Houston (on leave)
Cheryl Daniels Howell
Jeffrey A. Hughes

Joseph E. Hunt
Willow S. Jacobson
Robert P. Joyce
Kenneth L. Joyner
Diane M. Juffras
David M. Lawrence
Dona G. Lewandowski
James M. Markham
Janet Mason
Laurie L. Mesibov
Kara A. Millonzi
Jill D. Moore
Jonathan Q. Morgan
Ricardo S. Morse
C. Tyler Mulligan
David W. Owens
William C. Rivenbark

Dale J. Roenigk
John Rubin
John L. Saxon
Jessica Smith
Karl W. Smith
Carl W. Stenberg III
John B. Stephens
Charles A. Szypszak
Shannon H. Tufts
Vaughn Upshaw
A. John Vogt
Aimee N. Wall
Jeffrey B. Welty
Richard B. Whisnant
Gordon P. Whitaker
Eileen R. Youens

© 2008 School of Government
The University of North Carolina at Chapel Hill
Use of this publication for commercial purposes or without acknowledgment of its source is prohibited. Reproducing, distributing, or otherwise making available to a non-purchaser the entire publication, or a substantial portion of it, without express permission, is prohibited.
Printed in the United States of America
12 11 10 09 08   1 2 3 4 5
ISBN 978-1-56011-589-2
This publication is printed on permanent, acid-free paper in compliance with the North Carolina General Statutes.
Printed on recycled paper

# Contents

# Preface

*Social Services in North Carolina* provides a general description of social services agencies and programs in North Carolina and the state and federal laws that affect those agencies and programs. It is intended primarily as a resource for county social services directors, state and county social services employees, social services attorneys, and county social services board members, but also may be a useful guide for county commissioners, county managers, and others who want to better understand North Carolina's complex social services system.

*Social Services in North Carolina* completely revises, rewrites, updates, and supersedes the fourth edition of *A Guidebook to Social Services in North Carolina*, which was written by Mason P. Thomas Jr. and Janet Mason and was published by the Institute of Government in 1989. (Prior editions of *A Guidebook to Social Services in North Carolina* were published by the Institute of Government in 1968, 1972, and 1976.)

No book is ever the work of only one person, and this book is no exception.

*Social Services in North Carolina* draws on the work of Professor Thomas (who retired in 1992) and Professor Mason, a valued colleague, mentor, teacher, and friend whose experience and knowledge of social services far exceeds my own, as well as other current and former faculty colleagues at the Institute, now School, of Government, including Steve Allred, Fleming Bell II, Frayda Bluestein, Anita Brown-Graham, Joe Ferrell, Margaret Henderson, Diane Juffras, David Lawrence, Jill Moore, Vaughn Upshaw, and Gordon Whitaker. It also draws on the experience and knowledge of the hundreds of county social services directors, social services attorneys, social services board members, and state and county social services employees that I have had the pleasure to work with and teach since I joined the Institute of Government faculty in 1992.

In writing this I would be remiss if I did not express my special thanks to Janet Mason, who reviewed the entire manuscript for *Social Services in North Carolina*, and to Drake Maynard at the Office of State Personnel, Diane Juffras, Margaret Henderson, and Gordon Whitaker, who reviewed particular chapters and offered many valuable comments and suggestions.

It is my sincere hope that this book will be a useful resource for those who work for and with North Carolina's "state-supervised and county-administered" social services system and that it will contribute to the School of Government's long and proud tradition of practical scholarship that seeks to improve the lives and well-being of North Carolinians by helping public officials and citizens better understand and improve state and local government.

John L. Saxon
Professor of Public Law and Government
School of Government
The University of North Carolina at Chapel Hill
June 2008

# Chapter 1

# What Is "Social Services"?

In its broadest sense, the term "social services" refers to

- the broad array of services and assistance that public and private agencies provide to meet the social, economic, and human needs of children, families, senior citizens, disabled persons, and the poor;[1]
- the dozens of programs that are administered by state and county social services agencies and the assistance and services that are provided through these programs;
- the large and complex system of public and private agencies that establish, fund, supervise, and administer social services programs; and
- the intricate system of laws, policies, and procedures that govern social services agencies and programs.

For many years, the term "welfare" was used when referring to government assistance and social services programs and to the public agencies that administered these programs.[2] Over the past forty years, however, the term "social services" generally has replaced "welfare"

---

1. The term "human services" is sometimes used to refer to these services. In this context, human services includes not only the public assistance and social services provided by state and county social services agencies, but also clinical health services provided by public health departments; mental health, developmental disability, and substance abuse services provided through area mental health authorities; and a wide variety of other services (including homeless shelters, domestic violence prevention, housing assistance, child development, and services for children, youth, and senior citizens) that are provided by public and private agencies to meet the needs of families, children, youth, senior citizens, and others.

2. Until 1969 North Carolina's county departments, directors, and boards of social services were known as county departments, directors, and boards of public welfare.

in the law and in public discourse.[3] Today, social services programs that provide assistance to low-income individuals and families often are referred to as "public assistance," "means tested," or "safety net" programs—terms that generally do not carry the same social stigma as "welfare" and also reflect the U.S. Supreme Court's decisions holding that government assistance for the poor is, at least in some instances, a legal right or entitlement, not charity.[4] In addition, the change from "welfare" to "social services" reflects the fact that state and county social services agencies provide a broad range of social services for children, families, and the elderly (including adult and child protective services, adoption services, employment services, and child support enforcement services) as well as financial assistance or "welfare" payments for low-income individuals and families.

Negative public perceptions regarding "social services," however, persist.

> Many people view social services programs as being too costly; there is inadequate awareness of what many of them actually accomplish; and biases and myths about [social services] programs and recipients continue to exist.[5]

In addition, the "complexity of the social services system and . . . [social services] programs . . . contributes to public misunderstanding" of social services.[6] Social services programs and agencies, therefore, continue to be "affected by shifts in the availability of private and charitable resources, economic conditions, and the political climate."[7]

---

3. In 1996 Congress enacted, and President Clinton signed into law, federal "welfare reform" legislation that sought to "end welfare as we know it."

4. *See* Goldberg v. Kelly, 397 U.S. 254 (1970).

5. Mason P. Thomas Jr. and Janet Mason, *A Guidebook to Social Services in North Carolina*, 4th ed. (Chapel Hill: Institute of Government, The University of North Carolina, 1989), 1. Government programs for the poor have always raised public concern regarding personal responsibility versus social responsibility, government responsibility versus private-sector responsibility, costs, fiscal accountability, fraud, and distinctions between those who are "deserving" of assistance and those who are not.

6. Thomas and Mason, *A Guidebook to Social Services in North Carolina*, 1.

7. *Id.* at 1–2.

## Social Services Programs and Agencies

Broadly speaking, the goal of "social services" is to help children, families, the poor, disabled persons, and senior citizens achieve and maintain economic and social well-being. This broad purpose is reflected in the mission statements adopted by many state and county social services agencies. For example, North Carolina's Division of Social Services defines its mission as

- ensuring that individuals and families have sufficient economic resources to obtain the basic necessities of life;
- assisting individuals in achieving and maintaining self-sufficiency through employment if possible;
- ensuring that children and adults are protected from abuse, neglect, and exploitation; and
- assisting disabled and dependent adults while ensuring that they live in the most independent setting feasible with the least possible intrusion from public agencies.[8]

In addition, the objectives of particular social services programs often are reflected in statements of purpose that are contained in federal and state law. For example, federal law states that the purposes of the Temporary Assistance for Needy Families (TANF) program are to

- provide assistance to needy families so that children may be cared for in their own homes or in the homes of relatives;
- end the dependence of needy parents on government benefits by promoting job preparation, work, and marriage;
- prevent and reduce the incidence of out-of-wedlock pregnancies; and
- encourage the formation and maintenance of two-parent families.[9]

Social services programs and agencies provide a "safety net" for children, families, the poor, disabled persons, and senior citizens by addressing a wide range of economic and social problems that impair the ability of children, families, the poor, disabled persons, and senior citizens to function adequately in society—problems that include poverty, hunger and malnutrition, lack of medical care, homelessness,

---

8. N.C. Division of Social Services website, www.dhhs.state.nc.us/dss/about/mission.htm.

9. 42 U.S.C. § 601.

child abuse and neglect, elder abuse and neglect, teenage pregnancy, out-of-wedlock births, and unemployment. And, because these social problems affect the general welfare and well-being of the entire community, social services programs and agencies also serve the community, the county, and the state when they address the social, economic, and human needs of individuals and families.

To address these needs and problems, public social services agencies provide a wide range of assistance and services to children, families, the poor, disabled persons, and senior citizens. Some social services programs provide financial assistance, food, or health care to individuals and families with limited incomes. Others provide services to protect vulnerable children or adults from abuse or neglect, to collect child support from absent parents, or to assist individuals or families become more self-sufficient.

County social services departments administer dozens of social services programs. Each of these programs, however, has its own rules regarding eligibility, assistance, services, administration, and funding. And the rules that govern these programs are often incredibly detailed, complex, and confusing, filling hundreds of pages in social services policy and procedure manuals. Thus, a person or family might be eligible for assistance or services under one program, but ineligible for assistance or services under another. Some social services programs provide assistance only for children and families. Others serve only elderly or disabled persons. Some social services programs are "means tested" and provide assistance only to persons whose incomes and assets are low enough to be considered poor.[10] Other social services are not means tested and may be provided to individuals regardless of whether they are "poor."

---

10. The federal poverty level (FPL) provides one measure, but not the only measure, for determining whether an individual or family is poor. The FPL is established by the U.S. Department of Health and Human Services, is adjusted each year, varies based on the number of persons in the household, and attempts to provide a rough measure of the income a family needs in order to obtain adequate housing, food, and other basic necessities. In 2007 the FPL for a family of three living in North Carolina was $17,170 per year. In some instances, a family may be eligible for public assistance even if its income exceeds the FPL. But in other instances, a family cannot qualify for public assistance even though its income is below the FPL.

## North Carolina's Social Services System

North Carolina's social services system "is hard to summarize because it is so diverse and complex."[11]

In most states, social services programs are administered by state social services agencies—not by local governments—and are funded by federal and state tax revenues, without local government funding.

North Carolina, by contrast, has adopted a "county-administered and state-supervised" system of social services under which

- social services programs are administered primarily by county social services agencies under the supervision of state social services agencies, and
- counties are required to pay part of the cost of social services programs.

The social services system in North Carolina, therefore, involves "complicated relationships among the federal, state, and county governments."[12] All three levels of government—federal, state, and local—are involved in funding and administering social services programs. And at each of these levels of government, a number of agencies, boards, or commissions, as well as legislative or quasi-legislative bodies and (at the federal and state levels) the courts, exercise specific responsibilities with respect to the creation, funding, supervision, or administration of social services programs. Responsibility for social services, therefore, is shared by the federal, state, and county governments and is exercised through a complex network of government agencies.

The following chapters of this book describe North Carolina's social services system, social services agencies, and social services programs in greater detail, addressing the history of social services in North Carolina; the role and responsibilities of the federal government, the state, and counties with respect to social services; the state and county agencies that are responsible for administering social services programs in North Carolina; the types of public assistance and social services that are provided to individuals and families by state and county social services agencies; how public assistance and social services programs are financed; the rules that

11. Mason P. Thomas Jr., *A Guidebook to Social Services in North Carolina*, 3d ed. (Chapel Hill: Institute of Government, The University of North Carolina at Chapel Hill, 1976), i.

12. Thomas and Mason, *A Guidebook to Social Services in North Carolina*, 1.

govern the confidentiality of records regarding persons who apply for or receive public assistance and social services; and the legal liability of social services agencies, officials, and employees.

Chapter 2

# A Brief History of Social
# Services in North Carolina

The history of social services in North Carolina, like that of other states, is one of gradual evolution from limited government assistance for the poor, the infirm, and orphans to a modern and complex "welfare state" that provides not only a "safety net" for its citizens but also a wide variety of programs that address the social, economic, nutritional, and health care needs of elderly persons, disabled individuals, children, and families.[1]

"Social services," therefore, does not denote a static group of governmental functions. Indeed, it is somewhat misleading to talk about

---

1. This chapter incorporates and revises information included in Janet Mason and John Saxon, "Social Services," Chapter 12, in Charles D. Liner, ed., *State and Local Government Relations in North Carolina: Their Evolution and Current Status,* 2d ed. (Chapel Hill: Institute of Government, The University of North Carolina at Chapel Hill, 1995), 200–205. For additional information regarding the history of social services in North Carolina and the United States, *see* Roy M. Brown, *Public Poor Relief in North Carolina* (Chapel Hill: The University of North Carolina Press, 1928); A. Laurance Aydlett, "The North Carolina State Board of Public Welfare," *The North Carolina Historical Review* 24 (Jan. 1947): 1–33; Benjamin Joseph Klebaner, "Some Aspects of North Carolina Public Poor Relief: 1700–1860," *The North Carolina Historical Review* 31 (Oct. 1954): 479–492; Roddey M. Ligon Jr., *Public Welfare in North Carolina: A Guidebook for County Commissioners* (Chapel Hill: Institute of Government, The University of North Carolina at Chapel Hill, 1961), 1–6; Alan D. Watson, "Public Poor Relief in Colonial North Carolina," *The North Carolina Historical Review* 54 (Oct. 1977): 347–366; Walter I. Trattner, *From Poor Law to Welfare State: A History of Social Welfare in America,* 6th ed. (New York: Free Press, 1999).

"social services" in North Carolina before the twentieth century—or, perhaps, before the 1960s—because the limited public assistance provided to indigent or dependent citizens before that time bears very little resemblance to the social services that are provided to individuals and families today. Some functions that are included in the present-day concept of "social services," like financial assistance for the poor, were known by different names ("poor relief" or "public welfare") during the eighteenth and nineteenth centuries and have changed significantly over the years. Other functions, like mental health and juvenile delinquency services, used to be components of North Carolina's "public welfare" system but now are conceptually and organizationally distinct from the state's social services system. And many functions of the current social services system, like subsidized child day care and health insurance, were completely unknown in earlier times.

The history of social services in North Carolina, therefore, is characterized by change, including

- changes in public attitudes towards government responsibility for social services;
- dramatic increases in the public resources devoted to social services;
- a proliferation of new social services programs; and
- changes in intergovernmental relations and responsibility with respect to social services.

At least one aspect of North Carolina's social services system, though, has continued throughout the past two hundred years: the emphasis on local (county) administration of social services programs.

### Poor Relief in Colonial North Carolina: 1663 to 1776

Public assistance or "relief" for the poor in colonial North Carolina was patterned primarily on the English "poor laws" enacted during the sixteenth and seventeenth centuries.[2] These laws provided for (a) the public support of the "impotent" poor through the local parishes of the

---

2. Brown, *Public Poor Relief in North Carolina*, 7, 9, 21–22.

established church and (b) the placement and apprenticeship of orphans and dependent children.[3]

Following in this tradition, public assistance, care, and "relief" of the poor, the ill, orphans, and widows in colonial North Carolina were, in theory if not in actual practice, one of the implicit responsibilities of the Anglican Church, acting through the vestry of each of its parishes in the colony.[4] It was not until 1755, however, that North Carolina's colonial assembly enacted legislation requiring the church wardens of each parish to pay for the maintenance and care of poor persons who were sick or disabled.[5]

In 1759 the colonial legislature authorized the vestry of each parish to levy a poll tax for the support of the poor and other parish expenses.[6] The citizens of some North Carolina counties, however, were not "greatly impressed . . . by their duty to the poor" and "did not . . . see the need for public poor relief" despite the existence of pervasive poverty and need.[7] Vestries, therefore, were not established or did not function in some parishes.

In those parishes with functioning vestries, early records indicate that individuals sometimes appeared before the vestrymen to state that a poor person needed aid or to request reimbursement for the assistance or care they had provided to an indigent person and that

---

3. *Id.* at 1–9. The English poor laws, however, also distinguished sharply between the "deserving" and "undeserving" poor, viewed the poverty of the "undeserving" poor as morally culpable, and sought to protect society against the "undeserving" poor.

4. The Church of England was recognized as the "established" church of North Carolina under the 1663 and 1665 royal Charters to the Lords Proprietors by King Charles II and the Vestry Acts of 1701, 1704, 1711, 1715, and 1741 and remained such until it was "disestablished" under the North Carolina Constitution of 1776. The Vestry Acts enacted by North Carolina's colonial assemblies charged vestries with responsibility for erecting churches and chapels within each parish (whose territorial boundaries were coextensive with the boundaries of the precincts and counties that were the basic units of local government in colonial North Carolina), employing a minister, and collecting a poll tax to support the church. At first, vestrymen for each parish were appointed by colonial officials. Later, they were elected by the freeholders of each parish, precinct, or county. Stephen B. Weeks, *Church and State in North Carolina* (Baltimore: The Johns Hopkins Press, 1893), 14.

5. Brown, *Public Poor Relief in North Carolina*, 18–19.

6. *Id.* at 19–20.

7. *Id.* at 20.

the vestries provided some limited relief for the poor.[8] On the whole, though, there "was no great demand upon the public purse for relief of the poor" in colonial North Carolina.[9]

Following English law and custom, North Carolina's colonial government addressed the care of orphans and dependent children through apprenticeship—the placement of children with "foster" families who would not only provide for their care until they came of age but also teach them some skill or trade that they could pursue as adults.[10] North Carolina's colonial assembly enacted the colony's first apprenticeship law in 1715, allowing orphans to be apprenticed only by order of the county or precinct court.[11]

## Poor Relief in North Carolina Counties: 1776 to 1868

The North Carolina Constitution of 1776 made no provision for public relief of the poor. In 1777, however, North Carolina's General Assembly enacted legislation requiring the freeholders of each county to elect seven "overseers of the poor," who assumed the responsibilities for poor relief that formerly were imposed on parish vestries.[12] Some counties, however, failed to elect overseers of the poor and the overseers and wardens of the poor in some counties neglected their duties.[13] In 1846 the justices of the county courts were authorized to appoint wardens of the poor in each county and to levy property and poll taxes for poor relief.[14]

Public support and care for the poor was, at first, provided through "outdoor" relief—by making direct payments to a needy person, reimbursing individuals for the cost of their care of indigent persons, or

---

8. *Id.* at 22–24.

9. *Id.* at 10–17, 24.

10. Brown, *Public Poor Relief in North Carolina*, 146–149.

11. *Id.* at 147. Although apprenticeship remained an important means of providing care for orphans and dependent children well into the nineteenth century, the frequency of apprenticing or "binding out" children decreased with the rise of orphanages and child-placing institutions in the second half of the nineteenth century and the advent of modern public assistance programs for families with dependent children during the first half of the twentieth century.

12. *Id.* at 26; Acts of 1777, ch. VII.

13. *Id.* at 27, 28–29.

14. *Id.* at 35; 1846 N.C. Pub. Laws ch. 64.

contracting with individuals to care for the poor (a procedure known as "bidding out" the poor).

In 1785, however, the General Assembly enacted legislation authorizing seven counties to build almshouses for the care of poor, aged, infirm, and insane persons.[15] And in 1793 the General Assembly enacted a statewide law authorizing all North Carolina counties to provide "indoor" relief for the poor by erecting "proper buildings . . . for the reception, residence and employment of the poor."[16]

By 1848 at least thirty-two North Carolina counties maintained county poorhouses.[17] Often, these institutions housed vagrants, prostitutes, unwed mothers and their children, and insane persons, as well as individuals who were unable to support themselves due to age or illness.[18] Some provided minimally adequate care to their residents, but many did not.[19]

## The State's First Welfare Institutions: 1868 to 1917

In 1868 the General Assembly enacted legislation transferring responsibility and authority for poor relief from the county courts to the newly established boards of county commissioners.[20] The precise means of providing poor relief, however, were left to local discretion, and traditional practices did not change very much.[21]

Although counties retained primary responsibility for poor relief throughout the nineteenth century, the North Carolina Constitution of 1868 recognized, for the first time, the state's responsibility for public

------

15. Brown, *Public Poor Relief in North Carolina*, 28. During the period 1786 to 1830, the General Assembly enacted scores of local acts authorizing particular counties to establish almshouses or county poorhouses. *Id.* at 32–34.

16. *Id.* at 31, 33.

17. *Id.* at 65.

18. *Id.* at 28, 29–30, 32, 65.

19. *Id.* at 58–66.

20. 1868 N.C. Pub. Laws ch. 20, § 8 (24); *see also* N.C. CONST. of 1868 art. VIII, § 1. During the nineteenth century, each county was responsible, under the doctrine of "legal settlement," for the care of poor people who had resided in the county for at least one year. *See* McDowell County v. Forsyth County, 121 N.C. 295 (1897).

21. Brown, *Public Poor Relief in North Carolina*, 69–70; *see also* Copple v. Davie County Bd. of Comm'rs, 138 N.C. 132 (1905).

welfare, requiring the General Assembly to enact legislation providing for the beneficent care of "the poor, the unfortunate, and orphan[s]."[22]

In response to this constitutional mandate, the General Assembly established a five-member state Board of Public Charities in 1869.[23] The new board, however, ceased to function between 1873 and 1889.[24] When the board was revived in 1889, it focused most of its attention on visiting and reporting on the conditions of county poorhouses and "homes for the aged and infirm."[25]

Public welfare and assistance for the poor during this period were supplemented substantially, if not outweighed, by private charity and charitable organizations (sometimes focusing on special populations such as dependent children).[26] But greater links between the state and counties began to develop. The renewed Board of Public Charities, for example, facilitated the creation of voluntary county committees that visited county institutions and reported to the state board.

The period between 1868 and 1917 also saw some gradual expansion of the state's interest and involvement in public welfare, health, and social services.[27] The state built two additional hospitals for the insane in 1880 and 1883 (the present-day Cherry Hospital in Goldsboro and Broughton Hospital in Morganton), established additional residential schools for children who were deaf or blind, opened the Caswell Training School for the care of "feeble minded" and "mentally defective" children in 1911, established other state institutions for

---

22. N.C. CONST. of 1868 art. XI, § 7. The 1868 constitution also authorized the General Assembly to appropriate funds for the care of indigent citizens who were "deaf-mute, blind [or] insane," and directed it to establish one or more homes for "destitute orphans," to provide for the education of "idiots and inebriates," and to establish a state Board of Public Charities to study social problems and investigate and supervise charitable and penal institutions in the state.

23. 1868–69 N.C. Pub. Laws ch. 170; Brown, *Public Poor Relief in North Carolina*, 72.

24. *Id.* at 82.

25. *Id.* at 82–94.

26. The first orphanages in North Carolina were established in 1812 and 1813. *Id.* at 152. By 1926 there were twenty-three orphanages in North Carolina, twenty-one of which were operated by religious institutions or fraternal orders. *Id.* at 153.

27. In 1845 the state had established a school for blind children (the present-day Governor Morehead School in Raleigh). In 1856 the state had opened its first hospital for the care of the "insane" on the outskirts of Raleigh (which, in 1959, was renamed Dorothea Dix Hospital and operated until 2008, when it was replaced by a new Central Region Psychiatric Hospital in Butner).

the care of persons suffering from epilepsy and tuberculosis and for elderly or disabled confederate veterans and widows, paid pensions to elderly or disabled confederate veterans and widows, and provided some state support for orphanages operated by religious or charitable organizations.[28]

## The Beginnings of a State Public Welfare System: 1917 to 1937

Many features of North Carolina's contemporary social services system find their source in North Carolina's first statewide public welfare law. This law, which was enacted in 1917 and amended in 1919, marked the beginning of an organized system of state supervision and local administration of social services.[29]

Under these laws, the state Board of Public Charities was enlarged to seven members, was renamed the Board of Charities and Public Welfare, and was given expanded authority, including responsibility for promoting the welfare of dependent and neglected children and for inspecting child-caring institutions. The new laws also provided for a state commissioner of public welfare and for a professional staff to assist the commissioner and board.

During this period, the Board of Charities and Public Welfare established a state Division of Child Welfare, along with bureaus for County Organization, Institutional Supervision, Mental Health and Hygiene, and Promotion and Education. The state board and the commissioner of public welfare also were involved substantially in implementing the juvenile court law, which was enacted in 1919.[30]

The 1917 and 1919 laws also provided for the appointment of three-member county boards of charity and public welfare (in place of the unofficial boards of visitors), and for the appointment, by the board of county commissioners and the board of education in each county acting jointly, of a county superintendent of public welfare.[31] The superintendent acted both as agent of the state board and as administrator

---

28. Brown, *Public Poor Relief in North Carolina*, 94–97.

29. 1917 N.C. Pub. Laws ch. 170; 1919 N.C. Pub. Laws ch. 46.

30. 1919 N.C. Pub. Laws ch. 97.

31. Under the 1917 law, members of these county welfare boards were appointed by the board of county commissioners. In 1919 responsibility for appointing the members of county welfare boards was transferred from the county commissioners to the state Board of Charities and Public Welfare.

of public poor funds under the direction of the county commissioners—a dual role that exists for county social services directors today. The superintendent, who also served as the chief school attendance officer and juvenile probation officer for the county, was responsible for the oversight of dependent and neglected children, supervising prisoners on parole or probation in the county, and assisting in finding jobs for the unemployed. Although local officials appointed the superintendent, the state board was required to pass on his qualifications for the position.

By 1925, fifty-seven counties had county welfare departments, forty-six had full-time county superintendents, and eleven had part-time superintendents; in forty-three counties the school superintendent also served as the superintendent of welfare.[32]

Under this new structure the number of county homes increased and their quality and conditions tended to improve.[33] The distribution of poor relief funds, however, continued to be largely unsupervised and was subject to graft or political or personal influence.[34] Although state law made the county superintendent, under the county commissioners' control, responsible for the care and supervision of the poor and administration of the poor fund, the authority actually delegated to the superintendent varied greatly from county to county. Some boards of commissioners set general policy and determined amounts of money available but left administration of the policy up to the superintendent. Other boards ignored the law and continued to handle the discretionary handing-out of funds or only gradually shared administrative responsibility with the local superintendent.

In 1923 the General Assembly enacted a mothers' aid law to provide financial assistance to certain indigent mothers with children under the age of fourteen.[35] Forerunner of the federal Aid to Families with Dependent Children (AFDC) program, North Carolina's mothers' aid program was state-supervised and county-administered, and the cost of the program was divided equally between the state and counties that chose to participate. The standards set for the program and its supervision by the state created a noticeable contrast to the often arbitrarily administered and inadequately supervised poor-relief practices of the counties.

---

32. Aydlett, "The North Carolina State Board of Public Welfare," 1, 20–23.
33. Brown, *Public Poor Relief in North Carolina*, 100–132.
34. *Id.* at 133–145.
35. 1923 N.C. Pub. Laws ch. 260.

Although counties' participation in the program was optional, seventy-one counties were participating in the program by 1926.[36]

In some areas, North Carolina was becoming a leader in a national trend toward centralized, or state, fiscal and administrative responsibility for government functions. By 1934 the state was financing most of the services that had been major county functions in 1900—public schools, roads and highways, and prison camps. The state also had responsibility for administering roads, highways, and the prison system.

The state's role in public welfare also increased, but much more modestly. In contrast to, and perhaps partly because of, the state's assumption of other major responsibilities, both the funding and administration of public welfare remained primarily county responsibilities. Counties remained responsible for poor relief, for the care of the elderly poor, and for the care of dependent children. The state maintained various public health and welfare institutions, contributed to the mother's aid program, and established a fund for foster care for children.

## Development and Growth of the Modern Social Services System: 1937 to 1981

The widespread hardship brought on by the Great Depression led to a change in attitudes toward poverty. There was an increased awareness of the seriousness of local disparities that were based on levels of unemployment, agricultural conditions, and other economic factors. During and following the depression, public welfare activities by state and local governments expanded, and governmental involvement in addressing the problems of the poor took on a new legitimacy.

The federal government, which theretofore had resisted involvement in most public welfare efforts, seriously tackled unemployment and its effects. In 1935 Congress enacted the Social Security Act, which has been called "the cornerstone of the American welfare state" and marked the beginning of a drastic redefinition of government's role in public welfare and social services.[37]

---

36. The mothers' aid program, however, provided assistance to fewer than 300 North Carolina families in 1925–26. Brown, *Public Poor Relief*, 158.

37. Social Security Act, ch. 531, 49 Stat. 620 (1935); Edward D. Berkowitz, *America's Welfare State from Roosevelt to Reagan* (Baltimore: The Johns Hopkins University Press, 1991), 13.

The Social Security Act had several major components. The pension program for the elderly—old-age insurance—was funded by employment taxes on employers and employees. It was, and remains, a federally administered program. The unemployment insurance program, although also funded through employment taxes, used federal financial incentives to encourage states to administer programs in accordance with federal standards.

These social insurance programs were distinguished from the public assistance or "relief" programs that also were part of the Social Security Act—Old Age Assistance (OAA) and Aid to Dependent Children (ADC). Eligibility for these programs was based on financial need. Funding for these programs came from federal and state (and, sometimes, local) general tax revenues, and federal funding was conditioned on states' complying with federal standards.[38]

The Social Security Act brought federal child welfare funds to North Carolina in 1936 and triggered the development of legislation to qualify the state for federal funds for the OAA and ADC programs. Besides providing federal funding and creating important new federal–state relationships, the Social Security Act resulted in major changes in state–county relationships, with responsibility shifting from the county to the state level. The Social Security Act required that state OAA and ADC programs be approved by the federal government, be in effect in all political subdivisions of the state, and be administered by, or under the supervision of, a single state agency. When North Carolina chose to participate in the OAA and ADC programs, legislation was passed in 1937 to make participation by counties mandatory.[39]

In addition to accepting the provisions of the federal Social Security Act governing the OAA and ADC programs, the 1937 legislation specified the responsibilities of the state Board of Charities and Public Welfare, the new state director of public assistance, the county boards of charities and public welfare, and boards of county commissioners with

---

38. Initially, the federal government provided a dollar-for-dollar match for state funding for Old Age Assistance and $1 for every $2 spent by states for Aid to Dependent Children. James T. Patterson, *America's Struggle Against Poverty 1900–1980* (Cambridge: Harvard University Press, 1981), 67.

39. 1937 N.C. Pub. Laws ch. 288. Implementation of the OAA and ADC programs in North Carolina necessitated the organization of the thirty-one counties that still did not have full-time public welfare superintendents. By 1937 all 100 counties had full-time public welfare superintendents.

respect to these public assistance programs. The 1937 legislation also revised the procedures for appointing county welfare boards. Under the 1937 law, the board of county commissioners appointed one member of the county welfare board, the state Board of Charities and Public Welfare appointed a second member, and those two appointees appointed a third member.

Although the Social Security Act required state financial participation, the burden of providing matching funds fell largely on the counties.[40] Having so recently assumed a major portion of the cost for schools and highways, the state was not prepared to shoulder by itself the increased costs of public welfare. By 1945 many counties were seeking through special legislative acts to increase the limits on property taxation for general relief, and, in that year, state legislation was enacted to double the rate that counties could levy for general relief purposes.[41] In 1958, formulas were developed to distribute supplemental state funding to counties to offset, in part, their costs in providing public assistance for poor county residents.

After 1937 the availability of Old Age Assistance provided an alternative to county-operated "homes for the aged and infirm" as a means of caring for North Carolina's elderly poor. As a result, many county homes for the aged were closed, sold to private owners, or replaced by privately operated boarding homes (or "rest homes") for the elderly during the 1940s and 1950s.[42] By 1968 only nine North Carolina counties continued to operate county homes for the aged, and the last county-operated adult care home (in Beaufort County) closed in 2005.

The development of the social services system in North Carolina since 1937 largely has reflected initiatives and funding criteria at the federal level. From World War II through the 1960s, the social services system grew steadily in terms of programs, cost, personnel, people served, and complexity. In the 1960s and 1970s, public assistance and social services

---

40. *See* Clement Harold Donovan, "The Readjustment of State and Local Fiscal Relations in North Carolina, 1929–1938" (doctoral dissertation, The University of North Carolina, 1940), 185.

41. Aydlett, "The North Carolina State Board of Public Welfare," 1, 32.

42. In 1951 the General Assembly established a State Boarding Care Fund to pay the cost of care of elderly and disabled residents of domiciliary care facilities (boarding or rest homes, now known as adult care facilities). The Boarding Care Fund was abolished in 1969 and was replaced in 1973 by the State–County Special Assistance program.

programs multiplied at what some considered an uncontrollable rate and federal courts began to play an increasing role in defining and enforcing rights and responsibilities in the social services system.[43]

In 1964 Congress created the federal Food Stamp program.[44] The federal–state Medicaid program was established by Congress in 1965 and implemented by North Carolina in 1970.[45] The Work Incentive (WIN) program, started in 1967, began a string of efforts to tie work or training requirements to the receipt of public assistance.

In 1974 the federal Supplemental Security Income (SSI) program replaced the federal–state Old Age Assistance, Aid to the Blind, and Aid to the Totally and Permanently Disabled programs.[46] The same year, Congress enacted the Child Abuse Prevention and Treatment Act, which required states, as a condition of receiving federal funding for child welfare, to establish procedures for reporting and investigating suspected child abuse and neglect.[47] Titles IV-D and XX of the Social Security Act also were enacted in 1974, providing states with federal funds to pay for child support enforcement programs and a variety of social services.[48]

In 1980 Congress enacted the Adoption Assistance and Child Welfare Act (Title IV-E of the Social Security Act), which required state social services agencies to make "reasonable efforts" to keep abused and neglect children with their families by providing foster care prevention and family reunification services and to implement procedures govern-

---

43. *See* King v. Smith, 329 U.S. 309 (1968); Shapiro v. Thompson, 394 U.S. 618 (1969); Goldberg v. Kelly, 397 U.S. 254 (1970); Dandridge v. Williams, 397 U.S. 471 (1970); Wyman v. James, 400 U.S. 309 (1971).

44. U.S. Dept. of Agriculture, "A Short History of the Food Stamp Program," www.fns.usda.gov/fsp/rules/Legislation/about_fsp.htm (last visited April 9, 2008). Legislation amending the Food Stamp Act was enacted in 1971, 1973, and 1977.

45. N.C. Division of Medical Assistance, "History of [the] North Carolina Medicaid Program," www.dhhs.state.nc.us/dma/historyofmedicaid.pdf (last visited April 9, 2008). North Carolina's Medicaid program was established in 1969 and began operating on January 1, 1970.

46. *See* Social Security Amendments of 1972, Pub. Law 92-603, § 301, 86 Stat. 1715 (1972) (enacting Title XVI of the Social Security Act, 42 U.S.C. §§ 1381 through 1383f).

47. Pub. Law 93-247, 88 Stat. 4 (1974).

48. Social Security Amendments of 1974, Pub. Law 93-647, §§ 2, 101, 88 Stat. 2716, 2732 (1974).

ing child welfare case management, permanency planning, and foster care review.[49]

Since 1960 the state's role and responsibilities with respect to social services have grown significantly as a result of the creation and expansion of federally funded social services programs, increased federal funding for social services programs, federal requirements with respect to these programs, and other factors. Over the years, the state has assumed responsibility for paying a greater portion of the nonfederal share of the cost of most social services programs and has exercised greater responsibility with respect to the direction and supervision of county social services agencies. For the most part, however, North Carolina has retained a county-administered and state-supervised system of social services in which local (county) governments are responsible for administering most state social services programs and paying at least part of the cost of those programs from local tax revenues.

In 1969 the General Assembly rewrote the state's public welfare and social services laws, changed the name of the state Board of Public Welfare to the state Board of Social Services, and created a state Department of Social Services, headed by a state commissioner of social services (appointed by the state Board of Social Services).[50] These changes reflected both a change in philosophy and the fact that the programs' scope had become much broader than financial aid. State supervision of county administration occurred primarily through field representatives who were active in developing and coordinating public welfare work in the counties.

In 1970, North Carolina adopted a revised state constitution, which expressly recognized the state's responsibility to establish charitable and benevolent institutions to address "the needs of humanity and the public good."[51] The following year, the General Assembly transferred the authority and responsibilities of the state Board of Social Services, the state commissioner of social services, the state Department of Social Services, and other state boards, commissions, and departments responsible for health, mental health, social services, and related functions to a new Department of Human Resources, whose secretary was

---

49. Pub. Law 96-272, 94 Stat. 500 (1980) (enacting Title IV-E of the Social Security Act).

50. 1969 N.C. Sess. Laws ch. 546.

51. N.C. CONST. of 1971 art. XI, § 3.

appointed by the governor.[52] In 1973 the General Assembly created a new state Social Services Commission to adopt rules and regulations governing the state's social services programs.[53]

In 1974, North Carolina became one of the first states in the nation to enact an adult protective services law to address the problem of abuse, neglect, and exploitation of elderly and disabled people.[54]

## Social Services Today: 1981 to 2008

The history of social services over the past twenty-seven years has been one of continued expansion of social services programs balanced against ongoing efforts to contain costs and to reform the social services system.

North Carolina's present-day social services system continues to be shaped by federal policy and laws creating federal–state social services programs. But recent federal laws and policies also have given states more authority and responsibility regarding some social services programs, and the state, in turn, has given counties increased authority with respect to at least one social services program.

In 1981 the General Assembly again revised and recodified the state's public assistance and social services laws.[55]

The same year, Congress amended Title XX of the Social Security Act to establish the Social Services Block Grant (SSBG) program.[56] The SSBG program "capped" federal funding for a wide variety of social services programs but gave states greater flexibility in determining what services are provided through the SSBG program, who is eligible for social services, and how services are provided. In 1984, Congress enacted additional requirements for state child support enforcement programs.[57] The federal Family Support Act, enacted in 1988, replaced earlier work programs with the Job Opportunities and Basic Skills Training Program

---

52. 1971 N.C. Sess. Laws ch. 864, § 15.

53. 1973 N.C. Sess. Laws ch. 476.

54. 1973 (1974) N.C. Sess. Laws ch. 1378.

55. 1981 N.C. Sess. Laws ch. 275 (Chapter 108A of the North Carolina General Statutes [hereinafter G.S.]).

56. Omnibus Budget Reconciliation Act of 1981, Pub. Law 97-35, § 2352, 95 Stat. 867 (1981).

57. Child Support Enforcement Amendments of 1984, Pub. Law 98-378, 98 Stat. 1305 (1984).

(JOBS) for AFDC recipients.[58] In 1990, Congress created the Child Care and Development Block Grant to provide funding to states for subsidized child day care.[59]

In 1991 North Carolina's General Assembly enacted legislation creating a state Child Fatality Task Force and a state Child Fatality Review Team.[60] In 1993 the state legislature passed legislation creating a statewide child fatality and abuse prevention system and a new early childhood education and development initiative known as Smart Start. In 1995 the state extended automatic Medicaid eligibility to all recipients of Supplemental Security Income benefits, dropping its status as a "209(b)" Medicaid program that restricted Medicaid eligibility for the elderly and disabled.

In 1996, Congress enacted the Personal Responsibility and Work Opportunities Reconciliation Act (PRWORA).[61] PRWORA constituted the most drastic overhaul of America's welfare system since 1935—attempting to "end welfare as we know it." PRWORA replaced the federal–state Aid to Families with Dependent Children (AFDC) program with a new Temporary Assistance to Needy Families (TANF) block grant program; "capped" federal funding for TANF; gave states increased authority to establish their own rules for TANF; limited the length of time that families could receive TANF; required most parents who receive TANF to work or participate in work-related activities; and attempted to address welfare dependency by promoting marriage and discouraging out-of-wedlock births.[62] PRWORA also restricted eligibility under the Food Stamp and Supplemental Security Income programs, restricted the eligibility of non-citizens for federal and state public benefits, and strengthened the child support enforcement program.

North Carolina's General Assembly implemented PRWORA's TANF provisions in 1997 by enacting legislation to replace the state's AFDC

---

58. Pub. Law 100-485, 102 Stat. 2343 (1988).

59. Omnibus Budget Reconciliation Act of 1990, Pub. Law 101-508, § 5082, 104 Stat. 1388-236 (1990).

60. 1991 N.C. Sess. Laws ch. 689, § 233.

61. Pub. Law 104-193, 110 Stat. 2105 (1996).

62. The TANF provisions of the 1996 federal welfare reform law are discussed in greater detail in John L. Saxon, "Welfare Reform: What Will It Mean for North Carolina?" *Popular Government*, 62(4) (Summer 1997): 15–27.

program with a new Work First program for needy families.[63] Under the Work First program, all counties were given greater responsibility for developing Work First service plans, and some counties (known as "electing" counties) were given greater authority to establish local eligibility rules for the county's Work First program.

In 1997, Congress enacted the Adoption and Safe Families Act (ASFA), which resulted in significant changes in North Carolina's Juvenile Code.[64] ASFA addressed three general perceptions about America's child welfare system: that children remained in foster care too long; that the child welfare system emphasized family preservation at the expense of the safety and well-being of abused and neglected children; and that inadequate attention and resources were devoted to adoption as a permanent placement option for abused and neglected children. Under ASFA, North Carolina and other states were required to ensure that child safety, permanency, and well-being are of paramount concern in any child welfare decision and to expedite permanency decisions for children in foster care.

The state Department of Human Resources was renamed as the Department of Health and Human Services (DHHS) in 1997.[65] In 1998 the General Assembly created the Health Choice program to provide health insurance to children in uninsured, low-income families. In 1999, Medicaid eligibility was expanded to include all elderly and disabled persons with incomes below the federal poverty level.

In 2004, responsibility for social services for elderly and disabled adults was transferred from DHHS's Division of Social Services to the renamed DHHS Division of Aging and Adult Services. And in 2007 the General Assembly enacted legislation phasing-out counties' responsibility to pay part of the cost of providing medical care under the state Medicaid program.

---

63. N.C. Sess. Laws 1997-443 (G.S. 108A-27 through 108A-29.1). The 1997 Work First legislation is described in greater detail in John L. Saxon, "Welfare Reform: Legislation Enacted by the 1997 General Assembly," *Social Services Bulletin* No. 26 (Chapel Hill: Institute of Government, The University of North Carolina at Chapel Hill, 1997).

64. Pub. Law 105-89, 111 Stat. 2115 (1997).

65. SL 1997-443, § 11A.1.

# Chapter 3

# The Role and Responsibilities of the State, Counties, and the Federal Government

Government in the United States is an overlapping, interlocking web of relationships among the federal government, the states, and local governments. The states stand at the center of the web. Each state is primarily responsible . . . for providing [public education, highways, law enforcement, courts, and a wide array of other] public services . . . even though the federal government plays an increasingly important role in setting national policy and providing federal funds for [many of these services]. Each state is free to organize its own government . . . [and all] of the states have chosen to employ some form of local government[.] [In North Carolina and most other states] . . . the county is the basic unit [of local

government and its primary function is] . . . to serve as
a local administrative arm of the state government.[1]

In North Carolina, governmental authority and responsibility for social
services (and for many other governmental functions and services)
is shared among the three levels of American government—the federal government, the state government, and local governments—and
among dozens of government agencies at all three levels of government,
including

- legislative or quasi-legislative institutions (for example,
  Congress, the North Carolina General Assembly, and boards of
  county commissioners);
- executive or administrative agencies, departments, boards, or
  commissions (for example, the U.S. Department of Health and
  Human Services, the North Carolina Department of Health and
  Human Services, and county departments of social services);
  and
- federal courts, state courts, and quasi-judicial bodies.

In some instances, one level of government exercises complete and
exclusive responsibility with respect to a particular social services
program, while the other two levels of government have little or no
responsibility for that program. For example, the federal government is responsible for the administration and funding of the federal
Supplemental Security Income (SSI) program. In other instances,
responsibility for a particular social services program may be shared
by two or three levels of government—and by one or more branches,
departments, or agencies at each level. For example, the federal government, the state, and counties each have certain administrative, fiscal,
or policy-making responsibilities with respect to North Carolina's
Medicaid program.

As a result, social services generally involves complicated, complex, and often overlapping and potentially conflicting relationships
among and within the federal government, state government, and local
governments.

---

1. Joseph S. Ferrell, *Handbook for North Carolina County Commissioners*, 3d ed.
(Chapel Hill: School of Government, The University of North Carolina at Chapel
Hill, 2007), 1.

## The State's Role and Responsibilities

In North Carolina, the general role and responsibility of state government with respect to social services is spelled out in two sections of North Carolina's Constitution of 1970.

One of these provisions is similar to a section of North Carolina's Constitution of 1868. This provision recognizes the state's duty to provide "beneficent [care] for the poor, the unfortunate, and . . . orphan[s]."[2] The second provision requires the state to establish and operate, under such organization and in such manner as the General Assembly may prescribe, "such charitable [and] benevolent . . . institutions and agencies as the needs of humanity and the public good may require."[3]

The North Carolina Constitution, therefore, recognizes the state's authority and responsibility to create, administer, and fund social services programs and agencies to provide assistance and services to needy families, children, and individuals. But it does not prescribe

- the extent and scope of the state's responsibility for social services;
- what social services agencies (other than a state "board of public welfare") must be established;
- what social services programs must be created or funded;
- how state social services agencies must be organized; or
- how state social services programs must be administered or funded.

### THE GENERAL ASSEMBLY

Under the constitutional provisions discussed above, North Carolina's state legislature, the General Assembly, is primarily responsible for determining the extent and scope of the state's responsibility for social services and how the state will discharge its responsibility. To do so, the General Assembly enacts legislation that creates and funds state social services agencies and programs, authorizes the state to participate in federal–state social services programs, and prescribes how federal–state and state social services programs will be administered and funded.[4] More specifically state laws enacted by the General Assembly

---

2. N.C. CONST. art. XI, § 4.
3. N.C. CONST. art. XI, § 3.
4. *See* Martin v. Wake County, 208 N.C. 354, 180 S.E. 777 (1935) (care of indigent sick and afflicted poor is a proper function of the state's government, but the

- create and define the responsibilities of state social services agencies;
- create state social services programs;
- authorize the state to participate in federal–state social services programs;[5]
- appropriate state funding for federal–state and state social services programs;
- allocate federal social services funds received by the state;
- determine how state social services programs will be administered and funded;
- approve the state's Temporary Assistance for Needy Families (TANF) plan;[6]
- determine which counties will be designated as "electing" counties under the Work First program;
- determine who is eligible for Medicaid and what services will be provided under the state's Medicaid program;
- determine local governments' role, authority, and responsibility with respect to social services; and
- determine whether counties will be required to pay all or part of the nonfederal share of the cost of federal–state and state social services programs.

Much, but not all, of the social services legislation enacted by the General Assembly is codified in Chapter 108A of the North Carolina General Statutes [hereinafter G.S.], which includes laws regarding

---

General Assembly may require counties, as administrative agencies of the state, to perform this function within their territorial limits); James Walker Memorial Hosp. v. City of Wilmington, 237 N.C. 179, 74 S.E.2d 749 (1953); Craven County Hosp. Corp. v. Lenoir County, 75 N.C. App. 453, 331 S.E.2d 690 (1985); Rosie J. v. N.C. Dep't of Human Resources, 347 N.C. 247, 491 S.E.2d 535 (1997) (the General Assembly's restrictions on the funding of medically necessary abortions for indigent women did not violate the state's constitutional obligations to provide beneficent care for the poor).

5. See Section 108A-71 of the North Carolina General Statutes [hereinafter G.S.]. As discussed below, the state's authority to adopt policies governing eligibility and benefits with respect to federal–state social services programs, such as the Food Stamp, Temporary Assistance for Needy Families (TANF), and Medicaid programs, is limited by federal law and regulations. Federal law and regulations, however, give the state significant policy-making authority with respect to the Medicaid and TANF programs.

6. North Carolina's TANF program is known as "Work First."

county administration of social services programs, administration of specific social services programs (such as Work First, State–County Special Assistance, Foster Care and Adoption Assistance, Food and Nutrition Services, Medicaid, Health Choice, and adult protective services), confidentiality of social services records, and financing of social services programs. Other laws regarding social services agencies, employees, and programs are codified in Chapter 7B (Juvenile Code), Chapter 48 (Adoption), Chapter 110 (child day care and child support enforcement), Chapter 126 (State Personnel Act), and Chapter 153A (Counties) of the General Statutes.

Social services policies adopted by the General Assembly also are included in uncodified session laws, such as uncodified provisions of the state's biennial appropriations act, which specifies who is eligible for Medicaid and what services will be provided under the state's Medicaid program. The state's biennial appropriations act also allocates federal funding that is received by the state under the Social Services Block Grant, the TANF Block Grant, the Child Care and Development Block Grant, and the Low-Income Energy Assistance Block Grant, and appropriates money from the state's General Fund for social services agencies and programs.

The General Assembly also exercises general oversight authority over the state's social services agencies and programs by requiring state social services agencies to report to the General Assembly on a wide variety of subjects involving the administration of social services programs.[7] And, from time to time, the General Assembly authorizes studies of social services agencies and programs by the Legislative Research Commission, the Department of Health and Human Services, or other state study commissions.

Within the General Assembly, the House Appropriations Subcommittee on Health and Human Services, Senate Appropriations Committee for Health and Human Services, the House Committee on Children, Youth, and Families, and the Senate Committee on Mental Health and Youth Services exercise primary responsibility for proposed legislation regarding social services programs and agencies.[8]

---

7. The General Assembly abolished the Joint Legislative Public Assistance Commission in 2001. SL 2001-424, § 21.13(a) (repealing G.S. 120-225).

8. Standing committees of the North Carolina House and Senate are established at the beginning of each biennial legislative session. These committees

## THE DEPARTMENT OF HEALTH AND HUMAN SERVICES

As noted above, the North Carolina Constitution gives the General Assembly the authority to establish state agencies and institutions to "serve the needs of humanity and the public good."[9] Acting pursuant to this authority, the General Assembly has created the state Department of Health and Human Services (DHHS) and has designated DHHS as the single state agency that is responsible for administering or supervising the administration of state and federal–state social services programs.[10]

Under North Carolina's county-administered and state-supervised social services system, which is discussed in the next section of this chapter, DHHS and its constituent divisions are primarily responsible for the supervision of state and federal–state social services programs. DHHS, however, is responsible, directly or through contracts with private vendors, for some administrative functions, such as paying Work First Family Assistance benefits, processing and paying Medicaid claims, determining disability for the state's Medicaid program, operating the child support enforcement program in thirty of the state's counties, and hearing and deciding administrative appeals involving eligibility for social services programs.

DHHS and the Social Services Commission also are authorized, under state law, to adopt administrative rules and regulations regarding social services programs. These administrative rules, however, must be consistent with applicable state statutes and adopted in accordance with the state's Administrative Procedure Act.[11]

## OTHER STATE GOVERNMENT AGENCIES

Four other state agencies also exercise authority with respect to state and county social services agencies and their employees.

The state Personnel Commission and the Office of State Personnel administer the State Personnel Act, which governs the appointment, discipline, and dismissal of most employees of DHHS and all employees of

---

reflect the 2005 organization of the House and Senate.

9. N.C. CONST. art. XI, § 3.

10. G.S. 108A-71; G.S. Ch. 143B, Art. 3. DHHS and its constituent divisions are discussed in more detail in Chapter 4.

11. G.S. Ch. 150B, Art. 2A. Administrative rules adopted by DHHS and the Social Services Commission are published in the North Carolina Register and are codified in Title 10A of the North Carolina Administrative Code (NCAC).

county social services departments (except those in counties with a "substantially equivalent" personnel system).[12]

The state Office of Administrative Hearings (OAH) and the state Industrial Commission exercise quasi-judicial authority to hear and decide some legal proceedings involving social services agencies and employees. OAH hears and makes recommended decisions in cases involving the firing of most state and county social services employees.[13] The Industrial Commission acts as a "court" that hears and decides cases under the state Tort Claims Act, including tort claims involving state social services agencies, officials, or employees.[14]

## State Courts

State courts do not exercise direct policy-making, administrative, or fiscal responsibility for social services, but they do exercise judicial authority in legal proceedings involving social services agencies, employees, and programs.

North Carolina's court system, the General Court of Justice, is divided into three divisions: the Appellate Division, consisting of the North Carolina Supreme Court and the North Carolina Court of Appeals; the Superior Court Division; and the District Court Division.[15]

Most of the cases involving social services agencies and programs are initially heard and decided by the district court. District court judges have jurisdiction to hear and decide juvenile cases involving abused, neglected, dependent, or delinquent juveniles; termination of parental rights; paternity of illegitimate children; establishment, modification,

---

12. *See* G.S. Ch. 126.

13. *See* G.S. Ch. 126; G.S. Ch. 150B, Art. 3.

14. *See* G.S. Ch. 143, Art. 31. Tort claims against counties, county officials, or county employees involving social services agencies, officials, employees, or programs are heard and decided by the state's superior courts rather than the state Industrial Commission. *See* Meyer v. Walls, 347 N.C. 97, 489 S.E.2d 880 (1997).

15. North Carolina's court system is a unified, statewide, state-operated system. This means that all courts in North Carolina (other than federal courts) are part of the judicial branch of state government. Some state judicial districts are coextensive with particular counties and some judicial officials are elected by the voters of a particular county or judicial district. Some local government agencies exercise quasi-judicial authority. Strictly speaking, however, there is no judicial branch of local government and there are no local (county or city) courts in North Carolina. North Carolina's court system is described in more detail in Joan G. Brannon, *The Judicial System in North Carolina* (Raleigh: N.C. Administrative Office of the Courts, 2000).

and enforcement of child support obligations; and special proceedings involving adult protective services—as well as appeals from decisions by the clerk of superior court in proceedings involving the adoption of minor children.[16]

Uncontested adoption proceedings and proceedings to appoint a guardian for a minor child or an incapacitated adult are initially heard and decided by clerks (and assistant clerks) of superior court.

The superior court decides cases involving judicial review of administrative decisions (including final administrative decisions regarding the discharge of county social services employees who are subject to the State Personnel Act and final administrative decisions regarding eligibility for social services under G.S. 108A-79), judicial review of rules adopted by state social services agencies under the Administrative Procedure Act, appeals in guardianship proceedings, and tort claims against counties and county officials or employees involving social services agencies, officials, or employees.[17]

North Carolina's court of appeals hears appeals from district court decisions in juvenile, termination of parental rights, adoption, paternity, and child support cases; from superior court decisions involving social services agencies or employees; and from decisions of the Industrial Commission involving tort claims against state social services agencies, officials, or employees. The North Carolina Supreme Court reviews decisions of the court of appeals if one of the three judges who decided the case in the court of appeals dissented from the court's decision, the case involves a significant constitutional issue, the case involves an issue of significant public interest, the case involves legal principles of major significance, or the decision of the court of appeals conflicts with a prior decision by the supreme court.

---

16. Although North Carolina does not have a separate "juvenile court," district court judges generally hear juvenile cases at special sessions of the district court. The district court also acts as a "family court" in several judicial districts.

17. Tort claims against the state or state social services agencies involving state or county social services agencies, officials, employees, or programs are initially heard and decided by the state Industrial Commission. See G.S. Ch. 143, Art. 31.

## The Counties' Role and Responsibilities

Although the North Carolina Constitution speaks of the state's responsibility for social services, the state may delegate all or part of its responsibility for social services to counties.[18]

North Carolina's one hundred counties are political subdivisions of the state. Each North Carolina county was created by an act of the state General Assembly, which also has the power to abolish, subdivide, or consolidate existing counties, to create new counties, to determine each county's form of government, to authorize or limit each county's power to levy taxes, and to specify the nature and scope of each county's legal authority and responsibility.[19]

North Carolina counties, therefore, may exercise only those powers specifically conferred on them by state law—they have no inherent powers of self-government. And more importantly, counties in North Carolina must exercise those powers, duties, and responsibilities that are imposed on them by state law.[20] The authority and responsibility of North Carolina counties for social services, therefore, derives from state laws that authorize or require counties to administer or fund social services programs.

### NORTH CAROLINA'S STATE-SUPERVISED AND COUNTY-ADMINISTERED SOCIAL SERVICES SYSTEM

Most states operate a "state-administered" social services system. Under a state-administered social services system, counties have little or no responsibility for administering or funding state and federal–state social services programs. In states with state-administered social services systems, local social services offices generally are established by the state social services agency and the state social services agency

---

18. *See* Martin v. Wake County, 208 N.C. 354, 180 S.E. 777 (1935) (care of indigent sick and afflicted poor is a proper function of the state's government, but the General Assembly may require counties, as administrative agencies of the state, to perform this function within their territorial limits); James Walker Memorial Hospital v. City of Wilmington, 237 N.C. 179, 74 S.E.2d 749 (1953); Craven County Hospital Corp. v. Lenoir County, 75 N.C. App. 453, 331 S.E.2d 690 (1985).

19. Article VII of the North Carolina Constitution requires the General Assembly to provide for the organization and government of counties, cities, towns, and other political subdivisions of the state and, except as limited by the constitution, allows the General Assembly to give such powers and duties to counties and other local governments as the General Assembly deems advisable.

20. Duties that are imposed on counties by state law are called state "mandates."

exercises direct authority over the employees of local social services offices.

North Carolina, by contrast, is one of at least a dozen states that has a "state-supervised and county-administered" social services system.[21] This means that county social services agencies are primarily responsible for administering state and federal–state social services programs under the supervision of state social services agencies.[22] Under this system, local social services agencies are part of county, not state, government and employees of local social services agencies are county, not state, employees. County social services agencies, however, must comply with applicable state and federal requirements in administering state and federal–state social services programs. And, under North Carolina's county-administered social services system, counties are required to pay at least part of the cost of administering most state and state–federal social services programs and part of the cost of assistance and services provided under many state and federal–state social services programs.

North Carolina's state-supervised and county-administered system of social services reflects the state's long history of county responsibility for social services, the continuing role of counties as a primary means for providing basic government services to North Carolinians, and the strength of local government in North Carolina. But it also "represents an exception to the trend . . . to centralize at the state level the administration and funding of major government functions."[23] And the state's

---

21. Other states with state-supervised and county-administered social services systems include California, Colorado, Minnesota, New York, Ohio, Pennsylvania, Virginia, and Wisconsin.

22. State social services agencies retain some responsibility for administering some social services programs. For example, although county social services departments approve or deny applications for assistance under the state Medicaid program, the state Division of Social Services hears and decides appeals regarding Medicaid eligibility and the state Division of Medical Assistance, acting through a private vendor, processes Medicaid claims and makes Medicaid payments to hospitals, nursing homes, doctors, and other health care providers.

23. Janet Mason and John Saxon, "Social Services," in Charles D. Liner, ed., State and Local Government Relations in North Carolina 2d ed. (Chapel Hill: Institute of Government, The University of North Carolina at Chapel Hill, 1995), 199. During the 1930s, North Carolina's state government assumed primary responsibility for funding the operation of public schools and for administering and funding prisons, roads, and highways. The state also assumed some additional responsibility for social services programs following enactment of the federal Social Security Act, but required counties to administer and pay part of the cost of most of the

delegation to counties of administrative and fiscal responsibility for social services programs continues to generate some special problems and frustrations, as evidenced by recent debates regarding the fiscal impact of Medicaid on low-wealth counties.

### COUNTY AUTHORITY AND RESPONSIBILITY: STATE LAW AND MANDATES

The general parameters of the state–county relationship with respect to social services and the authority and responsibility of North Carolina counties for social services are set forth in several provisions of North Carolina's General Statutes.

G.S. 108A-1 requires every county in North Carolina to have a county board of social services (or in a county with a population of at least 425,000, a county social services board, a board of county commissioners that exercises the powers and duties of a county social services board, or a consolidated human services board). Similarly, G.S. 108A-12 requires every county social services board to appoint a county social services director, who is responsible for appointing the staff of the county department of social services, for administering state and federal–state social services programs as required by law, and for acting as the agent of the state Department of Health and Human Services (DHHS).[24]

G.S. 153A-255 authorizes counties to undertake, sponsor, organize, engage in, and support any social service program that will further the health, welfare, education, employment, safety, comfort, and convenience of its citizens.[25] State law also requires counties or county departments of social services to administer, or to assist in the administration of, a number of state and federal–state social services programs, including Medicaid,[26] Temporary Assistance for Needy Families,[27] Food and Nutrition Services (Food Stamps),[28] Low-Income

---

public assistance programs established under the Social Security Act. Since then, the state has significantly increased its administrative and fiscal responsibility for social services programs but continues to administer most social services programs through county social services agencies and to require counties to pay part of the cost of state and federal–state social services programs.

24. G.S. 108A-14(2), (3), (5).

25. See 40 Op. N.C. Att'y Gen. 704 (1969). Cf. Hughey v. Cloninger, 297 N.C. 86, 253 S.E.2d 898 (1979); Stam v. State, 302 N.C. 357, 275 S.E.2d 439 (1981).

26. G.S. 108A-25(b); G.S. 153A-255.

27. G.S. 108A-27(f), (g); G.S. 153A-255.

28. G.S. 108A-25(a)(3); G.S. 108A-51; G.S. 153A-255.

Energy Assistance,[29] State-County Special Assistance,[30] Foster Care and Adoption Assistance,[31] child protective services,[32] adult protective services,[33] guardianship services,[34] Health Choice,[35] and child support enforcement services.[36]

Counties, however, must administer state and federal–state social services programs in accordance with applicable requirements set forth in federal and state law and rules and under the supervision of the state DHHS.[37] And in at least one instance, state law expressly addresses the state's authority to supervise, direct, and control the county's provision of social services. G.S. 108A-74 allows the state to impose a corrective action plan on the county, to withhold federal and state funding for the administration of child welfare services, or to take control of a county's child welfare program and provide these child welfare services through direct administration by the state DHHS or through contracts with other public or private agencies if a county department of social services fails to provide child protective services, foster care services, or adoption services in accordance with applicable state laws and regulations.

G.S. 153A-257 allocates responsibility for social services among the state's counties based on the "legal residence" of persons who are entitled to public assistance or social services.[38] If two or more county departments of social services disagree with respect to a minor's residence in a child abuse, neglect, or dependency case, the state DHHS Division of Social Services may determine which county is responsible for providing protective services and financial support for the minor.[39]

---

29. G.S. 108A-25(a)(5); G.S. 153A-255.

30. G.S. 108A-25(a)(2); G.S. 108A-40; G.S. 153A-255.

31. G.S. 108A-25(a)(4); G.S. 153A-255.

32. G.S. 7B-302.

33. G.S. 108A-103.

34. G.S. 108A-15; G.S. 153A-255.

35. G.S. 108A-70.26(a); G.S. 153A-255.

36. G.S. 110-141.

37. *See* G.S. 108A-1, G.S. 108A-14(3), G.S. 108A-25.

38. A person's legal residence generally is in the county in which he or she resides. A minor's legal residence generally is that of the parent or other relative with whom the minor resides. A person who is in a hospital, mental institution, nursing home, adult care home, group home, foster home, confinement facility, or similar institution does not necessarily reside in the county in which the institution is located.

39. G.S. 153A-257(d).

State law also provides that the General Assembly may divide the nonfederal share of the cost of social services for county residents between the state and counties.[40] When state law or rules require counties to pay part of the nonfederal share of social services programs, G.S. 108A-90 requires boards of county commissioners to levy and collect property taxes in an amount sufficient to pay the county share. If a county fails to pay its full share of social services costs to the state, the state may withhold from the county any state social services funding or sales tax revenues that otherwise would be paid to the county by the state.[41]

North Carolina counties, therefore, have a substantial amount of responsibility for the administration and funding of state and federal–state social services programs. In many instances, this responsibility is discharged through the county department of social services under the supervision of the county social services director. In other instances, responsibility rests with the county social services board or the board of county commissioners. In every instance, however, the authority and responsibility of counties, county commissioners, county social services departments, county social services directors, and county social services boards ultimately is defined by and subject to state law, state supervision, and state control.

## Municipalities and Human Services

Unlike counties, cities and towns in North Carolina are not responsible for the administration or funding of state or federal–state social services programs.

Cities and towns, however, are authorized to administer and fund some "human services" programs for their residents. In its broadest sense, the term "human services" includes any program or service that addresses needs related to human survival and healthy functioning in society, including social services, health and mental health services, housing assistance, employment services, and parks and recreation programs, to name just a few.

State law expressly authorizes, but does not require, cities and towns to administer, fund, or administer and fund human services programs

---

40. G.S. 108A-87.
41. G.S. 108A-93.

concerned with employment, economic development, child care, health, or welfare needs of low- and moderate-income individuals and families,[42] as well as programs that provide in-home services, nutrition services, counseling, recreation, transportation, and other assistance or care for senior citizens.[43] State law also authorizes municipalities to appropriate funding for the state's mental health, developmental disability, and substance abuse program;[44] to construct, operate, fund, and maintain public hospitals;[45] to administer and fund drug abuse prevention and treatment programs;[46] and to undertake and fund human relations, community action, and manpower development programs.[47]

## The Federal Government's Role and Responsibilities

The U.S. Constitution allows, but does not require, the federal government to use federal tax revenues to establish and administer, or to assist state and local governments in administering, social services programs for the poor, the disabled, the elderly, and children.[48] Thus, unlike North Carolina's state government, the federal government does not have any constitutional obligation or responsibility to establish, administer, or fund social services programs. But it does have the legal authority to do so.

### CONGRESS

Responsibility for federal social services policy and law is vested primarily in the U.S. Congress, which enacts legislation creating federal and federal–state social services programs.[49]

---

42. G.S. 160A-456.
43. G.S. 160A-497.
44. G.S. 122C-115(b).
45. G.S. 131E-5; G.S. 131E-7.
46. G.S. 160A-494.
47. G.S. 160A-492.
48. Article I, Section 8, of the United States Constitution authorizes Congress to impose taxes and spend money to provide for the "general welfare" of the United States. The constitutionality of the federal government's authority to establish and fund social services programs was first upheld by the U.S. Supreme Court in 1937. *See* Helvering v. Davis, 301 U.S. 619 (1937).
49. Congress shares policy-making responsibility with the president, who may call on Congress to enact social services legislation or veto social services statutes passed by Congress; with federal agencies, which may adopt rules or regulations

Federal social services statutes enacted by Congress determine the nature and scope of the federal government's role and responsibility for social services, what federal social services programs and agencies will be established, whether federal social services programs will be administered by federal social services agencies or through state or local social services agencies, how much the federal government will spend for federal social services programs, who will be eligible to receive assistance or services under these programs, what requirements will apply to federal social services funding provided to state or local social services agencies, and how much flexibility states will have in administering federal–state social services programs. Examples of federal social services statutes include the Social Security Act, which created the Social Security, Supplemental Security Income, Medicare, and Medicaid programs; the Food Stamp Act; the Adoption and Safe Families Act; the welfare reform provisions of the Personal Work Opportunities and Responsibility Act of 1996; and the Indian Child Welfare Act. These federal social services statutes generally specify the persons who are eligible to receive assistance or services under each federal or federal–state social services program, specify the type of assistance or services that may be provided under each program, specify how each program will be funded, and specify who will be responsible for administering each program.

Congress also exercises primary fiscal authority for federal and federal–state social services programs by determining, through the federal budget and appropriations process, how much the federal government will spend on social services programs.

## THE U.S. DEPARTMENT OF HEALTH AND HUMAN SERVICES AND OTHER FEDERAL AGENCIES

At the federal level, administrative responsibility for federal and federal–state social services programs is exercised by the U.S. Department of Health and Human Services and other federal departments, agencies, bureaus, and offices.

Some federal social services programs are administered directly by federal agencies. The federal Social Security Administration, for

---

supplementing or implementing federal social services statutes; and with state governments, which may enact laws or adopt policies for some federal–state social services programs within the parameters set by Congress.

example, administers the Old Age, Disability, and Survivors Insurance (OASDI or "Social Security") program and the Supplemental Security Income (SSI) program. State and local governments have little or no responsibility for these federal social services programs.

Other federal social services programs are administered primarily through private contractors. The federal Medicare program, for example, is administered by private health insurance carriers (like Blue Cross and Blue Shield) under the supervision of the Center for Medicare and Medicaid Services.

But many federal social services programs (or, more accurately, federal–state social services programs), including the Medicaid, Food Stamp, Temporary Assistance for Needy Families, Low-Income Energy Assistance, Foster Care and Adoption Assistance, and child protective services programs, are administered by state and local social services agencies under the supervision of the U.S. Department of Health and Human Services or other federal agencies, which generally are responsible for

- reviewing and approving the social services plans that states submit to the federal government as a condition of receiving federal funding for these federal–state social services programs;
- distributing federal social services funding to states;
- issuing rules, regulations, and policies governing the states' administration of federally funded social services programs;
- collecting and analyzing data with respect to these programs;
- monitoring the states' compliance with federal law, regulations, policies, and requirements that apply with respect to these programs; and
- withholding federal funds or imposing other penalties or sanctions when states fail to comply with federal requirements.

## FEDERAL COURTS

Federal courts do not have any express policy-making, administrative, or fiscal responsibility for federal or federal–state social services programs. They do, however, exercise judicial authority with respect to these programs and their decisions often have a significant impact on state and county social services agencies.

The United States Supreme Court, for example, issued a series of decisions in the 1960s and 1970s striking down state welfare policies that were contrary to federal requirements.[50] And after persons who applied for Medicaid filed a lawsuit against North Carolina's Department of Human Resources, a federal judge in Charlotte issued a series of orders requiring state and county social services agencies to change their policies and procedures to ensure that all Medicaid applications were processed in a timely manner as required by federal law, to establish an ongoing monitoring process to ensure compliance with the federal time limits, to submit monthly reports to the court, and to pay monetary penalties if they failed to comply with the court's order.

### THE FEDERAL–STATE RELATIONSHIP: COOPERATIVE FEDERALISM AND FEDERAL "MANDATES"

As noted above, some federal social services programs are funded, in whole or part, by the federal government but are administered through state (or, in North Carolina, state and local) social services agencies.[51] These federal social services programs are more precisely referred to as federal–state social services programs, because the federal government and the states share responsibility for these programs and cooperate in providing assistance and services under these programs. Thus, the relationship between the federal government and states with respect to federal–state social services programs sometimes is described as one of "cooperative federalism."

The nature and terms of this cooperative federal–state relationship vary from program to program and are spelled out in the requirements and conditions of applicable federal laws and regulations; in the provisions of the "state plan" for each program; and in the terms of

---

50. *See* King v. Smith, 392 U.S. 309 (1968); Shapiro v. Thompson, 394 U.S. 618 (1969); Rosado v. Wyman, 397 U.S. 397 (1970); Wyman v. James, 400 U.S. 309 (1971); Townsend v. Swank, 404 U.S. 282 (1971).

51. The federal government's authority for social services relates primarily to federal and federal–state social services programs. The federal government does not have any direct policy-making, administrative, or fiscal responsibility for state or local social services programs that do not receive federal funding. Certain requirements of the U.S. Constitution and federal law, however, may apply with respect to state or local social services programs that don't receive federal funding. For example, the due process clause of the U.S. Constitution generally requires that state or county social services agencies give adequate notice and an opportunity for hearing to persons who are denied assistance or services regardless of whether the assistance or services are provided under a federally funded social services program.

federal grants, contracts, waivers, or agreements with the state. Generally, however, cooperative federalism means that the federal government

- pays all or part of the cost of federal–state social services programs;
- establishes some or all of the policies governing these programs; and
- allows states to administer these programs in accordance with federal requirements regarding eligibility, assistance, and program administration.[52]

Federal law, for example, requires that most federal–state social services programs be administered

- by a single state agency or by local social services agencies under the supervision of a single state agency;
- in all political subdivisions of the state under uniform, statewide policies;
- in a way that protects the legal rights and confidentiality of persons applying for or receiving assistance or services; and
- by employees who are selected and protected under a merit-based personnel system.

Some federal social services laws require states to pay part of the cost of federal–state social services programs based on federal "match"

---

52. It is important to note that the federal government also gives states some discretion with respect to the operation of some federal–state social services programs, as long as that discretion is exercised within the parameters of federal requirements. For example, federal law generally provides that families may not receive Temporary Assistance for Needy Families for more than sixty months, but allows states to adopt more stringent time limits or to allow a limited number of families to exceed the federal time limit. Similarly, the federal Medicaid statute requires states to cover certain categories of people and to provide certain medical services but gives states the option to cover other categories of people, to provide optional medical services, to determine the amount, scope, and duration of covered services, and to determine payment rates for covered services. Federal "mandates," therefore, do not dictate every aspect of every federal–state social services program.

or "maintenance of effort" formulas. And federal social services laws often specify

- who is eligible or ineligible for assistance and services under federal–state social services programs;
- what type of assistance must or may be provided to eligible persons;
- how much assistance must or may be provided; and
- how long assistance or services must or may be provided.

These federal requirements often are called federal "mandates." Strictly speaking, however, the federal government does not mandate or require any state to participate in or administer any federal–state social services program. Instead, federal social services mandates are more properly characterized as "strings" that are attached to federal social services funding, which is the "carrot" offered to induce states to participate in federal–state social services programs. North Carolina and other states, therefore, may decline to participate in any federal–state social services program and refuse to accept federal social services funding. But if the state chooses to participate in a federal–state social services program and to accept social services funding, it must comply with the federal requirements that are attached to the program and funding. And because states are required to comply with these federal requirements as a condition of receiving federal social services funding, these federal "mandates" affect and help shape state social services policies in an indirect, but nonetheless real, way.

There is no direct relationship between the federal government and counties with respect to federal–state social services programs. Instead, the federal government provides funding for these programs to each state—not directly to counties—and holds the state, rather than counties, accountable for complying with federal requirements and conditions. Federal social services mandates, however, affect the administration and funding of federal–state social services programs at the local level because the federal mandates that are imposed on the state are passed on to counties along with federal funding for social services programs.

# Chapter 4

# State Social Services Agencies

In North Carolina, most social services programs are administered through county departments of social services. State social services agencies, however, also play an important role in administering some social services programs, in establishing policies governing state and federal–state social services programs, in distributing funding for social services programs, and in supervising the local administration of social services programs. Most of these state social services agencies are located within the state Department of Health and Human Services (DHHS).

## The Department of Health and Human Services

The North Carolina Department of Health and Human Services (DHHS) is the largest department of state government, with approximately 20,000 employees and an operating budget of approximately $14 billion per year.[1]

The mission of DHHS is "to provide efficient services that enhance the quality of life of . . . individuals and families," to provide them with opportunities for healthier and safer lives, and to help them achieve economic and personal independence.[2]

---

1. North Carolina Department of Health and Human Services (DHHS) website (www.dhhs.state.nc.us/whoweare.htm#facts).

2. DHHS website (www.dhhs.state.nc.us/whoweare.htm#mission).

In 1970 the voters of North Carolina adopted a new state constitution, which became effective on July 1, 1971. One of the new
constitution's provisions required the General Assembly to allocate all
of the state's administrative departments, agencies, and offices and
their respective functions, powers, and duties among and within not
more than twenty-five principal administrative departments according
to their major purposes.[3]

In response to this mandate, the General Assembly enacted the Executive Organization Act of 1971, which created a new state Department
of Human Resources as one of seventeen principal departments of state
government.[4] Under the 1971 act, the Department of Human Resources
assumed the functions, powers, and duties previously exercised by the
state's Department of Social Services, the state Board of Social Services,
the Department of Mental Health, and twenty-eight other state commissions, boards, agencies, and offices.

In 1973 the General Assembly enacted the Executive Organization Act of 1973, which recreated and reorganized the Department of
Human Resources.[5] The 1973 act created a number of new commissions,
including the Social Services Commission, organized the department
into seven divisions, including the Division of Social and Rehabilitative
Services, the Division of Mental Health Services, and the Division of
Health Services, and gave the secretary of human resources the authority to create, with the governor's approval, additional divisions within
the department.

In 1997 the department was renamed the Department of Health and
Human Services.[6]

The head of DHHS is the secretary of health and human services.[7]
The secretary is appointed by the governor and serves at the governor's
pleasure.[8]

DHHS currently consists of ten divisions plus dozens of
commissions, offices, and agencies. See Figure 4.1. Each DHHS division
is headed by a director, who is appointed by the secretary and serves
at the secretary's pleasure. DHHS also oversees eighteen mental

---

3. N.C. Const. of 1971 art. III, § 11.
4. 1971 N.C. Sess. Laws ch. 864, Chapter 143A of the North Carolina General
Statutes [hereinafter G.S.].
5. 1973 N.C. Sess. Laws ch. 476, G.S. Ch. 143B.
6. SL 1997-443, G.S. Ch. 143B, Art. 3.
7. G.S. 143B-139.
8. G.S. 143B-9.

**Figure 4.1 Department of Health and Human Services Organizational Chart**

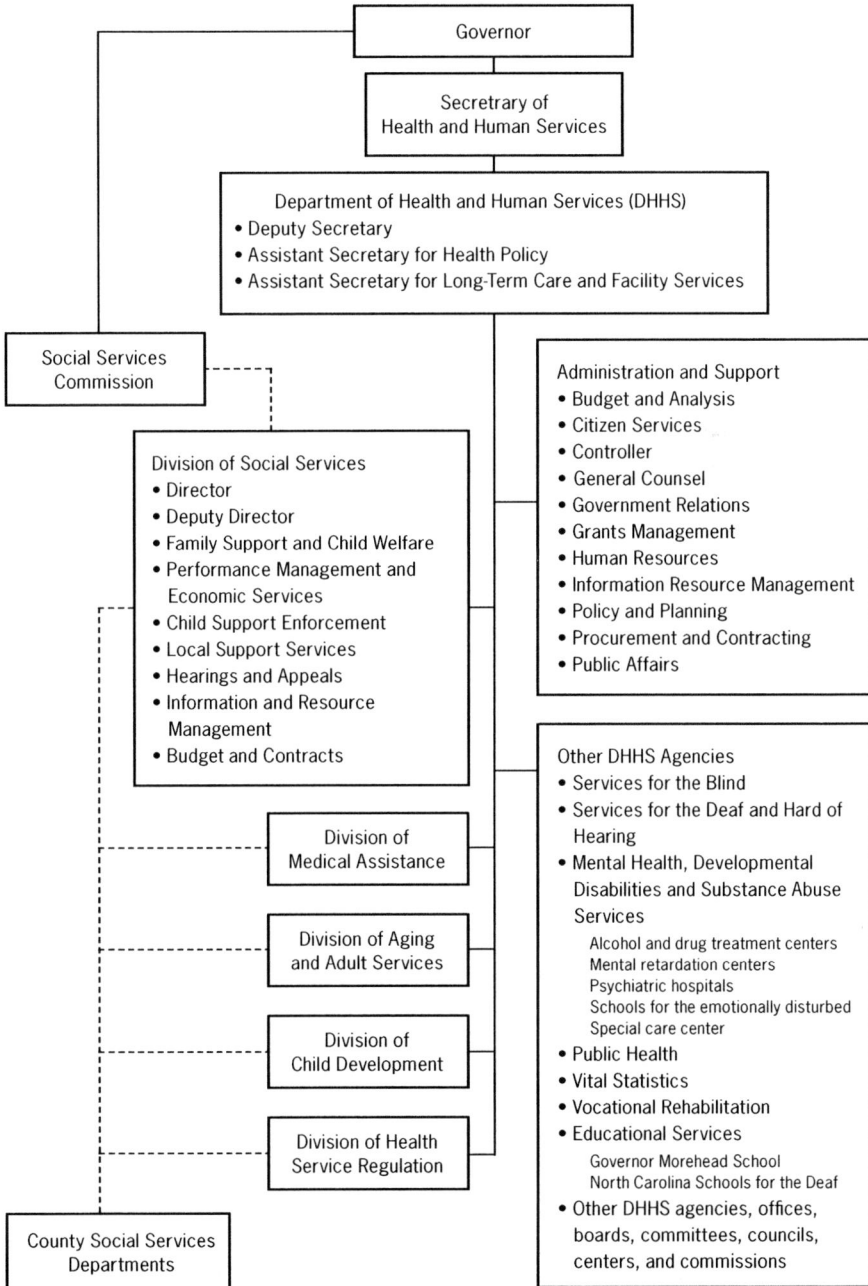

Note: This DHHS organizational chart does not include every office, division, institution, board, commission, or agency that is a part of DHHS.

retardation centers, psychiatric hospitals, alcohol and drug abuse treatment centers, schools, and other facilities.

## The Social Services Commission

The state Social Services Commission consists of thirteen members (one from each of the state's congressional districts) who are appointed by the governor for four-year terms.[9] Staff support for the commission is provided by the DHHS Division of Social Services.

The Social Services Commission has the authority to adopt rules and regulations governing social services programs (other than the state Medicaid program) that are administered under Chapter 108A of the North Carolina General Statutes [hereinafter G.S.].[10] The commission's rules must be adopted in accordance with the state's Administrative Procedure Act (G.S. Ch. 150B, Art. 2A) and may not be inconsistent with applicable federal or state law.

The commission also has the power to

- adopt rules governing the payment of state funds to private child-placing agencies and residential child care facilities for the care of children who are in the custody or placement responsibility of county departments of social services;
- adopt standards for the inspection and licensing of maternity homes and child-care institutions;
- adopt standards for the inspection and operation of jails and local confinement facilities;
- adopt standards for the regulation and licensing of charitable organizations, professional fund-raising counsel, and professional solicitors;
- investigate social problems in the state and conduct hearings and subpoena witnesses and documents in connection with such investigations; and
- adopt rules establishing rates and fees for the state's child support enforcement program.

---

9. G.S. 143B-154.
10. G.S. 143B-153.

The commission also appoints one or two members of each county's board of social services.[11]

## The Division of Social Services

The Division of Social Services (DSS) is one of the ten divisions of DHHS.

The mission of DSS is to assist needy individuals and families by providing them with economic support and helping them become self-sufficient and to protect the safety and promote the well-being of vulnerable, at-risk, abused, neglected, and dependent children.

DSS is responsible for administering or supervising the administration of a number of social services programs, including Work First (Temporary Assistance to Needy Families or TANF), food and nutrition services, energy assistance, refugee assistance, child support enforcement, foster care and adoption assistance, adoption services, child protective services, and child welfare services.

DSS currently consists of five primary sections: the child support enforcement section, the performance management section, the economic services section, the family support and child welfare services section, and the human resources section. DSS provides support, technical assistance, and supervision to county social services departments through a network of regional child support consultants, Work First, food assistance, and energy program representatives, children's programs representatives, program integrity representatives, and local operations and business liaisons. The hearings and appeals unit of DSS hears and decides administrative appeals from decisions by county social services departments regarding eligibility for Medicaid, Work First, food and nutrition services, and other public assistance and social services programs.

## The Division of Medical Assistance

The Division of Medical Assistance (DMA) is a division of DHHS. DMA was created in 1978.[12]

---

11. G.S. 108A-3.

12. North Carolina's Medicaid program was administered by the Division of Social Services from 1970 until 1978.

DMA's mission is "to provide access to high quality medically necessary health care to eligible North Carolina residents through cost-effective purchasing of health care services and products."[13]

DMA administers or supervises the administration of two social services programs: the North Carolina Medicaid program and the Health Choice program for uninsured children. County social services departments are responsible for determining the Medicaid eligibility of individuals who do not receive SSI benefits. DMA contracts with private companies to process and pay Medicaid claims, to operate the Medicaid Management Information System, to conduct quality assurance and utilization reviews for certain Medicaid services, and to process requests for prior approval for certain Medicaid services.

## The Division of Aging and Adult Services

The Division of Aging and Adult Services (DAAS) is a division of DHHS. The DHHS Division of Aging was created in 1977.[14] In 2003 responsibility for adult services was transferred from the Division of Social Services to the Division of Aging, which was renamed the Division of Aging and Adult Services.

The mission of DAAS is to promote the "independence and enhance the dignity of North Carolina's older and disabled persons and their families and ready younger generations to enjoy their later years."[15]

DAAS supervises the administration by local aging agencies and other aging services providers of social services programs for senior citizens that are funded under the federal Older Americans Act and the state's Home and Community Care Block Grant. DAAS also is responsible for the state's long-term care ombudsman and elder rights programs; the North Carolina Senior Games; certification of senior centers, adult day care programs, and adult health day care programs; senior center development; and the Older Americans Act health promotion and disease prevention program. The division's adult services section supervises the administration of guardianship services, adult protective services, adult placement services, adult care home case management

---

13. DMA website (www.dhhs.state.nc.us/dma/2006report/2006report.pdf).
14. G.S. 143B-181.1.
15. Division of Aging and Adult Services (DAAS) website at www.dhhs.state.nc.us/aging.

services, and the State-County Special Assistance program by county social services departments.

The Governor's Advisory Council on Aging consists of thirty-three members. It advises the governor, the secretary of health and human services, and DAAS on the needs of senior citizens and problems of the elderly.

## The Division of Child Development

The Division of Child Development (DCD) is a division of DHHS. DCD was created in 1993.

DCD is responsible for the licensure and monitoring of child day care facilities and for administering or supervising the administration of the state's subsidized child day care program. The subsidized child day care program is administered locally by county departments of social services or other local purchasing agencies.

The North Carolina Child Care Commission is responsible for adopting rules governing the licensure and operation of child day care facilities. Its fifteen members are appointed by the governor, the speaker of the house, and the president pro tempore of the North Carolina Senate.

## The Division of Health Service Regulation

The Division of Health Service Regulation (DHSR) is a division of DHHS. DHSR was formerly named the Division of Facility Services (DFS). DHSR's responsibilities include the licensure and regulation of adult care homes. County social services departments are responsible for the inspection and monitoring of adult care homes under DHSR's supervision.

DHSR also licenses or regulates a variety of other programs, institutions, and health care facilities, including hospitals, nursing homes, home health agencies, mental health group homes, jails, and emergency management services.

The state Medical Care Commission is a seventeen-member commission appointed by the governor. The commission adopts rules and regulations governing the licensure and operation of health care facilities.

The DHHS Penalty Review Committee reviews and makes recommendations to DHSR regarding administrative penalties against adult care homes for violations of state licensure requirements.

## The North Carolina Child Fatality Task Force

The state Child Fatality Task Force was created in 1991 by the General Assembly to study the incidence and causes of childhood deaths and to develop a system for the multidisciplinary review of child deaths. An eleven–member state Child Fatality Prevention Team is responsible for studying child deaths attributed to abuse or neglect and providing assistance to community child protection teams and community child fatality prevention teams.

# Chapter 5

# County Commissioners and Social Services

As elected local government officials, county commissioners have a strong interest in ensuring that county residents receive the help they need through social services programs. At the same time, however, county commissioners also must be concerned, at times, with the cost of social services programs and the financial impact of social services programs on local taxpayers. For both of these reasons, county commissioners—individually, as boards, and through the North Carolina Association of County Commissioners—have been, and continue to be, extremely interested, concerned, and involved with respect to social services in North Carolina.[1]

---

1. Historically, boards of county commissioners in North Carolina have always exercised, since the time of their creation in 1868, some authority and responsibility with respect to the provision of social services to county residents. In the 1800s, county commissioners were authorized to construct almshouses for the poor, to employ a public overseer of the poor, and to provide "poor relief" payments to the needy. In 1919 county commissioners were given the authority (acting jointly with the county board of education) to appoint a county superintendent of public welfare, and were responsible, under the 1923 mothers' aid law, for approving applications for financial assistance and determining the amount of assistance provided (on recommendation of the county superintendent and board of public welfare). In 1937 the board of county commissioners was authorized to appoint one of the members of the county board of public welfare and to review decisions by the county board of public welfare with respect to assistance granted under the Old Age Assistance and Aid to Dependent Children programs. More recently, county commissioners have been given the authority to determine whether or how the county will administer the child support enforcement (IV-D) program and to adopt the plan for the county's Work First program.

## The Board of County Commissioners

Each North Carolina county has a board of county commissioners.[2]

The board of county commissioners is the governing body for county government and, except as otherwise provided by law, exercises all of the legal rights, powers, duties, and responsibilities of the county.[3] The county commissioners' primary responsibilities with respect to county government include

- organizing and reorganizing the structure of county government to promote the orderly and efficient administration of county affairs;[4]
- appointing a county manager to serve as the chief administrator of county government;[5]

---

2. *See* Joseph S. Ferrell, *Handbook for North Carolina County Commissioners*, 3d ed. (Chapel Hill: School of Government, The University of North Carolina at Chapel Hill, 2007); David M. Lawrence, "City and County Governing Boards," Article 3, in *County and Municipal Government in North Carolina* (Chapel Hill: School of Government, The University of North Carolina at Chapel Hill, 2007). Also available online at www.sog.unc.edu/pubs/cmg/cmg03.pdf. All county commissioners (other than those appointed to fill a vacancy due to the death or resignation of a county commissioner during his or her term) are elected by the county's voters in partisan elections in even-numbered years. *See* Lawrence, "City and County Governing Boards," 2. The structure and composition of boards of county commissioners, however, vary widely across the state. *See* Section 153A-121 of the North Carolina General Statutes [hereinafter G.S.]. The size of boards ranges from three to eleven commissioners, the terms of county commissioners are either two or four years, and commissioners may be elected on at at-large or district basis. *See* Lawrence, "City and County Governing Boards," 2.

3. *See* G.S. 153A-34 and G.S. 153A-12. The board of county commissioners, however, does not have complete control over county government. It shares authority over some local governmental functions with other local officials and semiautonomous boards and agencies. And state law defines the nature, scope, and extent of the commissioners' authority, limiting the commissioners' powers in some instances and, in other instances, mandating certain activities, programs, or services.

4. *See* G.S. 153A-76.

5. *See* G.S. 153A-81. All of North Carolina's counties, except Swain County, operate under a county-manager form of government. State law requires county managers to direct and supervise the administration of all county offices, departments, boards, commissions, and agencies under the general control of the board of county commissioners and to prepare and submit a proposed annual county budget to the board of county commissioners. *See* G.S. 153A-82. State law authorizes county managers to appoint, with the approval of the board of commissioners or under authority delegated by the county commissioners, all

- appointing the county attorney;[6]
- establishing the county's fiscal policy, adopting the county budget, and levying county taxes as authorized by law;[7]
- regulating private conduct through their ordinance-making powers;[8]
- establishing general personnel policies governing the employment, dismissal, and compensation of county employees;[9] and
- supervising the maintenance, repair, and use of all county property, acquiring real and personal property for the county, and disposing of county property as authorized by law.[10]

## Legal Powers and Duties of County Commissioners
The powers and duties of boards of county commissioners with respect to social services agencies, employees, and programs are defined by statutes enacted by North Carolina's General Assembly.

### SOCIAL SERVICES ORGANIZATION, STRUCTURE, AND GOVERNANCE
State law gives the board of county commissioners broad authority to organize and reorganize county government in order to promote the orderly and efficient administration of county affairs.[11] This authority generally includes the power to

- create, change, abolish, and consolidate offices, positions, departments, boards, commissions, and agencies of county government;

---

county officers, employees, and agents (except those who are elected by the people or whose appointment is otherwise authorized by law) and to suspend or dismiss county officers, employees, and agents (except those who are elected by the people or whose appointment is otherwise provided by law) in accordance with general personnel ordinances, rules, and policies adopted by the board of commissioners. *See* G.S. 153A-82.

    6. *See* G.S. 153A-114.

    7. *See* G.S. 153A-101; G.S. 153A-146; G.S. 153A-149; G.S. 153A-151.

    8. *See* G.S. 153A-121. Zoning and land use and development ordinances are examples of the commissioners' regulatory authority. *See* G.S. Ch. 153A, Art. 18.

    9. *See* G.S. 153A-92 through G.S. 153A-94.

    10. *See* G.S. Ch. 153A, Art. 8.

    11. *See* G.S. 153A-76.

- impose ex officio the duties of more than one office on a single officer; and
- change the composition and manner of selection of county boards, commissions, and agencies.

The board of county commissioners, however, may *not*

- abolish the county department or board of social services or assign the powers and duties of the county social services director, department, or board to another official, department, or board;[12] or
- change the composition of the county social services board or the manner in which the county social services board is appointed.[13]

A board of county commissioners, however, may assign additional duties or responsibilities to the county social services board, department, or director, and may establish additional qualifications for the appointment of county social services board members or the county social services director.[14]

A board of county commissioners also may assume and exercise the powers and duties of the county social services board in counties with populations of at least 425,000.[15] Alternatively, a board of county commissioners of a county with a population of at least 425,000 may create a consolidated human services agency, director, and board that exercises most of the powers and duties that would otherwise be exercised by the county social services department, director, and board.[16]

In addition, state law gives county commissioners a number of powers and duties with respect to county social services boards:

- determining whether the county social services board will consist of three or five members;[17]

---

12. *See* G.S. 153A-76(1) and (3); 52 Op. N.C. Att'y Gen. 44 (1982).

13. *See* G.S. 153A-76(4).

14. G.S. 108A-9; G.S. 153A-25. The county commissioners may not waive any qualification for an appointive office that is fixed by state law.

15. G.S. 153A-77(a), (f). This provision currently applies only to Mecklenburg, Wake, and Guilford counties and has been implemented only by Mecklenburg County.

16. G.S. 153A-77(b) through (f). This provision currently applies only to Mecklenburg, Wake, and Guilford counties and has been implemented only by Wake County.

17. G.S. 108A-2.

- appointing one member of a three-member social services board or two members of a five-member board;[18]
- removing a social services board member from office if the board member was appointed by the county commissioners and there is "good cause" to remove the board member;[19] and
- establishing the *per diem* rates and policies for subsistence and travel reimbursement for social services board members.[20]

## SOCIAL SERVICES BUDGET AND FUNDING

The county commissioners' responsibility for social services is most visible in connection with their authority to approve, adopt, and amend the budget for the county department of social services.[21]

Because the county board and department of social services are not municipal corporations, are not part of the state's budgeting system, and do not have the authority to levy taxes, they are not "units of local government" as defined under the Local Government Budget and Fiscal Control Act (LGBFCA) and their budgets are, therefore, part of the county budget.[22] The LGBFCA requires that the county budget, including the budget for the county social services department, be approved by the board of county commissioners through the adoption of an annual county budget ordinance, which levies taxes and appropriates revenues for all county programs, functions, activities, and objectives other than capital or grant projects and internal or trust or agency funds.[23]

---

18. G.S. 108A-3.

19. *See* John L. Saxon, "The County Board of Social Services (Part III): Appointment, Terms, Term Limits, and Removal from Office," *Social Services Law Bulletin* No. 36 (Chapel Hill: Institute of Government, The University of North Carolina at Chapel Hill, 2002).

20. G.S. 108A-8.

21. Preparation and approval of the county social services budget is discussed in more detail in Chapter 12.

22. G.S. 159-7(b)(15). Preparation, review, and approval of the county budget is governed by the Local Government Budget and Fiscal Control Act (LGBFCA). *See* G.S. Ch. 159, Art. 3. The LGBFCA is discussed in detail in David M. Lawrence, *Local Government Finance in North Carolina,* 2d ed. (Chapel Hill: Institute of Government, The University of North Carolina at Chapel Hill, 1990).

23. G.S. 159-13(a); G.S. 159-8; G.S. 159-7(b)(2). Trust and agency funds are funds that a local government holds in a fiduciary, trust, or agency capacity on behalf of and for the benefit of an individual, association, or another governmental entity.

In general, county commissioners have substantial discretion regarding the funding for county government functions, and this is also true with respect to certain functions, activities, or programs of the county social services department. County commissioners, for example, have some discretion regarding the staffing levels for county social services departments and the funding levels for salaries and benefits for county social services employees. County commissioners also have discretion regarding the implementation and funding of "optional" social services programs.[24]

State law, however, imposes several requirements on boards of county commissioners with respect to county funding for social services programs. State law, for example, requires counties to provide certain social services programs (known as "mandated" programs) and to pay part of the cost of administering and providing assistance or services for some of these mandated social services programs.[25] When state law requires a county to pay part of the cost of these social services programs, the board of county commissioners must levy and collect property taxes in an amount sufficient to pay the county's share of the cost of these programs.[26] If a county fails to appropriate and pay its share of the cost of these social services programs, the state may withhold state social services funding or sales tax revenues that otherwise would be paid to the county.[27] State law also prohibits the transfer of county funding for social services programs from one program to another during the fiscal year without the approval of the state's Department of Health and Human Services, and prohibits the lapse or reversion of unexpended county appropriations for social services programs.[28]

### SOCIAL SERVICES EMPLOYEES AND PERSONNEL POLICIES

Employees of the county social services department are county, not state, employees.[29] County social services employees, though, are sub-

---

24. G.S. 153A-255; G.S. 153A-149(c)(30).

25. *See* G.S. 153A-255.

26. G.S. 108A-90; G.S. 153A-149(b)(8).

27. G.S. 108A-93.

28. G.S. 108A-91. These unexpended balances, however, may be considered by the county commissioners in making further county appropriations for social services programs.

29. Laws governing county social services employees are discussed in more detail in Chapter 8.

ject to the provisions of the State Personnel Act and to rules adopted by the State Personnel Commission governing the appointment, compensation, promotion, leave, discipline, and dismissal of state employees.[30]

If, however, a board of county commissioners has adopted rules and regulations governing the salary schedule and vacation and sick leave for county employees generally and files these rules with the state personnel director, the county's salary schedule and provisions regarding vacation and sick leave, rather than the salary schedule and leave provisions adopted under the State Personnel Act, will apply to county social services employees.[31]

State law also allows the board of county commissioners to adopt ordinances, rules, or policies or provide for the adoption of policies and rules governing the work schedules and holidays for county employees, service award and incentive award programs for county employees, the working conditions of county employees, and other personnel matters regarding county employees.[32] These county personnel policies apply to county social services employees to the extent that they are not inconsistent with the provisions of the State Personnel Act or rules adopted by the State Personnel Commission governing county social services employees.

State law also authorizes the board of county commissioners to purchase life and health insurance for county employees (including county social services employees), to participate in the Social Security insurance program and the Local Government Employees' Retirement System or another retirement plan for county social services employees, and to provide other fringe benefits for county employees.[33]

The county commissioners also have the legal authority to approve or disapprove the decision of the county social services board regarding the county social services director's salary.[34] Neither the board of county commissioners nor the county manager, however, has any

---

30. G.S. 126-5(a)(2)b. The State Personnel Act, however, does not apply to a county's social services employees to the extent that the county's board of commissioners has established and implemented a personnel system that has been determined to be "substantially equivalent" to the state personnel requirements governing county social services employees. G.S. 126-11.

31. G.S. 126-9(a).

32. G.S. 153A-94.

33. G.S. 153A-92(d); G.S. 153A-93; G.S. 153A-96.

34. G.S. 108A-13.

authority to appoint or dismiss the county social services director or other employees of the county social services department.[35]

### Social Services Programs, Policy, and Administration

County commissioners have some authority and responsibilities with respect to social services policy and the administration of social services programs.

The board of county commissioners, for example, has the legal authority to undertake, sponsor, organize, engage in, and support optional or nonmandated social services programs to further the health, welfare, education, safety, comfort, and convenience of county residents; to contract with other government agencies, nonprofit or community organizations, or private businesses or individuals to provide social services to county residents.[36] State law also authorizes counties, acting by or with the approval of the board of county commissioners, to develop a single portal of entry, common data base, and consolidated case management system for social services and human services programs.[37]

The board of county commissioners is responsible for

- providing adequate facilities for the county social services department;
- determining whether the county social services department will be represented by the county attorney, by a staff attorney employed by the county or the county social services department, by retained counsel, or by a special county attorney for social services;[38]
- approving or adopting procedures for the approval of contracts involving the county social services department; and
- approving, with the county social services board, a schedule of fees that may be charged for certain services provided by the county department of social services.[39]

The board of county commissioners also is responsible for

---

35. G.S. 108A-12(a); G.S. 108A-14(a)(2).
36. G.S. 153A-255; G.S. 153A-259.
37. G.S. 153A-77.1.
38. *See* G.S. 108A-16.
39. G.S. 108A-10.

- determining which county agency (or private contractor) will administer the local child support enforcement program in counties in which state-administered child support programs are not operated;[40]
- determining whether the county will provide financial assistance to certain disabled persons under the optional "general assistance" provisions of the State-County Special Assistance program;[41]
- appointing a committee to develop the county's Work First plan;[42]
- approving the county's Work First plan;[43] and
- assisting in the development of outcome and performance goals for the Work First program.[44]

State law also authorizes a board of county commissioners to request, by a three-fifths vote of the board, the state to designate that county as an "electing" Work First county.[45] If a county is designated as an "electing" county, the board of county commissioners is responsible for

- designing, implementing, and administering the county's Work First program;
- establishing eligibility criteria and methods for calculating Work First Family Assistance benefits;
- determining the eligibility of families for Work First assistance;
- making Work First payments to eligible families;
- developing and implementing an appeals process for Work First recipients;
- establishing outcome and performance goals for the Work First program;
- monitoring and evaluating the impact of Work First on families and children; and
- providing monthly progress reports to the state Department of Health and Human Services.[46]

40. G.S. 110-141.
41. G.S. 108A-45.
42. G.S. 108A-27.6(c).
43. G.S. 108A-27.6(d).
44. G.S. 108A-27.6(a)(1).
45. G.S. 108A-27(e).
46. G.S. 108A-27.3. The board of county commissioners may delegate any or all of these responsibilities, except establishing outcome and performance measures,

Except as noted above, the board of county commissioners does not have any authority to adopt local policies for federal or federal–state social services programs administered by the county social services department or to supervise or control the administration of social services programs that are administered by the county social services director pursuant to state law.[47] The county commissioners, however, may require the county social services director to make periodic or special reports to the board of county commissioners or the county manager regarding the director's administration of social services programs.[48]

---

adopting the county Work First plan, and ensuring compliance with applicable federal and state rules for the Work First program, to any public or private entity, but remains accountable to the state for all of its responsibilities with respect to the Work First program. G.S. 108A-27.3(b).

47. *See* G.S. 108A-1; G.S. 108A-14(a)(3).

48. G.S. 153A-104.

# Chapter 6

# The County Social Services Board

---

County social services boards have played an important role in the governance and administration of social services agencies and programs in North Carolina for the past ninety years.[1]

---

1. County social services boards are discussed in greater detail in John L. Saxon, "The County Social Services Board (Part I): Introduction and Overview," *Social Services Law Bulletin* No. 32 (Chapel Hill: Institute of Government, The University of North Carolina at Chapel Hill, 2001); John L. Saxon, "The County Social Services Board (Part II): Qualifications and Disqualifications," *Social Services Law Bulletin* No. 33 (Chapel Hill: Institute of Government, The University of North Carolina at Chapel Hill, 2002); and John L. Saxon, "The County Social Services

The state's 1917 public welfare law authorized, but didn't require, the board of county commissioners in each North Carolina county to appoint a three-member county board of charities and public welfare.[2] In 1919 the law was amended to require the state Board of Charities and Public Welfare to appoint a county board of charities and public welfare for each county.[3] In 1941 these county boards were renamed county boards of public welfare.[4] And in 1969 they were renamed county boards of social services.[5]

Until the 1960s, county social services boards were involved, directly and significantly, in the administration of social services programs.[6] The nature and scope of the board's role during this period reflected the fact that county social services departments administered far fewer programs than today, provided services to far fewer people, employed far fewer staff, and were subject to far less oversight and control by the state.

Today, by contrast, social services boards are rarely involved in the administration of social services programs. Instead, the role of the county social services board primarily focuses on the general direction, oversight, and supervision of the county social services department.[7]

---

Board (Part III): Appointment, Terms, Term Limits, and Removal from Office," *Social Services Law Bulletin* No. 36 (Chapel Hill: Institute of Government, The University of North Carolina at Chapel Hill, 2002). *See also* John L. Saxon, *Serving on the County Board of Social Services* (Chapel Hill: Institute of Government, The University of North Carolina at Chapel Hill, 2001).

2. 1917 N.C. Pub. Laws ch. 170.

3. 1919 N.C. Pub. Laws ch. 46, § 2.

4. 1941 N.C. Pub. Laws ch. 270, § 2 (C.S. § 5014).

5. 1969 N.C. Sess. Laws ch. 546 (G.S. 108-7).

6. For example, until 1953, the county board of social services had the exclusive authority to approve or deny all applications for old age assistance and aid to dependent children (subject to eligibility requirements established by state law) and to determine the amount of assistance provided to elderly persons and children under these programs (subject to maximum payment amounts established by state law and subject to review by the board of county commissioners).

7. *See* Vaughn Upshaw, "Essential Responsibilities of Local Governing Boards," *Popular Government* 71(2):14–25 (2006); John Carver, *Boards That Make a Difference*, 3d ed. (San Francisco: Jossey-Bass, 2006).

## The Board's Legal Status

State law requires that every North Carolina county have a county board of social services.[8]

County social services boards are established by state law and derive their legal status, powers, and duties from statutes enacted by the North Carolina General Assembly. County boards of social services, however, are not political subdivisions, departments, agencies, or units of state government.[9]

Instead, the county social services board is a local (county) government board. Unlike a county or city, the social services board is not a "municipal or public corporation" or a "body corporate and politic."[10] Nor is it a "public authority" or "unit of local government" under North Carolina's Local Government Budget and Fiscal Control Act.[11] The social services board, instead, is a functional board that serves a single county and, therefore, is a constituent part of the county and the county's

---

8. G.S. 108A-1. Although state law allows the creation of multi-county boards of public health and multi-county mental health authority boards, it does not allow the creation of multi-county boards of social services. In counties with populations that exceed 425,000, the board of county commissioners may function as the county social services board or may establish a consolidated human services department and a consolidated human services board in lieu of a county social services department and board. G.S. 153A-77. These alternative social services governance models are discussed in the penultimate section of this chapter.

9. See Meyer v. Walls, 347 N.C. 97, 489 S.E.2d 880 (1997) (holding that a county social services department is not a department, institution, or agency of the state). Cf. G.S. 122C-116(a) (a multi-county area mental health authority is a political subdivision of the state).

10. Cf. G.S. 153A-11 (describing counties as bodies "politic and corporate"). A municipal or public corporation is a unit of local government that has corporate status (for example, the authority to sue, be sued, contract, and hold property in its own name and legal capacity separate and distinct from other persons, corporations, or entities). See David M. Lawrence, Local Government Finance in North Carolina, 2d ed. (Chapel Hill: Institute of Government, The University of North Carolina at Chapel Hill, 1990), 101.

11. G.S. 159-7. See also Lawrence, Local Government Finance in North Carolina, 100–105.

government,[12] rather than an independent or autonomous local government board.[13]

This does not mean, however, that the board of county commissioners has the same authority over the county social services board as it has with respect to other county boards, commissions, or agencies. Although state law gives the board of county commissioners broad legal authority to "create, change, abolish, and consolidate offices, positions, departments, boards, commissions, and agencies of the county government," the commissioners' authority under this statute does not extend to the abolition of any county board, department, or agency—such as the county social services board—that is "established or required by [state] law."[14]

## The Board's Legal Powers and Duties

The legal powers and duties of county social services boards are defined primarily by statutes enacted by North Carolina's General Assembly.[15] County social services boards are

- required to exercise the duties and responsibilities that are imposed on them by state law;[16]

---

12. *See* Lawrence, *Local Government Finance in North Carolina*, 101–102. Because county social services boards and departments are not considered municipal corporations, they cannot fall within the definitions of "unit of local government" or "public authority" under the Local Government Budget and Fiscal Control Act (LGBFCA).

13. *See* Avery v. Burke County, 660 F.2d 111 (4th Cir. 1981); Meares v. Brunswick County, 615 F. Supp. 14 (E.D.N.C. 1985); Malloy v. Daniel, 58 N.C. App. 61, 293 S.E.2d 285 (1982).

14. G.S. 153A-76. *See also* 52 Op. N.C. Att'y Gen. 44 (1982).

15. State law (G.S. 108A-9(5)) provides that the state Social Services Commission, the state Department of Health and Human Services (DHHS), and the board of county commissioners may assign additional duties and responsibilities to county social services boards. When the Social Services Commission or DHHS assigns additional duties and responsibilities to county social services boards, these additional duties and responsibilities may be specified in administrative rules (codified in the North Carolina Administrative Code) or other statements of policy or procedure.

16. *See* G.S. 108A-9. Legal duties or responsibilities are mandatory in nature, though social services boards have some discretion with respect to the manner in which they will discharge their mandated duties or responsibilities. Mandated duties or responsibilities that are imposed on county social services boards pursu-

- authorized to exercise the powers that are expressly granted to them under state law;[17]
- authorized to exercise any power that is reasonably necessary to enable them to exercise the powers that are expressly granted to them under state law and to discharge the duties that are imposed on them by state law, is reasonably implied by, or incident to, their express powers and duties, or is essential to the accomplishment of their purpose;[18]
- prohibited from exercising powers that are not granted to them by state law or that are granted to another public entity or official under state law; and
- required to comply with applicable provisions of federal and state law in the discharge of their powers and duties.[19]

In some instances, the social services board's power with respect to a particular matter is exclusive.[20] In other instances, the board's power is shared and must be exercised jointly with another public official, board, or agency.[21]

The legal powers and duties of county social services boards include

- appointing the "third" member of the county social services board;[22]

---

ant to state law, however, generally may not be delegated to another public entity or official.

17. County social services boards generally have the discretion to exercise or not exercise their legal authority or powers, as opposed to their legal duties or responsibilities, and, unless prohibited by law, may delegate their legal authority to another public entity or official.

18. A social services board, for example, has the implied authority to adopt rules of procedure for board meetings.

19. Some state laws apply specifically to county social services boards. Others, such as the Open Meetings Law, apply more generally to local government boards and, thus, to county social services boards.

20. The county social services board, for example, has the exclusive power to dismiss the county social services director, but must do so in accordance with the requirements and limitations of the State Personnel Act. G.S. 108A-12(a).

21. The social services board's decision regarding the social services director's salary, for example, must be approved by the board of county commissioners. G.S. 108A-13.

22. G.S. 108A-3(a), (b). This authority is exercised by the board members who have been appointed by the board of county commissioners and the Social Services Commission, rather than by the board as a whole. The "third" board member

- removing the "third" member of the social services board for "good cause" during his or her term;[23]
- electing the board's chair;[24]
- adopting rules of procedure for board meetings;
- meeting at least once per month, or more often if a meeting is called by the chair;[25]
- appointing the county social services director;[26]
- disciplining or dismissing the county social services director;[27]
- evaluating the social services director's performance;
- determining, with the approval of the board of county commissioners, the social services director's salary;[28]
- advising and consulting with the social services director about problems involving the social services director or department;[29]
- approving the board of county commissioners' appointment of the county attorney or a licensed attorney to serve as a special county attorney for social services matters;[30]
- assisting the county social services director in planning the social services department's proposed budget and transmitting or presenting the proposed budget to the board of county commissioners;[31]
- establishing county policies for social services programs that are consistent with applicable federal and state laws, rules, and policies;[32] and

---

is the board member who is appointed by the two, or four, social services board members who were appointed by the Social Services Commissioner and the board of county commissioners.

23. This authority is exercised by the board members who have been appointed by the board of county commissioners and the Social Services Commission, rather than by the board as a whole.

24. G.S. 108A-7.

25. *Id.*

26. G.S. 108A-9(1); G.S. 108A-12(a).

27. G.S. 108A-12(a).

28. G.S. 108A-13.

29. G.S. 108A-9(3).

30. G.S. 108A-16.

31. G.S. 108A-9(3), (4).

32. G.S. 108A-1.

- advising county and municipal authorities with respect to developing policies and plans to improve the community's social conditions.[33]

By contrast, state law does not give a county social services board the legal authority, power, or duty

- to hire, supervise, promote, discipline, or fire employees of the county social services department other than the director;
- to establish personnel policies for county social services employees;
- to determine the salary schedule and employment benefits for county social services employees;
- to approve or execute contracts involving the county social services department.

## Size and Composition of the Board

State law provides that a county social services board may consist of either three or five members, as determined by the board of county commissioners.[34]

Before 1963 almost all county social services boards consisted of three members. Today, almost all North Carolina counties have five-member boards of social services and only a few counties have three-member boards.

If a county has a three-member board of social services, the board of county commissioners may increase the size of the social services board from three to five members.[35] State law also allows the board of county commissioners to decrease the size of the county social services

---

33. G.S. 108A-9(2).

34. G.S. 108A-2.

35. If the county commissioners expand the social services board from three to five members, the commissioners appoint one additional social services board member for a term that expires at the same time as the term of the incumbent social services board member who was appointed by the state Social Services Commission; the state Social Services Commission appoints an additional social services board member for a term that expires at the same time as the term of the incumbent social services board member who was appointed by the board of county commissioners. The expansion of the social services board becomes effective when both of the additional social services board members have been appointed.

board from five to three members.[36] A resolution decreasing the size of the social services board from five to three members becomes effective on the first day of July following adoption of the resolution.[37] On that date, the following two seats on the county social services board cease to exist:

- the seat held by the social services board member appointed by the state Social Services Commission for a term expiring on June 30, 2007 (or triennially thereafter);
- the seat held by the social services board member appointed by the board of county commissioners for a term expiring June 30, 2008 (or triennially thereafter).[38]

State laws governing local public health, mental health, and human services boards specify the composition of those boards in great detail.[39] By contrast, the state laws governing county social services boards are virtually silent regarding the composition of these boards.[40] Instead, the only express requirement for appointment to the county social services board is that the appointee be a *bona fide* resident of the county.[41]

State law does not require that the social services board include a county commissioner, though at least one county commissioner serves on many, if not most, social services boards.

---

36. G.S. 108A-5(c).

37. *Id.* The commissioners' action to decrease (or increase) the size of the social services board is not subject to approval by DHHS, the state Social Services Commission, the county social services board, or the county social services director.

38. *Id.*

39. G.S. 130A-35, for example, requires that the composition of a county public health board "reasonably reflect the population makeup of the county" and include a physician, a dentist, an optometrist, a veterinarian, a registered nurse, a pharmacist, a professional engineer, a county commissioner, and three representatives of the general public.

40. A Social Services Commission rule formerly provided that county social services boards should include men and women from representative ethnic groups and from various geographical sections of the county. Former 10 N.C. ADMIN. CODE 24A .0302. The rule, however, was repealed effective March 1, 1990. More importantly, it is not at all clear that the state Social Services Commission has the legal authority to adopt rules regarding the composition of county social services boards or the qualifications of county social services board members. *See* N.C. Att'y Gen. Advisory Op. to Dr. Sarah Morrow (July 1, 1983).

41. *See* G.S. 108A-3(c). The legal qualifications required for appointment to the county social services board are discussed in the following section of this chapter.

The county social services director is the board's executive officer and acts as the board's secretary.[42] The social services director, however, is not a member of the county social services board.

## Appointment of Social Services Board Members

In counties that have three-member boards of social services, the board of county commissioners appoints one member of the county social services board, the Social Services Commission appoints one board member, and those two board members appoint the third board member.[43] In counties with five-member social services boards, the board of county commissioners and the state Social Services Commission each appoint two members of the social services board and those four board members appoint the remaining board member.[44]

Appointments to fill vacancies on the social services board caused by the death, resignation, or removal of a social services board member before the end of his or her term are made in the same manner as "regular" appointments to the board.[45]

When the Social Services Commission, a board of county commissioners, or county social services board members appoint a person to the social services board, the appointment must be made by majority vote in open session at an official meeting at which a quorum is present.[46]

Regular appointments to the county social services board are made on a three-year schedule, as indicated in Figure 6.1.[47]

---

42. G.S. 108A-14(a)(1).

43. G.S. 108A-3(a). The appointment by the other two board members must be unanimous. The incumbent "third" member of the board is not entitled to vote. If the other two board members cannot agree, the appointment is made by the senior resident superior court judge.

44. G.S. 108A-3(b). At least three of the other four board members must agree regarding the appointment of the "third" member. The incumbent "third" member of the board is not entitled to vote. If a majority of the other four board members cannot agree, the appointment is made by the senior resident superior court judge.

45. G.S. 108A-6.

46. *See* G.S. 143-318.11(6). The Open Meetings Law also prohibits the appointment of social services board members by "secret ballot." G.S. 143-318.13(b).

47. G.S. 108A-5.

## Figure 6.1  Appointment of Social Services Board Members

| Date of Appointment | Three-Member Board | Five-Member Board |
| --- | --- | --- |
| July 1, 2007 (and triennially thereafter) | County Commissioners (Board member No. 1) | County Commissioners (Board member No. 1) |
| | | Social Services Commission (Board member No. 4) |
| July 1, 2008 (and triennially thereafter) | Social Services Commission (Board member No. 2) | Social Services Commission (Board member No. 2) |
| | | County Commissioners (Board member No. 5) |
| July 1, 2009 (and triennially thereafter) | Social Services Board (Board member No. 3) | Social Services Board (Board member No. 3) |

State law does not specify the procedure through which the senior resident superior court judge should be asked to appoint the "third" social services board member when the two, or a majority of the four, social services board members appointed by the Social Services Commission and county commissioners are unable to agree regarding the appointment. Nor does it specify the procedure by which the judge should make the appointment. It seems clear, though, that the judge is not required to hold a public hearing with respect to the appointment, to make findings of fact or explain the basis for his or her decision, or to enter a court order making the appointment.

When the Social Services Commission, the board of county commissioners, the social services board members, or the senior resident superior court judge makes an appointment to the social services board, the action is final and may not be revoked or rescinded.[48]

### QUALIFICATIONS FOR APPOINTMENT TO THE BOARD

State law establishes only one, express legal qualification for appointment to the county social services board—that an appointee be a *bona fide* resident of the county on whose social services board he or she will

---

48. N.C. Att'y Gen. Advisory Op. to the North Carolina Board of Public Welfare (July 29, 1966).

serve.[49] Although state law does not specify what it means to be a *bona fide* resident, *bona fide* residence probably is equivalent to "legal residence" or "domicile," requiring actual residence in the county coupled with an intent to make the county one's home on a permanent, or at least indefinite, basis.[50]

State law gives boards of county commissioners the authority to establish "qualifications for any appointive office" within county government.[51] County commissioners, therefore, may establish additional qualifications for county social services board members, including social services board members who are appointed by the state Social Services Commission, by members of the social services board, or by a resident superior court judge, as long as those additional qualifications are not inconsistent with state law.

State law does not allow county social services boards, the state Social Services Commission, or the state Department of Health and Human Services to establish additional legal qualifications for county social services board members.[52]

Although county residency is the only legally required qualification for appointment to the county social services board, the Social Services Commission, board of county commissioners, social services board members, or senior resident superior court judge may, and should, consider a number of other factors, characteristics, and qualities when appointing individuals to the social services board. These factors, characteristics, and qualities are not, strictly speaking, additional qualifications for appointment to the county social services board, but

---

49. G.S. 108A-3(c). State law does not require a person to have been a county resident for any minimum period of time (for example, for one month or one year) before he or she may be appointed to the social services board.

50. *See* Hall v. Wake County Bd. of Elections, 280 N.C. 600, 606, 187 S.E.2d 52, 55 (1972).

51. G.S. 153A-25. In exercising this authority, however, the county commissioners may not waive any qualifications that are fixed by state law.

52. *See* N.C. Att'y Gen. Advisory Op. to Dr. Sarah Morrow (July 1, 1983). A Social Services Commission rule formerly provided that county social services board members should be public-spirited citizens with demonstrated concern for the social needs of the county, that social services board members should be people who have the time to attend board meetings regularly, and that social services board members should not be selected specifically to represent any organization and should not use their membership to promote the interest of political candidates or political groups. Former 10 N.C. ADMIN. CODE 24A .0302. The rule, however, was repealed effective March 1, 1990.

merely reflections of the standards, characteristics, and qualities that are desirable in persons who will serve on the social services board. For example, an appointing authority might expect persons who are appointed to the county social services board to be

- motivated by a sincere and demonstrated concern for the welfare of the citizens of their community;
- impartial, fair, open-minded, objective, and willing to listen to other points of view;
- critical and practical thinkers who can act independently, engage in creative problem-solving, and provide leadership and a sense of vision and direction for the county department of social services;
- able communicators who can work effectively and cooperatively with other board members, the county director of social services, the county commissioners, community groups, citizens, and state and local government agencies;
- honest and of unquestioned integrity; and
- willing to devote the time and effort necessary to fulfill the responsibilities of a board member.

## OATH OF OFFICE

As public officers, county social services board members are required to take an oath in which they swear or affirm that they will faithfully discharge the duties of their office and will support and maintain the constitutions and laws of the United States and of North Carolina.[53] Failure to take the oath, however, does not affect the validity of a social services board member's appointment or the actions he or she takes as a social services board member.

Although newly appointed social services board members often take their oaths of office at the first social services board meeting following the beginning of their terms, the oath may be taken at any time between the date a member is appointed and the date he or she assumes office after the beginning of his or her term. The oath of office may be administered anywhere within the state by a judge, a magis-

---

53. N.C. CONST. art. VI, § 7; G.S. 128-5. If a county social services board member is reappointed for a second consecutive term, he or she should take a new oath of office. A county commissioner who is appointed to serve ex officio on the county social services board generally is not required to take a separate oath of office as a social services board member.

trate, a clerk of superior court, a state legislator, a county or city clerk, a mayor, a chair of a board of county commissioners, a notary public, or other specified public officials.[54] A written copy of the oath subscribed by a newly appointed social services board member must be filed with the clerk of the board of county commissioners.[55]

## Term of Office

The "regular" term of office for all county social services board members—including county commissioners who are appointed ex officio to the social services board—is three years.[56]

Regular terms of county social services board members begin on July 1 (or on the date of appointment if the appointment is made after July 1) and end on June 30 of the third year thereafter.[57] If, however, an incumbent board member is not reappointed and no one is appointed to take his or her place on the board prior to the end of his or her term, the incumbent board member continues to hold office as a social services board member after June 30 and until he or she is reappointed or a successor is appointed and assumes office.[58]

When a person is appointed to fill a vacancy on the social services board resulting from the death, resignation, or removal of a social services board member before the end of the former board member's term, the newly appointed board member's appointment is for the remainder of the former board member's term.[59]

---

54. *See* G.S. 11-7.1.

55. G.S. 153A-26.

56. G.S. 108A-4. The term of a county commissioner who is appointed to the social services board is not concurrent with his or her term as a county commissioner, and his or her term on the social services board is unaffected by his or her continuation or termination in office as a county commissioner. John L. Saxon, "Stay or Go? County Commissioners on Social Services Boards," *Popular Government* 65(2) (Winter 2000): 30–31; State *ex rel.* Pitts v. Williams, 260 N.C. 168, 132 S.E.2d 329 (1963).

57. G.S. 108A-5.

58. *See* N.C. Const. art. VI, § 10.

59. G.S. 108A-6.

## Term Limits

State law provides that a person generally may not serve more than two consecutive three-year terms on the county social services board.[60]

The two-consecutive-term limit, however, does not apply to a social services board member who

1. was a county commissioner at any time during his or her first two consecutive terms on the social services board; and
2. is a county commissioner at the time he or she is reappointed to the social services board.[61]

## Removal from Office

North Carolina's social services law is silent with respect to the removal of county social services board members from office during their terms. Nonetheless, it is clear that, under general legal principles, a social services board member may be removed from office during his or her term if there is "good cause" to remove him or her from the board.

Good cause for removing a social services board member generally means a significant failure to perform the member's duties or other grounds that render the member's continuance in office contrary to the public interest, including

- conviction of a felony or a crime involving moral turpitude, even if the crime is unrelated to his or her official duties as a social services board member;
- bribery, corruption, extortion, or other criminal misconduct in office;
- other unlawful or grossly inappropriate conduct in office (including unlawful disclosure of confidential information);
- significant, persistent, or irreconcilable conflicts of interest;
- holding another public office that is incompatible with service on the social services board;
- misfeasance or malfeasance in office (willful or intentional neglect or failure to discharge official duties);

---

60. G.S. 108A-4. When a social services board member is appointed to serve the remainder of an unexpired term of a former board member, the unexpired term is not counted in applying the two consecutive term limit. G.S. 108A-6.
   61. G.S. 108A-104.

- neglect, inefficiency, or incompetence in performing official duties (including persistent, unexcused absences from board meetings);
- physical or mental incapacities that preclude the performance of official duties;
- any other act or omission that brings one's public office into disrepute or that significantly and detrimentally affects a member's ability to carry out his her official duties or that significantly and detrimentally affects the ability of the social services board, the county director of social services, or other government agencies to carry out their official duties.

On the other hand, good cause does not include

- differences between a board member's political affiliation or social, economic, or political views and those of the board of county commissioners, the Social Services Commission, the other members of the social services board, or the county director of social services;
- disagreements between a board member and the board of county commissioners, the Social Services Commission, the county director of social services, or other members of the county social services board about particular social services issues; or
- problems, difficulties, or personality clashes encountered in communicating, relating, or dealing with a board member that do not unduly disrupt the board's work.

Legal authority to remove a social services board member from office is vested in the commission, board, or public officials who appointed the board member (the "appointing authority").[62] The removal of a social services board member by an appointing authority is a quasi-judicial action that may be reviewed by a superior court judge through a writ of recordari or certiorari.[63] A social services board member who has been removed from office also may seek judicial review of his or her

---

62. This means, for example, that a social services board member who was appointed by the Social Services Commission may be removed only by the Social Services Commission, while a board member appointed by the county commissioners may be removed only by the board of county commissioners.

63. G.S. 1-269; Russ v. Brunswick County Bd. of Educ., 232 N.C. 128, 59 S.E.2d 589 (1950).

removal through a *quo warranto* proceeding (an action brought to try the successor's right to hold office) in superior court.[64]

## Multiple Office-Holding Limitations

County social services board members are subject to North Carolina's law regarding multiple office-holding.[65]

State law generally allows a person to hold concurrently

- one appointive office in state or local government and one elective office in state or local government; or
- two appointive public offices in state or local government.[66]

Because the position of county social services board member is an appointive public office in county government,[67] a county social services board member also may hold

- one elected office (such as city council member, school board member, county commissioner, register of deeds, sheriff, judge, or state legislator), or
- one additional appointed public office (such as public health director, public health board member, county manager, tax collector, military officer on active duty, or postmaster).[68]

---

64. G.S. 1-515 through G.S. 1-532; State *ex rel.* Pitts v. Williams, 260 N.C. 168, 132 S.E.2d 329 (1963).

65. Multiple office holding is discussed in more detail in A. Fleming Bell, II, *Ethics, Conflicts, and Offices: A Guide for Local Officials* (Chapel Hill, N.C.: Institute of Government, The University of North Carolina at Chapel Hill, 1997), 91–121.

66. G.S. 128-1.1.

67. *See* 40 Op. N.C. Att'y Gen. 571 (1969); 42 Op. N.C. Att'y Gen. 116 (1972); 44 Op. N.C. Att'y Gen. 342 (1975); 45 Op. N.C. Att'y Gen. 5 (1975); 60 Op. N.C. Att'y Gen. 50 (1990).

68. A social services board member's appointment to another local government board or committee (for example, the county Work First committee or a community child abuse prevention team) generally does not "count" in determining the number of offices he or she may hold if the responsibility of the other board or commission is purely advisory. Bell, *Ethics, Conflicts, and Offices*, 106–107; 40 Op. N.C. Att'y Gen. 572 (1969); 40 Op. N.C. Att'y Gen. 588 (1970). Regardless of the multiple office-holding limits, a county social services board member may not serve as the director, acting director, or interim director of the county social services department. Bell, *Ethics, Conflicts, and Offices*, 123–141 (discussing incompatible office-holding).

State law, however, also establishes a limited exception to these limits. Unless the resolution of appointment provides otherwise, the appointment by a board of county commissioners of one of its own members to another board or commission is considered an ex officio appointment and does not "count" as a separate appointed office in determining the number of appointed offices he or she may hold.[69] So, for example, a county commissioner could hold office as a county commissioner and, at the same time, serve as an ex officio member of both the county social services board and the public health board without violating the state's multiple office-holding rules.

If a person is appointed to the county social services board in violation of North Carolina's laws limiting multiple-office holding, his or her appointment to the board is absolutely and automatically null and void as a matter of law.[70]

### Ethics and Conflicts of Interest

The term "conflict of interest" generally refers to a conflict between an individual's personal, family, business, professional, or financial interests and his and her role, responsibilities, duties, or actions as a public official.

State law prohibits and punishes some conflicts of interest involving public officials. G.S. 14-234, for example, makes it a crime for a public official—including a county social services board member—to derive any "direct benefit" from a contract with a public agency if he or she is involved in "making or administering" the contract.[71] This particular provision, however, will rarely apply to county social services board members because social services boards have little or no authority

---

69. G.S. 128-1.2.

70. G.S. 128-2; 43 Op. N.C. Att'y Gen. 306, 308 (1974); Bell, *Ethics, Conflicts, and Offices*, 99–103.

71. G.S. 14-234 also makes it unlawful for a public official who derives a direct benefit from a contract with a public agency to attempt to influence any other person who is involved in making or administering the contract, and prohibits public officials from soliciting or receiving any gift or thing of value in exchange for recommending, influencing, or attempting to influence the award of a contract with the public agency he or she serves.

to make or administer contracts involving the county social services department.[72]

State law generally does not prohibit a social services board member or the board member's business or spouse from receiving payment for assistance or services that are provided to needy individuals and families through a program administered by the county social services department if

- the program is open to other providers of assistance or service on a nondiscriminatory basis;
- the agency does not have any control over the selection of providers by the agency's clients; and
- the amount of the payment is the same as that paid to other providers.[73]

Two statutes, however, expressly prohibit payments under the State–County Special Assistance and Medicaid programs on behalf of persons who are residents or patients in adult care or nursing homes that are owned or operated, in whole or in part, by a county social services board member or his or her spouse.[74] Although these statutes do not, strictly speaking, prevent the owner or operator of a nursing home or adult care home from serving on the social services board, they do so indirectly.

Similarly, a rule adopted by the Social Services Commission prevents some licensed foster parents from serving as county social services board members.[75] Under this rule, a county social services board member may not be licensed as a foster parent through the social services

---

72. If a social services board is involved in making or administering a contract involving the employment of a board member's spouse or payment of the board member or spouse for goods or services provided to needy persons served by the county social services department, the board member may avoid the conflict by refraining from participating in or attempting to influence the board's deliberations or action with respect to the contract. G.S. 14-234(b)(3), (b)(4), (b1); see also G.S. 14-234(d1).

73. See G.S. 14-234(b)(4); see also G.S. 14-234(b1).

74. G.S. 108A-47; G.S. 108A-55(d). These statutes also apply to adult care or nursing homes owned or operated by county commissioners, members of the state Social Services Commission, state and county social services employees, and the spouses of these persons. The statutes apply even if an individual operates a nursing home in county A and is appointed to the social services board in county B.

75. See 10A N.C. Admin. Code 41F .0702(j).

department in the county in which he or she lives, and may not be supervised or considered as a placement resource by his or her county's social services department. The rule, however, does not absolutely preclude the appointment of a foster parent to a county's social services board.[76]

## Compensation

Under state law, county social services board members are entitled to receive a per diem payment for the time they spend with respect to their duties as social services board members, and reimbursement for subsistence and travel expenses incurred as a result of their service as county social services board members.[77]

## The Board Chair

G.S. 108A-7 requires the county social services board, at its July meeting, to elect one of its members as the board's chair.[78] The social services board chair serves a term of one year (or until a new chair is elected).[79]

The board chair's powers and duties include

- presiding at social services board meetings;
- calling board meetings in addition to the board's regular monthly meeting;[80]
- appointing a social services board member to serve on the county's child protection or child fatality prevention team;[81] and

---

76. *See* 10A N.C. ADMIN. CODE 41F .0702(j)(5).

77. G.S. 108A-8. The board of county commissioners is responsible for determining the amount of the per diem payment for social services board members and county policies governing reimbursement for subsistence and travel.

78. The board's discussion of nominees for board chair and the election of the board chair must take place in open session at an official board meeting. A board member who has been nominated for board chair is not disqualified from voting in the election.

79. A board member who has been elected as board chair may be reelected for one or more additional, consecutive one-year terms as board chair.

80. *See* G.S. 108A-7.

81. G.S. 7B-1407(b)(6).

- exercising any other powers and duties (for example, preparing a proposed agenda for board meetings) specified under the board's rules of procedure.

Although state law does not require a social services board to elect a vice-chair, the board may do so if it wishes. If the board has elected a vice-chair, the vice-chair is generally authorized to preside at board meetings and exercise the board chair's powers and duties in the event of the chair's absence, disability, death, resignation, removal, or expiration of term.

If the board has not elected a vice-chair, or if the vice-chair and the chair are both absent or unable to perform the chair's duties, the remaining board members, by majority vote, may designate another board member to exercise the chair's powers and duties or authorize the social services director to preside at a social services board meeting.

## The Board's Relationship to the Director

State law provides that the county social services director is the social services board's secretary and executive officer.[82]

As the board's secretary, the social services director generally is responsible for taking minutes at social services board meetings.[83] The director's authority as the board's secretary does not include responsibility for preparing the proposed agenda for social services board meetings unless the board has directed the director to do so.

As the board's executive officer, the county social services director is generally responsible for executing the board's policies and directives and administering the county social services department and social services programs under the board's general supervision and oversight.[84]

---

82. G.S. 108A-14(a)(1). The county social services director, however, is not a member of the county social services board.

83. In practice, this responsibility generally is delegated to another social services employee who acts under the director's supervision. If the social services director is unable to attend a social services board meeting or is excluded from a closed session of a board meeting, the social services board or board chair may designate another social services board member or a social services employee to act as the board's secretary.

84. The legal powers and duties of the county social services director are discussed in more detail in Chapter 7. *See also* Carver, *Boards That Make a Difference* (providing one model for the relationship between a government or nonprofit

## Board Meetings and Rules of Procedure

State law requires the county social services board to meet at least once per month or more often if a meeting is called by the board chair.[85] The date, time, and place of the board's monthly meeting may be determined by a majority vote of the board or by the board chair if the board fails to do so.

### THE STATE OPEN MEETINGS LAW

All official meetings of the county social services board and any board committees are subject to the requirements of North Carolina's Open Meetings Law.[86] The Open Meetings Law requires a county social services board to:

- give public notice of all of its official meetings;[87] and
- allow members of the public to attend all of its meetings, except executive or closed sessions that are authorized under the Open Meetings Law.[88]

---

board and the director or chief executive officer of a government or nonprofit agency).

85. G.S. 108A-7. A board may adopt a policy under which special or additional board meetings will be called by the chair upon the request of one or more social services board members, by a majority of the social services board, or by the county social services director.

86. G.S. Ch. 143, Art. 33C. An official meeting occurs whenever a majority of a social services board's members meet, in person or by electronic means (such as a telephone conference call), in order to conduct a hearing, deliberate, take action, or transact public business. G.S. 143-318.10(d). *Deliberation* includes not only collective discussion, but also the collective acquisition and exchange of facts before a body makes a decision. A social services board cannot avoid the requirements of the Open Meetings Law simply by calling a meeting a "briefing session," "information session," "working session," or "retreat." But a *bona fide* social gathering or training session for social services board members is not an official meeting. The Open Meetings Law is discussed in more detail in David M. Lawrence, *Open Meetings and Local Governments in North Carolina*, 7th ed. (Chapel Hill: School of Government, The University of North Carolina at Chapel Hill, 2008).

87. G.S. 143-318.12. The Open Meetings Law does not allow the social services board to hold a secret meeting. Public notice must be given with respect to all official meetings of the board—even if the only subject that will be considered at a meeting is a subject that will be considered during an executive or closed session.

88. G.S. 143-318.10(a). The Open Meetings Law allows anyone to photograph or tape-record social services board meetings, other than closed sessions. The law, however, does not give the public the right to address a county social services board or participate in the board's deliberations. Nonetheless, at least some social

If a county social services board has a regular meeting schedule that provides that it will meet at the same time and place each month, it may comply with the public notice requirements of the Open Meetings Law by filing a notice with the clerk of the board of county commissioners stating the regular date, time, and place of the board's monthly meeting.[89] The Open Meetings Law does not require the social services board to file or post a copy of its proposed agenda for regular board meetings, but the board may make copies of its proposed agenda available to the press and public before its meetings if it chooses to do so.

If a board does not have a regular meeting schedule or if it meets at any time or place other than that specified in the regular meeting notice filed with the clerk, the meeting is considered a special meeting. The Open Meetings Law requires

- that public notice of a special meeting be given at least forty-eight hours before the meeting;
- that the notice state the date, time, place, and purpose of the special meeting; and
- that the notice be posted on the principal bulletin board of the county department of social services or at the door of the board's usual meeting place.[90]

Other requirements apply with respect to public notice of emergency and recessed board meetings.[91]

Under the Open Meetings Law, a social services board may exclude the public from a closed session of a board meeting when a closed session is required to

---

services boards set aside time during their meetings for comments and questions from the public.

89. G.S. 143-318.12(a). The board does not have to file this notice every month. If the board makes a permanent change with respect to the date, time, or place of its regular meetings, it must file a notice of its new schedule with the clerk at least seven calendar days before the next regular meeting to which the new schedule applies.

90. G.S. 143-318.12(b)(2). The notice also must be mailed, faxed, or delivered to each person or agency who has filed a written request with the board asking for notice of special board meetings.

91. G.S. 143-318.12(b)(1), (3).

- prevent the disclosure of privileged or confidential information that is protected under federal or state law;[92]
- preserve the attorney-client privilege with respect to consultations with the board's attorney;[93]
- consider the qualifications, competence, or performance of the county social services director, persons applying for appointment as the county social services director, or county social services employees;[94] or
- hear or investigate a complaint, charge, or grievance by or against the county social services director, a county social services employee, or another public officer or employee.[95]

A social services board, however, may not consider general personnel policy issues during a closed session; consider the qualifications, competence, performance, appointment, or removal of a social services board member during a closed session; or appoint or dismiss the county social services director during a closed session.[96]

In order to discuss a matter during a closed session, a board member must make, and the board must adopt during a public meeting of the board, a motion to meet in closed session.[97] The motion must state the statutory basis for meeting in closed session.[98]

When a social services board meets in closed session, it may not consider or discuss any matter other than that for which the closed session was called. All social services board members have the right to attend a closed session of the board. The board may allow the social services director, its attorney, or others to attend a closed session if their

---

92. G.S. 143-318.11(a)(1).

93. G.S. 143-318.11(a)(3). The board may not discuss general policy matters during a closed session, and the mere participation of the board's attorney at a board meeting is not a sufficient basis for a closed session.

94. G.S. 143-318.11(a)(6).

95. Id. G.S. 143-318.11 specifies several additional bases for holding a closed session.

96. G.S. 143-318.11(a)(6).

97. G.S. 143-318.11(c).

98. If the purpose of the closed session is to prevent the disclosure of privileged or confidential information, the motion must cite the law that makes the information confidential. If the purpose of a closed session is to discuss a pending lawsuit, the motion must identify the parties to the litigation.

presence will be useful to the board's discussion or consideration of the matter.

The Open Meetings Law requires that full and accurate minutes be kept of closed sessions.[99] The law also requires that the board prepare a "general account" of a closed session.[100] The minutes and general account of a closed session, however, may be withheld from public inspection for "so long as public inspection would frustrate the purpose of a closed session."[101]

## Quorum

Although state law does not expressly state the number of social services board members who must be present at a board meeting to conduct business or take action, most social services boards consider a quorum to be a majority of the board's membership (at least two members of a three-member board or at least three members of a five-member board) and some social services boards include their quorum requirements in their local rules of procedure.

If a quorum is not present, a social services board may meet, but it cannot transact any official business or take any official action as a board. If board members act without a quorum present, their actions are invalid unless subsequently ratified or confirmed by the board acting at a duly called meeting at which a quorum is present.

Absent a board policy to the contrary, an absent board member may participate in a social services board meeting via a telephone conference call or other electronic means and be counted as present for purposes of determining a quorum. An absent social services board member, however, may not vote by proxy.[102]

## Agenda and Order of Business

Unless otherwise provided by local rules, the proposed agenda for board meetings should be prepared by the board chair with input from the county social services director and members of the social services board. If possible, a copy of the proposed agenda and additional background information regarding proposed agenda items should be pro-

---

99. G.S. 143-318.10(e).
100. *Id.*
101. *Id.*
102. *See* 49 Op. N.C. Att'y Gen. 67 (1979).

vided to all board members at least two or three days before each board meeting.

By adopting and following an agenda, social services boards control

- what they discuss,
- how they discuss and act on matters that concern the board, and
- when they will discuss issues that concern the board.

The board's agenda may include a wide variety of subjects, issues, and other items, including

- reports from the director and staff;
- adoption of board policies and procedures;
- actions related to hiring, evaluating, or dismissing the social services director;
- discussion of issues affecting the county social services department; and
- discussion of social and economic problems affecting the community.

Every item on the board's agenda, however, should relate, in some way, to the board's role and responsibilities.[103]

Although some county social services boards may have had a tradition of beginning their meetings with a prayer or invocation, this practice may violate the U.S. Constitution's prohibition against state-establishment of religion.[104]

## MINUTES

"Full and accurate" minutes of social services board minutes must be preserved in writing or, at the board's option, in the form of sound or video recordings.[105]

When social services board minutes are kept in written form, they should be signed by the county social services director as the board's

---

103. When a social services board relies on the social services director to prepare the proposed agenda, it runs the risk that the agenda will focus on the director's job and responsibilities rather than the board's job and responsibilities.

104. A moment of silence at the beginning of board meetings during which individuals could silently reflect, meditate, or pray might not raise the same constitutional concerns.

105. G.S. 143-318.10(e).

secretary and note the date on which the minutes were approved by the board.[106]

At a minimum, the board's minutes must accurately reflect the substance of all actions taken by the board and the vote by which the action was taken. It is not necessary for the minutes to summarize the comments of each board member with respect to an issue. Nor is it necessary for the minutes to reflect the name of the board member who offered a motion or to record the names of the board members voting for or against a motion or proposal.[107] If the previously approved minutes of a board meeting are found to be incomplete or inaccurate, the board may, by majority vote, amend or correct the minutes to ensure that they are "full and accurate" as required by state law.

The minutes of social services board meetings are public records and must be made available for public inspection and copying under the state's Public Records Law, except to the extent that they contain privileged or confidential information that is protected from public disclosure under federal or state law.[108] An original set of the board's minutes must be preserved until they have no further official or historical value and their destruction is authorized pursuant to a records retention and disposition schedule established by the North Carolina Department of Cultural Resources and the county.

## RULES OF PROCEDURE

A county social services board has implicit legal authority to adopt rules of procedure governing its meetings, as long as its rules are not inconsistent with the requirements of the Open Meetings Law or other applicable state laws.

---

106. Although state law does not explicitly require that social services boards formally approve the minutes of their meetings, it is common, and good, practice to do so.

107. In some circumstances, though, it might be desirable to include this information in the minutes.

108. G.S. 132-1. As noted above, the Open Meetings Law permits a social services board to withhold from public inspection the minutes and general account of a closed session for "so long as public inspection would frustrate the purpose of a closed session." G.S. 143-318.10(e).

Other than the Open Meetings Law, however, state law provides little or no guidance regarding the procedures that govern meetings of the county social services board.[109]

Adopting written rules of procedure ensures a "level playing field" on which all social services board members have an equal and fair opportunity to participate in the board's business. When conflicts or crises arise, they can be resolved by reference to the board's rules rather than being decided on an ad hoc, arbitrary, or personal basis. Adopting and following rules of procedure also may facilitate the efficient functioning of a governing board.

Rules of procedure adopted by social services boards should be based on several fundamental principles:

- the board must act as a body;
- the board should proceed in the most efficient manner possible;
- the board must act by at least a majority vote;
- every board member must have an equal opportunity to participate in decision-making;
- the board's rules of procedure must be applied fairly and followed consistently;
- the board's actions should be the result of a decision on the merits and not a manipulation of procedural rules.[110]

Rules of procedure adopted by county social services boards generally should address the following subjects:

- Procedure for calling special board meetings
- Process for adopting the agenda for board meetings
- Public comment at board meetings
- Order of business at board meetings
- Election and responsibilities of the board chair (and vice-chair)
- Motions and voting
- Quorum
- Absences

---

109. The School of Government's suggested rules of procedure for small local government boards, however, may provide a useful starting point for developing rules of procedure for a county social services board. *See* A. Fleming Bell, II, *Suggested Rules of Procedure for Small Local Government Boards*, 2d ed. (Chapel Hill: Institute of Government: The University of North Carolina at Chapel Hill, 1998).

110. Bell, *Suggested Rules of Procedure for Small Local Government Boards*, 1.

- Minutes
- Appointment of the "third" board member
- Committees
- Amendment or revision of the rules

## Social Services Governance in Mecklenburg and Wake Counties

Under state law, counties with populations in excess of 425,000 (currently, Mecklenburg, Wake, and Guilford counties) may exercise social services governance through a county social services board established under G.S. 108A-1, through the board of county commissioners, or through a consolidated county human services board.[111]

### MECKLENBURG COUNTY

In 1984, acting under the authority granted by G.S. 153A-77(a), the Mecklenburg County Board of Commissioners adopted a resolution assuming the powers and duties of the county social services board. Since that time, Mecklenburg County has not had a separate county social services board,[112] and the board of county commissioners has been responsible for appointing the county social services director and exercising all of the other powers and duties that, in other counties, are exercised by the board of social services.

---

111. G.S. 153A-77. If it chose to do so, the General Assembly could amend G.S. 153A-77 to make its alternative social services governance models available to all North Carolina counties regardless of their populations, or make them applicable to other North Carolina counties that meet specific criteria with respect to population, location, or other factors.

112. G.S. 153A-77(a) provides that if the board of county commissioners assumes the powers and duties of the county social services board, it may appoint one or more advisory boards, committees, or councils to study social services issues, develop community support and cooperation with respect to social services programs, and advise the county commissioners with respect to social services matters. The county commissioners, however, may not delegate any of the commissioners' powers or duties regarding social services to these advisory boards, committees, or councils. 52 Op. N.C. Att'y Gen. 44 (1982). In Mecklenburg County, the board of county commissioners has established an advisory human services council to advise the board of county commissioners with respect to social services, public health, and mental health.

G.S. 153A-77(a), however, does not authorize a board of county commissioners

- to assume or exercise the statutory authority or responsibilities of the county social services director;
- to abolish, subdivide, consolidate, or reorganize the county social services department; or
- to assign the social services director's or department's statutorily mandated responsibilities or authority to other county agencies.[113]

## WAKE COUNTY

In Wake County, social services governance is exercised by a consolidated county human services board and the county manager under G.S. 153A-77(b).[114]

Wake County's consolidated human services board exercises all of the powers and duties formerly exercised by the county social services board (and the powers and duties formerly exercised by the county's public health and mental health boards) except the power to appoint and dismiss the county social services director.[115] Instead, Wake County's director of human services, who directs, administers, and supervises the county's consolidated human services agency, is appointed, and may be dismissed, by the county manager, with the advice and consent of the county's human services board.[116]

Members of Wake County's consolidated county human services board are appointed by the board of county commissioners upon nomination by the human services board and may serve a maximum of two consecutive four-year terms.[117] The human services board may not exceed twenty-

---

113. *See* 52 Op. N.C. Att'y Gen. 44 (1982).

114. G.S. 153A-77(b) was enacted by the General Assembly in 1996 at the request of Wake County's board of county commissioners based on a year-long human services "reengineering" process to study reorganization and streamlining of the county's human services agencies and programs. 1996 N.C. Sess. Laws ch. 690.

115. G.S. 153A-77(c).

116. G.S. 153A-77(d). The county human services director exercises the legal powers and duties formerly exercised by the county's directors of social services, public health, and mental health, and supervises a consolidated county human services agency that administers the programs and provides the services formerly administered or provided by the county's departments of social services, public health, and mental health. G.S. 153A-77(b)(3), (e).

117. G.S. 153A-77(c).

five members and must include a county commissioner, a psychiatrist, another licensed physician, a social worker, a psychologist, a registered nurse, consumers of human services (or public advocates for or relatives of human services clients), and persons representing other specified interests or professions.[118]

## The North Carolina Association of County Boards of Social Services

The North Carolina Association of County Boards of Social Services is a voluntary, private, nonprofit association of county social services boards, members of county social services boards, former social services board members, and other persons interested in local social services governance in North Carolina.[119]

The association's purposes, as set forth in its by-laws, are

- to serve as an advocate for the interests of county boards of social services, county departments of social services, employees of county departments of social services, and the clients of county departments of social services at the county, state, and federal levels of government;
- to plan, develop, and provide education and training programs for members of county boards of social services;
- to provide information to members of county boards of social services regarding issues affecting the administration and financing of public assistance and social services programs, and to provide a forum for the exchange of information and ideas among county boards of social services;
- to increase public understanding, acceptance, and support of public assistance and social services programs in North Carolina; and
- to promote closer working relationships between county boards of social services and county boards of commissioners, the state

---

118. G.S. 153A-77(c).

119. The vast majority, but not all, of North Carolina's county social services boards are members of the association. County social services boards, county social services board members, and others may become members of the association by submitting a membership application and paying an annual membership fee.

Social Services Commission, the state Department of Health and Human Services, and other public and private human services agencies and associations.[120]

The association publishes a newsletter and maintains a website for members, helps plan statewide education and training programs and conferences for county social services board members, and participates in several statewide human services coalitions and advocacy groups.

The association is governed by a board of directors consisting of a president, secretary, treasurer, and regional directors elected by the association's members. The association's annual business meeting generally is held each fall in conjunction with the annual Social Services Institute conference sponsored by the North Carolina Association of County Directors of Social Services.

---

120. N.C. Association of County Social Services Boards website at www.ncacbss.org (last visited April 14, 2008).

# Chapter 7

# The County Social Services Director

Every North Carolina county (except Wake County) has a county director of social services who is the head of the county department of social
services and the secretary and chief executive officer of the county
social services board.[1]

## Legal Status

The county social services director is a public official.[2]

---

1. *See* G.S. 108A-14. In Wake County, the county director of human services
exercises most of the powers and duties of the county social services director.
*See* Section 153A-77(e) of the North Carolina General Statutes [hereinafter G.S.];
G.S. 108A-15.1(c). State law authorizes two or more county social services boards
to employ one person to serve as the social services director of both (or all) of
the participating counties. G.S. 108A-12(b). Currently, no one serves as the social
services director for two or more counties.

2. *See* Eliason v. Cooper, 86 N.C. 236, 239–240 (1882) (defining "public official"). *See also* Hare v. Butler, 99 N.C. App. 693, 394 S.E.2d 231 (1990); Meyer v.
Walls, 122 N.C. App. 507, 471 S.E.2d 422 (1996), *aff'd.* 347 N.C. 97, 489 S.E.2d
880 (1997); Hobbs v. N.C. Dep't of Human Resources, 135 N.C. App. 412, 520
S.E.2d 595 (1999).

Although the county social services director acts as an agent of the state Department of Health and Human Services, the director is a county official and employee, not a state official or employee. Unlike the heads of most county departments, however, the county social services director is not appointed or directly supervised by the county manager or board of county commissioners and, instead, is primarily accountable to the county board of social services and to the state.

## Powers and Duties

The powers and duties of county social services directors are defined by state law.

In exercising his or her powers and duties, the director may delegate to one or more staff of the county social services department the authority to act as the director's representative and may limit the delegated authority of his or her representative to specific tasks or areas of expertise.[3] Ultimately, however, the county social services director remains responsible and accountable for the administration of the department and the actions of the department's staff.

### ADMINISTRATION OF SOCIAL SERVICES PROGRAMS

The county social services director is responsible for administering the state and federal–state social services programs established by Chapter 108A of the General Statutes [hereinafter G.S.] in accordance with applicable federal and state rules.[4] State law also expressly authorizes or requires the county social services director to

- assess reports of child abuse and neglect and take appropriate action to protect abused, neglected, or dependent children pursuant to North Carolina's Juvenile Code;[5]

---

3. G.S. 108A-14(b).

4. G.S. 108A-14(a)(3). These programs include, but are not limited to, Work First, Medicaid, Food and Nutrition Services (Food Stamps), State–County Special Assistance, Low-Income Energy Assistance, and Foster Care and Adoption Assistance. In "electing" counties, the board of county commissioners may direct that the Work First program be administered by a public official or public or private entity other than the county social services director and department. G.S. 108A-27(f); G.S. 108A-27.3(b).

5. G.S. 108A-14(a)(11). *See also* G.S. 7B-300; G.S. 7B-302; G.S. 7B-307; G.S. 7B-320; G.S. 7B-304; G.S. 7B-500.

- accept children for placement in foster homes and supervise foster care placements;[6]
- investigate proposed adoptive placements and supervise adoptive placements;[7]
- file legal proceedings seeking termination of parental rights with respect to certain juveniles placed in the custody of the department of social services;[8]
- receive and evaluate reports of abuse, neglect, or exploitation of disabled adults and take appropriate action to protect disabled adults from abuse, neglect, or exploitation;[9]
- supervise the operation of adult care homes;[10]
- conduct and make decisions in local hearings in appeals by persons who have applied for or are receiving public assistance or social services;[11]
- review requests for expunction from the list of persons who have been determined to be responsible for the abuse or serious neglect of a juvenile;[12]
- administer the state program of aid for the blind if requested by the board of county commissioners;[13]
- administer the county's child support enforcement program if designated by the board of county commissioners;[14] and
- act as the agent of the state Social Services Commission and the state Department of Health and Human Services with respect to their work in the county.[15]

---

6. G.S. 108A-14(a)(12). *See also* G.S. 7B-505; G.S. 7B-903; G.S. 7B-904; G.S. 7B-905; G.S. 7B-910; G.S. 7B-1905; G.S. 7B-2503; G.S. 7B-2506.

7. G.S. 108A-14(a)(6); G.S. 108A-14(a)(13). *See also* G.S. 48-1-109; G.S. 48-2-501; G.S. 48-3-201; G.S. 48-3-203; G.S. 48-3-204; G.S. 48-3-303; G.S. 48-3-309; G.S. 48-3-601.

8. G.S. 7B-1103.

9. G.S. 108A-14(a)(14). *See also* G.S. 108A-103 through G.S. 108A-106; G.S. 108A-108; G.S. 108A-109.

10. G.S. 108A-14(a)(8). *See also* G.S. 131D-2(b); G.S. 131D-26.

11. G.S. 108A-79(f).

12. G.S. 7B-321.

13. G.S. 111-35.

14. G.S. 110-130; G.S. 110-130.1(c); G.S. 110-141. *See also* G.S. 49-5; G.S. 49-16(2).

15. G.S. 108A-14(a)(5).

## Budget Preparation and Administration

State law requires the county social services director to develop, with the assistance of the county social services board, a planned budget for the county department of social services.[16] State law also provides that the county social services director is responsible for administering funds provided by the board of county commissioners for the care of indigent county residents under policies approved by the county social services board.[17]

## Approval and Execution of Contracts

North Carolina's General Statutes do not expressly authorize county social services directors to enter into contracts on behalf of the county social services department.[18] A county social services director, however, may enter into or execute a contract on behalf of the county or the county social services department if authorized to do so under a county ordinance or policy or pursuant to a specific state rule.

## Social Services Board's Secretary and Executive Officer

The county social services director is the secretary and executive officer of the county social services board.[19]

At a minimum, the director's responsibilities as the board's secretary include taking minutes at the board's meetings, preparing proposed minutes for the board's approval, and maintaining custody of the official minutes of the board.[20] If directed by the board or board chair, however, the director also may perform additional secretarial duties,

---

16. G.S. 108A-9(3). *See also* G.S. 108A-88. The budget of the county social services department, however, must be approved by the board of county commissioners as part of the county budget ordinance adopted in accordance with the Local Government Budget and Fiscal Control Act (LGBFCA). County social services budgets and funding are discussed in more detail in Chapter 12.

17. G.S. 108A-14(a)(4). The county social services department's budget, however, must be administered in accordance with the LGBFCA. County social services budgets and funding are discussed in more detail in Chapter 12.

18. *Cf.* G.S. 130A-41(a)(13) (authorizing local health directors to enter into contracts on behalf of local health departments subject to the authority of the board of county commissioners and in accordance with the LGBFCA).

19. G.S. 108A-14(a)(1).

20. In practice, the county social services director usually delegates these responsibilities to his or her administrative assistant or another county social services employee.

such as ensuring that proper public notice of county social services board meetings is given; maintaining copies of the board's policies, procedures, correspondence, and other official records; distributing reports and information to board members; facilitating communication among board members and between the board and other public officials or agencies; and notifying appropriate state or local authorities when there is a vacancy on or appointment to the county social services board.

As the board's executive officer, the director is responsible for implementing the board's policies and directives, assisting the board in discharging the board's powers and duties if requested to do so, and serving as the head of the county department of social services.

### APPOINTMENT, SUPERVISION, DISCIPLINE, AND DISCHARGE OF COUNTY SOCIAL SERVICES EMPLOYEES

The county social services director has exclusive authority to appoint, supervise, promote, discipline, and discharge all employees of the county social services department.[21] The director's authority to appoint, discipline, or discharge county social services employees, however, must be exercised in accordance with the requirements of the State Personnel Act and other applicable federal and state laws.[22]

### OTHER POWERS AND DUTIES

State law also authorizes or requires county social services directors to

- serve as the guardians of incompetent adults when required to do so by the clerk of superior court;[23]
- serve as the temporary guardian of minor children who are abandoned or have no natural guardians and need services from the county social services department;[24]

---

21. G.S. 108A-14(a)(2). *See also In re* Brunswick County, 81 N.C. App. 391, 344 S.E.2d 584 (1986) (holding that the county social services board has no authority to hire or fire county social services employees even in instances in which the department is headed by an "acting" or "interim," rather than a "permanent," county social services director).

22. The appointment, supervision, discipline, and discharge of county social services employees is discussed in more detail in Chapter 8.

23. G.S. 108A-15; G.S. 35A-1201(4); G.S. 35A-1213(d).

24. G.S. 35A-1220.

- serve on local community child protection and child fatality prevention teams;[25]
- arrange for the burial or cremation of unclaimed bodies of deceased persons;[26]
- issue certificates authorizing the employment of youth between the ages of twelve and eighteen in accordance with applicable federal and state child labor laws;[27]
- serve on the county's juvenile crime prevention council;[28]
- serve on the drug court treatment management committee for a judicial district if appointed by the district's senior resident superior court judge;[29]
- assist the state Department of Correction in the supervision of paroled ex-prisoners upon request by the state Post-Release Supervision and Parole Commission;[30] and
- perform functions specified under local emergency management plans.[31]

## Qualifications

The minimum education and experience qualifications for county social services directors are established by North Carolina's Office of State Personnel (OSP).

These qualifications for county social services directors currently require

- a master's degree in social work and two years of supervisory experience in the delivery of client services;[32]

---

25. G.S. 7B-1407(b)(1); G.S. 7B-1409.

26. G.S. 130A-415.

27. G.S. 95-25.5; G.S. 108A-14(a)(7).

28. G.S. 143B-544(a)(7).

29. G.S. 7A-796(11).

30. G.S. 148-56; G.S. 108A-14(a)(9).

31. *See* G.S. 166A-7.

32. If a social services director does not meet these requirements, he or she must have a bachelor's degree in social work and three years of supervisory experience in the delivery of client services, one of which must have been in social services; have graduated from a four-year college or university and have had at least three years of supervisory experience in the delivery of client services, two of which must have been in social services; or have an equivalent combination of training and experience.

- a thorough knowledge of the legal and philosophical basis for public welfare programs;
- considerable knowledge of principles and practice of social work;
- a thorough knowledge of management principles, techniques, and practices;
- knowledge of the agency's organization, operation and objectives and applicable federal and state laws, rules, and regulations;
- the ability to exercise sound judgment in analyzing situations and making decisions;
- the ability to direct employees and programs in the various areas of responsibility; and
- the ability to develop and maintain effective working relationships with the general public, and with federal, state, and local officials.[33]

## Recruitment and Appointment

The county social services board has the exclusive authority to appoint the county social services director.[34] In appointing the social services director, however, the board must follow the procedures specified by the State Personnel Act and rules adopted by the State Personnel Commission.[35]

The social services board may appoint an acting or interim social services director if the director's position is vacant and the board is unable to fill the director's position immediately.[36]

County social services boards should always consult with and request assistance from the county's personnel or human resources office or the local government staff of the Office of State Personnel to ensure that

---

33. N.C. Office of State Personnel website at www.osp.state.nc.us/ CLASS_SPECS/Spec_Folder_09000-09999/PDF_Files/09929.pdf (last visited April 14, 2008).

34. G.S. 108A-9(1); G.S. 108A-12.

35. *See* 25 N.C. ADMIN. CODE 01I .1901 through 01I.1905.

36. *See* 25 N.C. ADMIN. CODE 01I .2002(d) and (g). An emergency appointment generally may not exceed sixty work days. A temporary appointment generally may not exceed twelve months. An incumbent county social services board member may not serve as the acting or interim director of social services. The acting or interim social services director has the same powers and duties as a permanent social services director. *See In re* Brunswick County, 81 N.C. App. 391, 344 S.E.2d 584 (1986).

the board's process for advertising the position, screening applications, interviewing applicants, and selecting a new social services director complies with applicable requirements of federal and state law and enables board members to make informed judgments about applicants and to identify the most qualified applicants for the position.[37] State rules require that the board's procedures for recruiting and selecting a new county social services director be validly related to the duties and responsibilities of the director's position and applied consistently to all applicants.[38] State rules also require that the board's selection of a social services director be based upon a relative consideration of the qualifications of the applicants for the position and that the board adequately document the basis for the board's decision regarding the selection and appointment of the county social services director.[39]

Although the county social services board may discuss the qualifications of applicants for the director's position during closed session, the board's decision to appoint an individual as the county social services director must be made during an open session of an official board meeting.[40]

Individuals who are appointed as county social services directors generally are required to serve a probationary appointment of three to nine months.[41]

## Salary

State law provides that the salary of the county social services director is determined by the county social services board with the approval of the board of county commissioners.[42] The director's salary, however, must fall within the county's state-approved salary plan and schedule for county social services employees, which must establish a minimum

---

37. *See* Kurt Jenne and Margaret Henderson, "Hiring a Director for a Nonprofit Agency: A Step-by-Step Guide," *Popular Government* 65(4) (Summer 2000): 25.

38. 25 N.C. ADMIN. CODE 01I .1905(a).

39. *Id.*

40. G.S. 143-318.11(a)(6).

41. 25 N.C. ADMIN. CODE 01I .2002(a). County social services boards should verify the credentials and check the references of an individual who is appointed as the county social services director before the individual is appointed or, if this is not possible, before the expiration of the probationary period. *See* 25 N.C. ADMIN. CODE 01I .1905(a)(2); G.S. 126-30(b).

42. G.S. 108A-13.

salary that is at least 20 percent and not more than 60 percent more than the minimum salary for the highest position (other than deputy director or attorney) supervised by the director.[43]

In 2007 the annual salaries of county social services directors in North Carolina ranged from approximately $52,000 to approximately $164,000.[44]

## Supervision and Evaluation

The county social services director is directly accountable to the county social services board. And the board, in turn, is responsible for providing general supervision of the director and general oversight of the county social services department. State law, therefore, expressly requires the board to advise or "consult with" the director about "problems" relating to the director's office or the department.[45] But the board does not have the authority to overrule the director's decisions or interfere with the director's management of the department when state law vests authority for the department's management or administration in the director.

The county social services board also has the implied legal authority or responsibility to evaluate the director's performance and to develop a process for evaluating the director's performance.[46]

## Dismissal

The county social services board has the exclusive authority to discipline or dismiss (fire) the county social services director.[47] County social

---

43. N.C. Office of State Personnel website at www.osp.state.nc.us/ExternalHome/ Group5/LocalGovmt/0809SalaryReporting/Guidelines%20for%20Submission%20 of%20Local%20Salary%20Plans%202008-2009.pdf (last visited April 14, 2008).

44. *County Salaries in North Carolina 2008* (Chapel Hill: School of Government, The University of North Carolina at Chapel Hill, 2008), available at www.sog.unc .edu/pubs/electronicversions/pdfs/cosal2008/health.pdf.

45. G.S. 108A-9(3).

46. Procedures for evaluating the director's performance are discussed in Margaret S. Carlson, "How Are We Doing? Evaluating the Performance of the Chief Administrator," *Popular Government* 59(3) (Winter 1994): 24; and Margaret S. Carlson, "Board-Manager Performance Evaluations: Questions and Answers," *Popular Government* 62(4) (Summer 1997): 50.

47. *See* G.S. 108A-12(a).

services directors who have obtained "career" status may be disciplined or dismissed only for "just cause."[48]

In addition, social services boards must follow the procedures set forth in the State Personnel Act and State Personnel Commission rules when disciplining or dismissing a county social services director. If the board disciplines or dismisses a social services director who has attained "career" status, the director may appeal the board's decision to the State Personnel Commission and seek judicial review in superior court of a final board decision regarding disciplinary action or dismissal.[49]

## The North Carolina Association of County Directors of Social Services

The North Carolina Association of County Directors of Social Services was established in 1976. Membership in the association is open to all county social services directors.

The association works in cooperation with the state Department of Health and Human Services, the North Carolina Association of County Commissioners, the North Carolina Association of County Boards of Social Services, and a wide range of other public and private agencies to help county social services departments respond to the challenges facing the individuals and families that they serve and to address public policies affecting social services agencies and programs.[50]

The association sponsors the Social Services Institute, an annual conference and training event for county social services directors and employees of county social services departments.

The association employs a staff and maintains an office in Raleigh.

---

48. *See* G.S. 126-1.1 (as amended by SL 2007-372, superseding the decision in Early v. Durham County Department of Social Services, 172 N.C. App. 344, 616 S.E.2d 553 (2005) and G.S. 126-35(a)). A county social services director or employee attains "career" status if he or she is in a permanent position and has been continuously employed by the state or a county agency subject to the State Personnel Act for a period of at least twenty-four months immediately prior to being disciplined or dismissed. "Just cause" for disciplining or dismissing county social services employees is discussed in Chapter 8.

49. G.S. 108A-12(a); G.S. 126-34.1(a)(1). These procedures are discussed in Chapter 8.

50. N.C. Association of County Directors of Social Services website (www.ncacdss.org).

# Chapter 8

# The County Department of Social Services

Ninety-nine of North Carolina's one hundred counties have a county department of social services that operates under the direction and supervision of the county social services director and administers public assistance and social services programs in accordance with state law under the general supervision of the state Department of Health and Human Services.[1]

The functions, powers, and responsibilities of county social services departments are specified by state law. In some cases, these statutes expressly refer to the "county department of social services." For example, Section 108A-25 of the North Carolina General Statutes

---

1. In Wake County, the responsibilities of the county social services department are exercised by a consolidated human services department that operates under the direction of a county human services director. *See* G.S. 108A-15.1(c).

[hereinafter G.S.] and G.S. 108A-27.6 authorize or require the county department of social services to administer several social services programs.[2] In other instances, these laws refer to the powers or duties of the county social services director, rather than the county social services department, but recognize, explicitly or implicitly, that the director will hire and supervise employees of the county social services department and that the director's powers and duties will be delegated to and exercised by the staff of the county social services department.[3]

Because county social services departments are required to administer state and federal–state social services programs in accordance with federal and state requirements and procedures and under the supervision of state social services agencies, there is a significant degree of statewide uniformity and consistency with respect to the types of services provided by county social services departments and the manner in which these services are provided. County social services departments, however, do vary somewhat with respect to the type and scope of the services they provide, how they provide the services to county residents, how they are structured or organized, and the size of their staffs and budgets.

## Purpose and Mission

The primary function of the county social services department is to administer state and federal–state social services programs for the benefit of county residents.[4] The purpose or mission of county social services departments, however, goes far beyond the efficient administration of social services programs. The Catawba County Department of Social Services, for example, has defined its mission as improving the quality of life for county residents by preventing social problems; protecting adults, children and families from abuse and neglect; ensuring that children have permanent families; enabling adults and older foster children to become self-sufficient; ensuring that parents financially support their children; giving elderly and disabled persons a choice

---

2. *See also* Section 48-1-101 of the North Carolina General Statutes [hereinafter G.S.] (placement for adoption) and G.S. 131D-26 (monitoring of adult care home licensure requirements).

3. *See* G.S. 108A-14(a) and G.S. 108A-14(b).

4. Public assistance and social services programs are discussed in more detail in Chapter 11.

to remain in their homes rather than enter an adult care or nursing home; and connecting needy individuals and families with food, shelter, utilities, and medical attention.[5]

## Legal Status

Like other county departments or agencies, the county department of social services is a part of county government—not a separate or independent unit of local government.[6] This means that, absent specific statutory authorization, the county social services department does not have the legal capacity to sue or be sued in its own name, to enter into contracts in the department's name, to own property in the department's name, or to receive and spend money as a legal entity separate and apart from the county. Instead, legal proceedings involving the county social services department generally should be brought by or against the county and in the county's name.[7] Similarly, contracts involving the county social services department generally should be executed in the county's name, rather than the department's, and property purchased for the county social services department should be titled in the county's name, rather than the department's. And because the county social services department is not a separate unit of local government, its budget and expenditures are subject to approval by the county commissioners under the Local Government Budget and Fiscal Control Act (LGBFCA).[8]

Like other county departments and agencies, the county social services department is subject to the general oversight and direction of the board of county commissioners and county manager and, except as otherwise provided by state law, is subject to the same county ordinances, policies, and procedures that govern the operation and administration of other county departments and agencies.

---

5. Catawba County Department of Social Services website at www.catawbacountync.gov/dss/Mission.asp (last visited April 14, 2008).

6. *See* Malloy v. Durham County Dep't of Social Services, 58 N.C. App. 61, 293 S.E.2d 285 (1982); Meyer v. Walls, 347 N.C. 97, 489 S.E.2d 880 (1997); Craig v. Chatham County, 143 N.C. App. 30, 545 S.E.2d 455 (2001).

7. Some statutes authorize the county social services director to bring a legal proceeding in the director's name and capacity as a public official or through the county social services department.

8. The social services budget process is discussed in detail in Chapter 12.

In some respects, however, the county social services department is
unlike most other county departments and agencies. Unlike most other
county departments, the county social services department may not be
abolished by the board of county commissioners, nor may the county
commissioners merge the social services department with another
county department or agency or transfer any of the department's functions, powers, and duties to another county department or agency.[9]
Unlike most other department heads, the county social services director
is appointed and may be dismissed by the county social services board,
not by the county manager or county commissioners.[10] And unlike most
other county employees, employees of the county social services department are subject to the State Personnel Act and may be appointed
(employed) and may be dismissed (fired) only by the county social services director, not by the county manager or county commissioners.[11]

## Multi-County Social Services Agencies

State law authorizes two or more county social services boards to
establish a joint, multi-county social services agency operating under
the direction and supervision of a single social services director who
is appointed jointly by the participating social services boards.[12] Currently, however, there are no joint, multi-county social services agencies
in North Carolina.

## Consolidated Human Services Agencies

State law allows the board of county commissioners of a county with a
population in excess of 425,000 to create a consolidated county human
services agency that exercises the functions that otherwise would be
exercised by the county's social services department, health department, and mental health, developmental disabilities, and substance

---

9. *See* G.S. 153A-76.

10. *See* G.S. 108A-12(a). *Cf.* G.S. 153A-82(1) and G.S. 153A-87.

11. *See* G.S. 126-5(a)(2)b; G.S. 108A-14(a)(2). *Cf.* G.S. 153A-82(1) and
G.S. 153A-87. Personnel policies governing county social services employees are
discussed in a subsequent section of this chapter.

12. *See* G.S. 108A-12(b); G.S. 160A-462 through G.S. 160A-466. The creation of
a multi-county social services agency also would require the approval and cooperation of the boards of county commissioners of the participating counties.

abuse authority.[13] Wake County is the only North Carolina county that has created a consolidated human services agency under this law.

## Facilities and Offices

Each county is required to provide adequate physical facilities for the offices of the county social services department as well as adequate furnishings and equipment for the department's use. All facilities occupied by county departments of social services must meet certain state standards with respect to the types and amount of office space, privacy, accessibility, and storage.[14]

The size, location, and condition of office facilities of county social services departments, however, vary greatly from county to county. In some counties, the department of social services is located in a publicly owned building. Other counties lease office space for the social services department. In some counties, the social services department shares a facility with other county departments or offices. In other counties, the department occupies a separate building. In most counties, the social services department is located in one, central facility. Some county social services departments, however, operate one or more additional satellite or outreach offices.

State law allows the board of county commissioners to prescribe the office hours, workdays, and holidays observed by county departments of social services.[15] The board of county commissioners also has the authority to prohibit smoking in buildings occupied by the county social services department.[16]

## Organizational Structure

The county department of social services consists of the county social services director and all individuals who are appointed or supervised by the director.

---

13. *See* G.S. 153A-77(b)(3).

14. 10A N.C. Admin. Code 67A .0103.

15. *See* G.S. 153A-94(b). The board of county commissioners, however, usually delegates authority regarding the office hours for county social services departments and employees to the county manager, the county social services director, or the county social services board.

16. *See* G.S. 130A-498 and G.S. 143-599(5).

The county social services director is the head of the county social services department and is responsible for the department's overall operation and administration, for administering the funds appropriated for the department by the board of county commissioners, and for appointing and supervising the department's employees.[17]

Because state law does not mandate a uniform, statewide organizational structure for county social services departments, the administrative structure and organization of county social services departments varies somewhat from county to county.

State law, however, does require that all county social services departments separate their "income maintenance" functions from their "social services" functions.[18] And as a result of this requirement, all county social services departments are formally or informally subdivided into at least two administrative or organizational parts:

- an income maintenance (or "economic services") unit, section, or division; and
- a social services (or "adult, family, and children's services") unit, section, or division.

The organizational structure of smaller social services departments is relatively simple. In Tyrrell County, for example, the county social services department is informally subdivided into two parts—one that is responsible for Food and Nutrition Services (or Food Stamps), Medicaid, and financial assistance cases and the other that is responsible for other social services and administrative support. The department's Medicaid and Food Stamp eligibility workers are directly supervised by two income maintenance supervisors who, in turn, are supervised by the county social services director. The social services director directly supervises the department's two social workers, child day care coordinator, and three clerical workers.

---

17. *See* G.S. 108A-14(a)(2), G.S. 108A-14(a)(3), G.S. 108A-14(a)(4), and G.S. 108A-14(b).

18. *See* 10A N.C. Admin. Code 67A .0102. This means, at a minimum, that social services employees who provide child protective services, adult protective services, or other social services to individuals and families may not determine whether individuals and families are eligible for Food and Nutrition Services, Medicaid, Work First Family Assistance, and other financial assistance programs.

The organizational structure and management systems of mid-sized and large social services departments are more complex. See Figure 8.1. Some departments employ a deputy (or assistant) social services director who is responsible for one or more of the department's divisions or sections and for managing the department during the director's absence. Others employ assistant directors or program or services managers who are responsible for managing particular divisions or sections of the department. Some mid-sized and large departments establish a separate administrative services office that is responsible for matters involving personnel, budget, contracting, and information technology or employ departmental finance or personnel officers. Many mid-sized and large social services departments have one section that provides social services for adults and a separate section that provides social services for children and families, as well as separate sections for particular programs such as Medicaid or child support enforcement. And many of these departments create smaller teams, units, or subdivisions within their primary sections to perform specialized functions, such as case intake, case review, quality assurance, investigation, prevention, or placement.

By way of example, the organizational and management structure of the Forsyth County Department of Social Services is typical of that of many mid-sized or large social services departments. It consists of the county social services director, an assistant director, a human services planner, a staff development and training coordinator, a business office, an information technology office, a human resources office, an adult services division, a family and children's services division, and a temporary economic assistance and maintenance division. Each of the three major divisions is headed by a division director and is subdivided into sections or units that are headed by program managers or supervisors.

The department's adult services division includes units that investigate reports regarding the abuse, neglect, or financial exploitation of disabled adults, monitor the compliance of adult care homes with state licensing requirements, provide guardianship services to incapacitated adults, determine whether elderly or disabled individuals are eligible for Medicaid, provide in-home aides for disabled adults who need assistance with activities of daily living in order to remain in their homes, and assist elderly or disabled adults and their families in identifying appropriate placements in adult care or nursing homes in the community.

**Figure 8.1 Organizational Structure of a Large County Social Services Department**

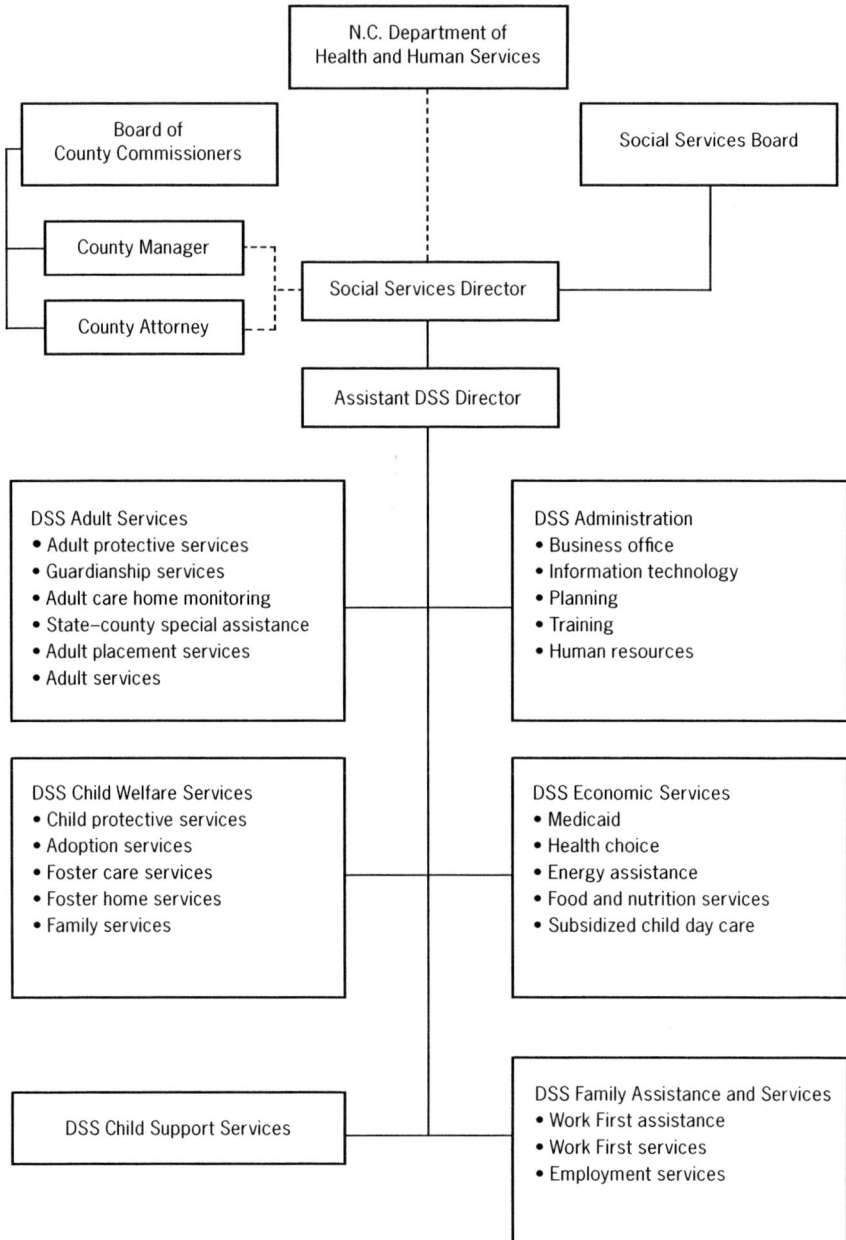

```
                        ┌─────────────────────────┐
                        │  N.C. Department of      │
                        │  Health and Human Services│
                        └─────────────────────────┘

┌──────────────────┐                              ┌──────────────────┐
│ Board of         │                              │ Social Services  │
│ County Commissioners│                           │ Board            │
└──────────────────┘                              └──────────────────┘

┌──────────────────┐      ┌──────────────────────┐
│ County Manager   │      │ Social Services Director│
└──────────────────┘      └──────────────────────┘
┌──────────────────┐
│ County Attorney  │
└──────────────────┘
                          ┌──────────────────────┐
                          │ Assistant DSS Director│
                          └──────────────────────┘
```

**DSS Adult Services**
- Adult protective services
- Guardianship services
- Adult care home monitoring
- State–county special assistance
- Adult placement services
- Adult services

**DSS Administration**
- Business office
- Information technology
- Planning
- Training
- Human resources

**DSS Child Welfare Services**
- Child protective services
- Adoption services
- Foster care services
- Foster home services
- Family services

**DSS Economic Services**
- Medicaid
- Health choice
- Energy assistance
- Food and nutrition services
- Subsidized child day care

**DSS Child Support Services**

**DSS Family Assistance and Services**
- Work First assistance
- Work First services
- Employment services

The family and children's services division includes a child protective services intake and investigation unit that receives and investigates reports of child abuse, neglect, and dependency, a case planning and management unit that provides social services to abused, neglected, or dependent children who are living at home, a foster care unit that provides assistance and services to children living in foster homes, an adoptions unit that assesses prospective adoptive parents, places children in adoptive homes, and provides assistance to adoptive families, a foster home services unit that recruits, licenses, and trains foster parents, and a family counseling unit that provides therapeutic counseling for children and families.

The department's economic assistance division determines the eligibility of families and children for Medicaid and the Health Choice insurance programs, provides child support enforcement services, provides employment services to families with dependent children, administers the child day care subsidy program, and determines the eligibility of individuals and families for Temporary Assistance for Needy Families, food and nutrition services, and energy assistance.

## Employees

The number of persons employed by county social services departments varies significantly from county to county.[19] At one extreme, the Camden County Department of Social Services has about a dozen employees. At the other extreme, the staff of the Mecklenburg County Department of Social Services consists of more than 1,200 employees.

### Legal Status

All employees of the county social services department are county, not state, employees. But unlike most other county employees, employees of the county social services department generally are subject to most of the provisions of the State Personnel Act, which governs the hiring,

---

19. The absolute and relative number of persons employed by a county social services department is affected by a number of factors, including the county's population, the type and scope of programs and services provided by the department, the number of persons who receive assistance or services from the department, state laws and policies governing maximum caseload limits, fiscal decisions by local officials, and staff efficiency and productivity.

classification, promotion, compensation, and dismissal of most state employees.[20]

The State Personnel Act, however, provides that county social services employees are exempt from its requirements (other than the equal employment opportunity requirements of G.S. 126-16) if the county's board of commissioners establishes and maintains a county personnel system that is approved by the State Personnel Commission as "substantially equivalent" to the State Personnel Act's standards for county social services employees.[21]

In addition, the State Personnel Act allows a board of county commissioners to adjust the salary ranges for employees of county social services departments based on local financial ability and fiscal policy and provides that if a board of county commissioners adopts rules and regulations governing administration of the county's pay plan and annual leave, sick leave, work hours, and holidays for county employees and files those rules with the State Personnel Commission, the county's rules supersede the State Personnel Commission's rules regarding leave, work hours, holidays, and pay plan administration for county social services employees.[22]

Because county social services employees are county employees, they are subject to other state laws governing county employees and to county personnel ordinances and policies governing other county employees as long as those other state laws and county personnel ordinances and policies do not conflict with the requirements and limita-

---

20. *See* G.S. 126-5(a)(2)b. The State Personnel Act does not apply to the employees of a consolidated human services agency established pursuant to G.S. 153A-77(b). Several federal statutes require that state and local social services agencies that administer federally funded social services programs use "competitive" or "merit-based" systems of personnel administration in recruiting, hiring, and retaining employees who are involved in the administration of these programs. *See* 7 U.S.C. § 2020(e)(6)(B) (Food Stamp program). Federal standards for state merit personnel systems are set forth in rules adopted by the U.S. Office of Personnel Management. *See* 29 C.F.R. § 900.603.

21. *See* G.S. 126-11. *See also* 25 N.C. ADMIN. CODE 01I .2401 through .2410. The State Personnel Commission has determined that the following counties have personnel systems that are, partially or completely, "substantially equivalent" to the personnel provisions of the State Personnel Act that apply to county social services employees: Caldwell, Catawba, Durham, Gaston, Guilford, Lincoln, Mecklenburg, New Hanover, Orange, Rockingham, and Rowan.

22. *See* G.S. 126-9(b); G.S. 126-9(a).

tions of the State Personnel Act that apply to county social services employees.

### CLASSIFICATION AND QUALIFICATIONS

State law requires the State Personnel Commission to establish a position classification plan for employees who are subject to the State Personnel Act.[23] The state personnel classification plan groups positions into a number of position classes based on the type of work involved; differentiates and ranks positions in each class based on the difficulty of the work, educational or certification requirements, supervisory responsibility, accountability, and other factors; and develops a class specification for each position that includes the title of the position (for example, Social Worker II), a description of the work required for the position, examples of duties performed in the job, and the minimum education and experience requirements for the position.[24]

Because county social services employees are subject to the State Personnel Act, the position of each employee of the county social services department must be allocated to one of the position class specifications included in the state personnel classification plan.[25] Social services position class specifications under the state personnel classification plan include child support agent, child support supervisor, social services program administrator, income maintenance caseworker, income maintenance investigator, income maintenance supervisor, income maintenance program administrator, social worker, social work supervisor, social work program manager, social services program administrator, and county social services director.

Because county social services employees are subject to the State Personnel Act, a person who is employed by the county social services department must possess at least the education, training, and experience that meets or is equivalent to the minimum requirements set forth in the state personnel classification plan for the position he or she fills.[26] For example, a person who is hired as a Social Worker I must have a bachelor's degree in a human services field from an accredited

---

23. *See* G.S. 126-4(1).

24. G.S. 126-4(3); Stephen Allred, *Employment Law: A Guide for North Carolina Public Employers,* 3d ed. (Chapel Hill: Institute of Government, The University of North Carolina at Chapel Hill, 1999), 192–193.

25. *See* 25 N.C. ADMIN. CODE 01I .1804.

26. *See* 25 N.C. ADMIN. CODE 01I .1905(b)(1).

college or university (or a bachelor's degree from an accredited college
or university and one year of directly related experience); a working
knowledge of basic social work principles, techniques, and practices
and their application to specific casework, group work, and community
problems; knowledge of governmental and private organizations
and resources in the community; knowledge of behavioral and
socioeconomic problems and their treatment; the ability to establish
and maintain effective working relationships with administrative
supervisors, with clients and their families, and with care providers and
various community organizations; the ability to express ideas clearly
and concisely; and the ability to plan and execute social work with
individuals and families.[27]

### Appointment and Supervision

All employees of the county social services department are appointed
and supervised by the county social services director.[28] Neither the
county social services board, the county manager, the board of county
commissioners, the state Social Services Commission, nor the state
Department of Health and Human Services has any authority to
appoint the staff of the county social services department or to approve
or disapprove the director's decision to hire a person as an employee of
the social services department.[29]

The director, however, must comply with applicable federal and state
statutes and rules in recruiting, appointing, supervising, promoting,
demoting, disciplining, and dismissing the staff of the county social
services department.

The State Personnel Act and rules adopted by the State Personnel
Commission, for example, require that notices of job vacancies for
which there is open recruitment be posted in the department's personnel office and in the unit in which the vacancy occurs.[30]

State rules also specify the types of appointments that the director may make in hiring county social services employees. Emergency

27. N.C. Office of State Personnel website at www.osp.state.nc.us/CLASS_SPECS/
Spec_Folder_03100-04099/PDF_Files/04011.pdf (last visited May 1, 2008).

28. G.S. 108A-14(a)(2).

29. *See In re* Brunswick County, 81 N.C. App. 391, 344 S.E.2d 584 (1986).

30. *See* G.S. 126-7.1. If the department will consider outside applicants, the
notice also must be posted with the Employment Security Commission for a
period of at least seven days. 25 N.C. Admin. Code 01I .1902.

appointments, for example, may be made only when an emergency situation requires the services of an employee before it is possible to identify a qualified applicant through the regular selection process.[31] State rules also allow the social services director to make temporary or time-limited appointments under certain conditions.[32] When the director hires an employee for a permanent position, state rules generally require the new employee to serve a probationary period of three to nine months.[33]

County departments of social services are also subject to federal and state laws prohibiting discrimination on the basis of race, gender, age, or disability in the recruitment, hiring, and employment of employees.[34]

### CRIMINAL HISTORY CHECKS

County social services departments are allowed, with the approval of the board of county commissioners, to obtain from the State Bureau of Investigation a criminal history record check on persons who have applied for employment with the county social services department or who are employed by the county social services department.[35]

### DRUG TESTING

It is unclear whether a county social services department may require all applicants for employment to undergo pre-employment drug testing.[36]

The rules are clearer with respect to persons who are currently employed by county social services departments.

---

31. 25 N.C. ADMIN. CODE 01I .2002(g). When an emergency appointment is required, all other requirements regarding recruitment, selection, and appointment are waived. When an emergency appointment is made, the appointment may not exceed sixty work days. State rules also provide for "trainee" and "work-against" appointments in certain situations. 25 N.C. ADMIN. CODE 01I .2002(b); 25 N.C. ADMIN. CODE 01I .2002(i).

32. 25 N.C. ADMIN. CODE 01I .2002(d); 25 N.C. ADMIN. CODE 01I .2002(e).

33. 25 N.C. ADMIN. CODE 01I .2002(a).

34. Federal and state employment discrimination laws are discussed in detail in Allred, *Employment Law.*

35. *See* G.S. 114-19.14; G.S. 153A-94.2. Criminal history record checks are discussed in detail in James C. Drennan, "Obtaining Records Checks to Reduce Risk," *Popular Government* 64(2) (Winter 1999): 30.

36. Drug testing by state and local government employers is discussed in detail in Diane M. Juffras, "Safety vs. Privacy: When May a Public Employer Require a Drug Test?" *Popular Government* 68(2) (Winter 2003): 4.

> First, a public employer may engage in random drug
> testing only of employees in safety-sensitive positions.
> It may not require employees whose primary duties are
> not likely to endanger the public or other employees
> to submit to random drug testing. Second, a public
> employer may ask *any* employee—in a safety-sensitive
> position or not—to take a drug test if it has a reason-
> able, individualized suspicion that the employee is
> using illegal drugs.[37]

The federal Drug-Free Workplace Act of 1988 does not authorize or
require drug testing of persons who apply for employment with or are
employed by a county social services department and the act's requirements regarding employer policies to ensure drug-free workplaces do
not apply to a county social services department unless it receives a
grant directly from a federal agency or contracts directly with a federal
agency.[38]

## POLITICAL ACTIVITIES

County social services employees whose activities are funded in whole
or in part by federal grants are subject to the federal Hatch Act.[39] Under
the Hatch Act, a county social services employee retains his or her
right to vote as he or she chooses and to express his or her opinions on
political subjects and candidates but may not be a candidate for elective
office in a partisan election, use his or her official authority or influence to interfere with or affect the result of an election or a nomination
for office, or directly or indirectly coerce, attempt to coerce, command,
or advise any other state or local employee who is subject to the act to
make any contribution to a party, committee, organization, agency, or
person for political purposes.[40]

---

37. *Id.* at 4, 5.

38. State social services agencies are the grantees for most federal social services grants. And while federal social services grant funds may be distributed by
the state to county social services departments, the county social services departments are, at most, subgrantees and therefore not covered by the act's requirements. *See* Allred, *Employment Law*, 254; 54 Fed. Reg. 4948 (Jan. 31, 1989).

39. 5 U.S.C. § 1501; Oklahoma v. U.S. Civil Service Comm'n, 330 U.S. 127
(1947); Broadrick v. Oklahoma, 413 U.S. 601 (1973).

40. *See* 5 U.S.C. § 1502.

State law also restricts the political activities of county social services employees, including those who are not covered by the Hatch Act.
The State Personnel Act prohibits a county social services employee
from engaging in any political activity while on duty and from using his
or her position to support or oppose any candidate, party, or issue in
an election.[41] State law also prohibits county social services employees
from soliciting political or partisan contributions from other employees
and using county funds, supplies, or equipment for partisan or political
purposes.[42]

### PERSONNEL POLICIES

State personnel rules prohibit county social services employees from
engaging in any other employment that conflicts with their employment responsibilities with the county social services department and
restrict the employment of two or more immediate family members
within a county social services department.[43]

State law authorizes boards of county commissioners to adopt or
provide for additional personnel policies governing county social services employees.[44] A board of county commissioners, for example, might
adopt an ordinance requiring all county employees to be residents of
the county or allow the county manager to adopt a policy governing
the use of county-owned computers and computer systems by county
employees.[45] Or the board of county commissioners might allow,
expressly or implicitly, the county social services director to adopt a

---

41. *See* G.S. 126-13(a).

42. *See* G.S. 153A-99. *See also* G.S. 126-14 and G.S. 126-14.1.

43. 25 N.C. ADMIN. CODE 01I .1703; 25 N.C. ADMIN. CODE 01I .1702. This
nepotism restriction applies to employees who are related as spouses, parents and
children, step-parents and step-children, parents-in-law and sons- and daughters-
in-law, siblings, step-siblings, half-siblings, and grandparents and grandchildren.
If the employment of immediate family members within the department cannot
be avoided, state rules prohibit the supervision of an employee by a member of
his or her immediate family or the employment of an individual in a position
that allows the exercise of influence over the employment, promotion, salary, or
supervision of an immediate family member.

44. *See* G.S. 153A-94.

45. Residency requirements by local government employers are discussed in
detail in Allred, *Employment Law*, 238–240. Computer, email, and Internet policies
of local government employers are discussed in Allred, *Employment Law*, 260–261.

"dress code" or other personnel policies governing county social services employees.

## SALARY AND COMPENSATION

State law requires the State Personnel Commission to establish a compensation plan for employees who are subject to the State Personnel Act.[46] Under the state compensation plan, each position included in the state personnel classification plan is assigned a salary plan grade (ranging from grade 50 to grade 96). The state salary plan specifies salary ranges for each salary grade, including hiring rates, minimum rates, midpoint rates, and maximum rates.[47] For example, under the state salary plan the position of Income Maintenance Caseworker I is assigned to salary grade 61 with an annual salary range of approximately $22,219 to $34,562, while the position of social worker II is assigned to salary grade 67 with an annual salary range of approximately $27,882 to $44,571.

Although the state salary plan applies to county social services employees as well as to most state employees who work for the state Department of Health and Human Services, the State Personnel Act expressly provides that, subject to the approval of the State Personnel Commission, a board of county commissioners may adjust the state salary plan in order to make the salaries of county employees who are subject to the State Personnel Act conform to local financial ability and fiscal policy.[48] In practice, therefore, the salary schedules for county social services employees are determined by the salary plans that are adopted by boards of county commissioners and approved by the Office of State Personnel, rather than the salary schedules for state employees.

When a board of county commissioners adopts a compensation plan for county social services employees, the county's salary schedule must

- use appropriate position classifications that are based upon differences in the difficulty and responsibility of the work;
- maintain the relative difference between and among classes in class series and between significantly related classes within occupational groupings under the state classification plan;

46. *See* G.S. 126-4(2).
47. The 2004 annual rates for grade 50 ranged from $17,957 to $22,611. The 2004 annual rates for grade 96 ranged from $101,201 to $172,157.
48. *See* G.S. 126-9(b); 25 N.C. ADMIN. CODE 01I .2101.

- establish a salary range for each grade, with minimum, maximum, and intermediate rates of pay; and
- provide for a vertical increase between consecutive salary grades within the schedule.[49]

Because state law gives county commissioners a fair amount of discretion in adopting salary schedules for county social services employees, there is a fair amount of variation in salary ranges and average salaries for county social services employees across the state. Average annual salaries for income maintenance caseworkers, for example, range from about $20,000 to $40,000, while average annual salaries of social services employees who are classified as Social Worker II range from about $27,000 to $51,000 per year.[50]

Although the federal Fair Labor Standards Act applies to all county social services employees, some salaried executive, professional, or administrative employees may be exempt from the act's overtime and minimum wage requirements.[51]

### EMPLOYEE BENEFITS AND RETIREMENT

Because county social services employees are county, not state, employees, they are not covered by the Teachers' and State Employees' Retirement System or by the State Health Plan for state employees. Instead, the board of county commissioners is primarily responsible for determining whether to provide fringe benefits, including health insurance and retirement benefits, for county social services employees and, if so, the type and extent of those benefits.[52]

Although coverage of county employees under North Carolina's Local Government Employees' Retirement System (LGERS) is optional, all North Carolina counties participate in LGERS and all eligible employees

---

49. *See* 25 N.C. ADMIN. CODE 01I .2106; 25 N.C. ADMIN. CODE 01I .2102. The salary of each county social services employee must fall between the minimum and maximum steps of the salary range of the class to which his or her position is assigned.

50. *County Salaries in North Carolina 2008* (Chapel Hill: School of Government, The University of North Carolina at Chapel Hill, 2008), available at www.sog.unc .edu/pubs/electronicversions/pdfs/cosal2008/envir.pdf.

51. *See* Allred, *Employment Law*, 198–212.

52. *See* G.S. 153A-92(d); G.S. 153A-93.

of county social services departments are covered by LGERS.[53] County social services employees also are covered by North Carolina's workers compensation and unemployment compensation statutes and by the federal Family and Medical Leave Act.

Boards of county commissioners are authorized to adopt or provide for rules governing vacation leave, sick leave, holidays, and other paid or unpaid leave for county employees, and these rules govern the leave and holidays of county social services employees when they are filed with the State Personnel Commission.[54]

### EMPLOYEE INTERCHANGE

County social services departments are authorized to participate in programs that involve the interchange of county social services employees with other state and local government agencies in accordance with the North Carolina Interchange of Governmental Employees Act of 1977.[55]

### PERSONNEL RECORDS

Information in the personnel files of county social services employees, former county social services employees, or persons who apply for employment with the county social services department is not subject to disclosure under North Carolina's Public Records Law.[56] State law, however, requires that the following information regarding county social services employees be disclosed to any member of the public when requested:

- the employee's name and age;
- the date of the employee's original employment or appointment;
- the office or station to which the employee is currently assigned;
- the employee's current position title and salary;

---

53. *See* G.S. 153A-93(a); G.S. Ch. 128, Art. 3. All, or virtually all, local government employees, including county social services employees, are also covered under the federal Social Security Act's Old Age, Survivors', and Disability Insurance system.

54. *See* G.S. 153A-94; G.S. 126-9(a).

55. *See* G.S. Chapter 126, Art. 10.

56. *See* G.S. 126-22; G.S. 153A-98(a). The term "personnel file" is defined broadly to include "any information in any form gathered by the [employer] . . . relating to [the employee's] application, selection or nonselection, promotions, demotions, transfers, suspension, and other disciplinary actions, evaluation forms, leave, salary, and termination of employment."

- the date and amount of the most recent increase or decrease in the employee's salary; and
- the date of the employee's most recent promotion, demotion, transfer, suspension, separation, or other change in position classification.[57]

Information from an employee's personnel file also may be disclosed to the employee's immediate supervisor and other county employees or officials who exercise supervisory authority with respect to the employee.[58] And the county manager, with the concurrence of the board of county commissioners, may inform any person of the termination, transfer, suspension, demotion, or other disciplinary action against a county employee and the reasons for that personnel action if the manager determines in writing that release of the information is essential to maintaining public confidence in the administration of county services or to maintaining the level and quality of county services.[59]

An employee or former employee of a county social services department has the right to review information contained in his or her personnel file, other than letters of reference that were solicited before he or she was hired and medical information that a prudent physician would not disclose to a patient.[60] If an employee or former employee believes that information in his or her personnel file is inaccurate or misleading, he or she may request that it be removed or place a statement in his or her file disputing the allegedly inaccurate information.[61]

57. G.S. 126-23; G.S. 153A-98(b). These requirements apply to personnel information regarding former employees of the county social services department but not to persons who have applied for employment with the county social services department but were not hired. See Elkin Tribune Inc. v. Yadkin County Bd. of County Comm'rs, 331 N.C. 735, 417 S.E.2d 465 (1992).

58. See G.S. 153A-98(c)(3). See also North Carolina Dep't of Correction v. Myers, 120 N.C. App. 437, 462 S.E.2d 824 (1995).

59. G.S. 153A 98(c)(7). Information from a county social services employee's personnel file also may be disclosed with the employee's consent, pursuant to court order, or as otherwise allowed by state law. See G.S. 153A-98(c)(4), (5), (6).

60. See G.S. 153A-98(c)(1).

61. See G.S. 153A-98(d). See also Nailing v. Univ. of North Carolina at Chapel Hill, 117 N.C. App. 318, 451 S.E.2d 351 (1994).

### DISCIPLINE, DEMOTION, SUSPENSION, AND DISCHARGE

A career employee of the county social services department may be given a disciplinary warning, demoted, suspended without pay, or fired by the county social services director only for unsatisfactory job performance or for unacceptable personal conduct.[62]

Unsatisfactory job performance is defined as "work-related performance that fails to satisfactorily meet job requirements as specified in the [employee's] job description, work plan or as directed by the [employee's supervisor or agency management]."[63]

Unacceptable personal conduct is defined as (1) conduct for which no reasonable employee should expect to receive prior warning; (2) work-related conduct that violates federal or state law; (3) the conviction of a felony or criminal offense involving moral turpitude that is detrimental to or impacts the employee's service to the agency; (4) willful violation of known or written work rules; (5) conduct unbecoming an employee that is detrimental to the agency's service; (6) abuse of a client, patient, student, or other person for whom the employee has charge or responsibility; (7) falsification of an employment application or other employment documentation; (8) willful failure or refusal to carry out a reasonable order from an authorized supervisor; or (9) absence from work after all authorized leave credits and benefits have been exhausted.[64]

A warning for unsatisfactory job performance or unacceptable personal conduct must be given to the employee in writing; inform the employee that it is a written disciplinary warning and not some other non-disciplinary process such as counseling; inform the employee of the specific incident of unsatisfactory job performance or unacceptable personal conduct that is the basis for the warning; inform the employee what specific actions, changes, or improvements, if any, must be taken

---

62. *See* G.S. 126-35(a) and G.S. 126-1.1 (as amended by SL 2007-372). A county social services employee is a career employee if he or she is in a permanent position appointment and has been continuously employed by a county agency that is subject to the State Personnel Act for a period of at least twenty-four months immediately preceding the date on which he or she is disciplined or discharged. *See also* 25 N.C. ADMIN. CODE 01I .2301. County social services employees who are not career employees may or may not be protected from discipline or dismissal under county personnel policies.

63. 25 N.C. ADMIN. CODE 01I .2302(a). *See also* Camp and Walker v. Dep't of Human Resources, 100 N.C. App. 498, 397 S.E.2d 350 (1990).

64. 25 N.C. ADMIN. CODE 01I .2304(b).

to correct or address the unsatisfactory job performance or unacceptable personal conduct; advise the employee of the time frame within
which the employee must take corrective action; advise the employee of
the consequences of failing to take the required corrective action; and
advise the employee of his or her right, if any, to contest or appeal the
warning.[65]

A county social services employee may be suspended without pay
for disciplinary purposes for a period of one day to two weeks.[66] An
employee, however, may not be suspended without pay for unsatisfactory job performance (other than grossly inefficient job performance)
unless he or she has received at least one prior disciplinary warning,
suspension, or demotion.[67] Before suspending an employee without pay,
the county social services director or a designated management representative must conduct a pre-disciplinary conference with the employee
in accordance with the rules adopted by the State Personnel Commission.[68] If a county social services employee is suspended without pay,
the employee must be given a written statement that sets forth the specific acts or omissions that are the basis for the suspension and advises
the employee of his or her right to appeal the suspension.[69]

A county social services employee may be demoted for unsatisfactory
job performance, grossly inefficient job performance, or unacceptable

65. 25 N.C. ADMIN. CODE 01I .2305.

66. 25 N.C. ADMIN. CODE 01I .2306(a). A county social services employee
may be placed on investigatory status (that is, removed from work status with
pay) when such action is necessary to investigate allegations of performance or
conduct deficiencies that would constitute just cause for disciplinary action, to
provide time within which to schedule and conduct a pre-disciplinary conference,
or to avoid disruption of the workplace or to protect the safety of persons or
property. 25 N.C. ADMIN. CODE 01I .2308(c).

67. 25 N.C. ADMIN. CODE 01I .2306(a). A previous disciplinary action may not
be used to support the dismissal of a county social services employee for unsatisfactory job performance if the employee's supervisor notes in the employee's
personnel file that the reason for the disciplinary action has been resolved or corrected or if eighteen months have passed since the action, additional disciplinary
action has not been taken against the employee during the past eighteen months,
and the agency did not, prior to expiration of the eighteen-month period, extend
the period and give the employee written notice of the reasons for extending the
period. 25 N.C. ADMIN. CODE 01I .2309(b).

68. 25 N.C. ADMIN. CODE 01I .2306(a); 25 N.C. ADMIN. CODE 01I .2308(2).

69. 25 N.C. ADMIN. CODE 01I .2306(a); 25 N.C. ADMIN. CODE 01I .2308(2).

personal conduct.[70] An employee, however, may not be demoted for unsatisfactory job performance (other than grossly inefficient job performance) unless he or she has received at least one prior disciplinary warning, suspension, or demotion.[71] Before demoting an employee, the county social services director or a designated management representative must conduct a pre-disciplinary conference with the employee in accordance with the rules adopted by the State Personnel Commission.[72] If a county social services employee is demoted for disciplinary reasons, the employee must be given a written statement that sets forth the specific acts or omissions that are the basis for the demotion and advises the employee of his or her right to appeal the demotion.[73]

A county social services employee may be fired for unacceptable personal conduct even if he or she has not received any prior warning regarding his or her conduct and the agency has not taken any prior disciplinary action against him or her.[74] By contrast, a county social services employee generally may not be dismissed for unsatisfactory job performance unless he or she has already received two disciplinary warnings, suspensions, or demotions.[75] State rules, however, allow a county social services employee to be dismissed for unsatisfactory job performance without having received a prior warning regarding his

---

70. 25 N.C. ADMIN. CODE 01I .2307(a).

71. 25 N.C. ADMIN. CODE 01I .2307(b). A previous disciplinary action may not be used to support the dismissal of a county social services employee for unsatisfactory job performance if the employee's supervisor notes in the employee's personnel file that the reason for the disciplinary action has been resolved or corrected or if eighteen months have passed since the action, additional disciplinary action has not been taken against the employee during the past eighteen months, and the agency did not, prior to expiration of the eighteen-month period, extend the period and give the employee written notice of the reasons for extending the period. 25 N.C. ADMIN. CODE 01I .2309(b).

72. 25 N.C. ADMIN. CODE 01I .2307(g); 25 N.C. ADMIN. CODE 01I .2308(3).

73. 25 N.C. ADMIN. CODE 01I .2307(e); 25 N.C. ADMIN. CODE 01I .2308(3).

74. 25 N.C. ADMIN. CODE 01I .2304.

75. 25 N.C. ADMIN. CODE 01I .2302(c). A previous disciplinary action may not be used to support the dismissal of a county social services employee for unsatisfactory job performance if the employee's supervisor notes in the employee's personnel file that the reason for the disciplinary action has been resolved or corrected or if eighteen months have passed since the action, additional disciplinary action has not been taken against the employee during the past eighteen months, and the agency did not, prior to expiration of the eighteen-month period, extend the period and give the employee written notice of the reasons for extending the period. 25 N.C. ADMIN. CODE 01I .2309(b).

or her job performance if his or her failure to perform his or her work satisfactorily results in or creates a risk of death or serious harm to the agency's clients, other employees, members of the public, or persons for whom the employee has responsibility or results in loss or damage to agency property or funds that seriously impacts the agency.[76]

Before a county social services employee is dismissed for unsatisfactory job performance or unacceptable personal conduct, the employee's supervisor must discuss the proposed firing with the county social services director or designated management representative, who must conduct a pre-disciplinary conference with the employee.[77] The employee must be given advance notice of the conference and the basis for the proposed disciplinary action.[78] The purpose of the pre-disciplinary conference is to ensure that a dismissal decision is sound and not based on misinformation or mistake.[79] At the conference, the director or designated management representative must give the employee oral or written notice of the recommended dismissal, the specific reasons for the proposed dismissal, and a summary of the information supporting the recommended dismissal.[80] The employee must be given an opportunity to respond and to offer information or arguments in support of the employee's position.[81] No witnesses or attorneys, however, may attend the conference.[82]

After the conference, the director or designated management representative must make a decision regarding the proposed dismissal. If the director or designated management representative decides to dismiss the employee, a written letter of dismissal stating the specific reasons for dismissal, the effective date of the dismissal, and the employee's

---

76. 25 N.C. ADMIN. CODE 01I .2303. This ground for dismissal is commonly referred to as "grossly inefficient job performance."

77. 25 N.C. ADMIN. CODE 01I .2308(4)(a).

78. 25 N.C. ADMIN. CODE 01I .2308(4)(c).

79. 25 N.C. ADMIN. CODE 01I .2308(4)(d).

80. 25 N.C. ADMIN. CODE 01I .2308(4)(e).

81. *Id.*

82. 25 N.C. ADMIN. CODE 01I .2308(4)(d); 25 N.C. ADMIN. CODE 01I .2308(4)(e). A second management representative may be present at management's discretion. Security personnel may be present when, in the discretion of the person conducting the conference, a need for security exists.

appeal rights must be delivered to the employee in person or by
certified mail.[83]

### EMPLOYEE GRIEVANCES AND APPEALS

A career county social services employee who is suspended, demoted, or
dismissed for unsatisfactory job performance or unacceptable personal
conduct has the right to appeal his or her suspension, demotion, or dismissal.[84] See Figure 8.2.

Except in cases in which a social services employee alleges discrimination in connection with a disciplinary action, the employee must
file his or her appeal within fifteen days of his or her receipt of written notice of the suspension, demotion, or dismissal in accordance
with the county's grievance policy for social services employees.[85] A
county's grievance policy for social services employees may allow the
county social services board, a county personnel advisory committee,
the county manager, or another public official or board to issue a recommended decision with respect to the employee's appeal. The county
social services director, however, retains exclusive authority to make
all final decisions regarding the suspension, demotion, or dismissal of
county social services employees.[86]

After the county social services director makes a final decision to
suspend, demote, or dismiss a county social services employee, a career

---

83. 25 N.C. ADMIN. CODE 01I .2308(4)(f). The letter may not be sent before the
beginning of the next business day following the conclusion of the pre-dismissal
conference or after the end of the second business day following the completion
of the pre-dismissal conference.

84. 25 N.C. ADMIN. CODE 01I .2310(a). Disciplinary warnings may not be
appealed unless allowed under the county's grievance policy for social services
employees. 25 N.C. ADMIN. CODE 01I .2309(e)(2). A probationary employee does
not have the right to file an appeal claiming that he or she was disciplined or
dismissed without just cause. 25 N.C. ADMIN. CODE 01I .2002(a)(3). A county
social services employee who is not a career employee may or may not have a right
to appeal his or her dismissal pursuant to the county's personnel ordinance or
policies.

85. 25 N.C. ADMIN. CODE 01I .2010(a). An employee who alleges discrimination in connection with disciplinary action may "bypass" the county grievance
procedure and file an appeal with the North Carolina Office of Administrative
Hearings within thirty days of receipt of notice of the suspension, demotion, or
dismissal. 25 N.C. ADMIN. CODE 01I .2010(b).

86. See G.S. 108A-14(a)(2). See also In re Brunswick County, 81 N.C. App. 391,
344 S.E.2d 584 (1986).

**Figure 8.2 Grievance and Appeal Process for County Social Services Employees**

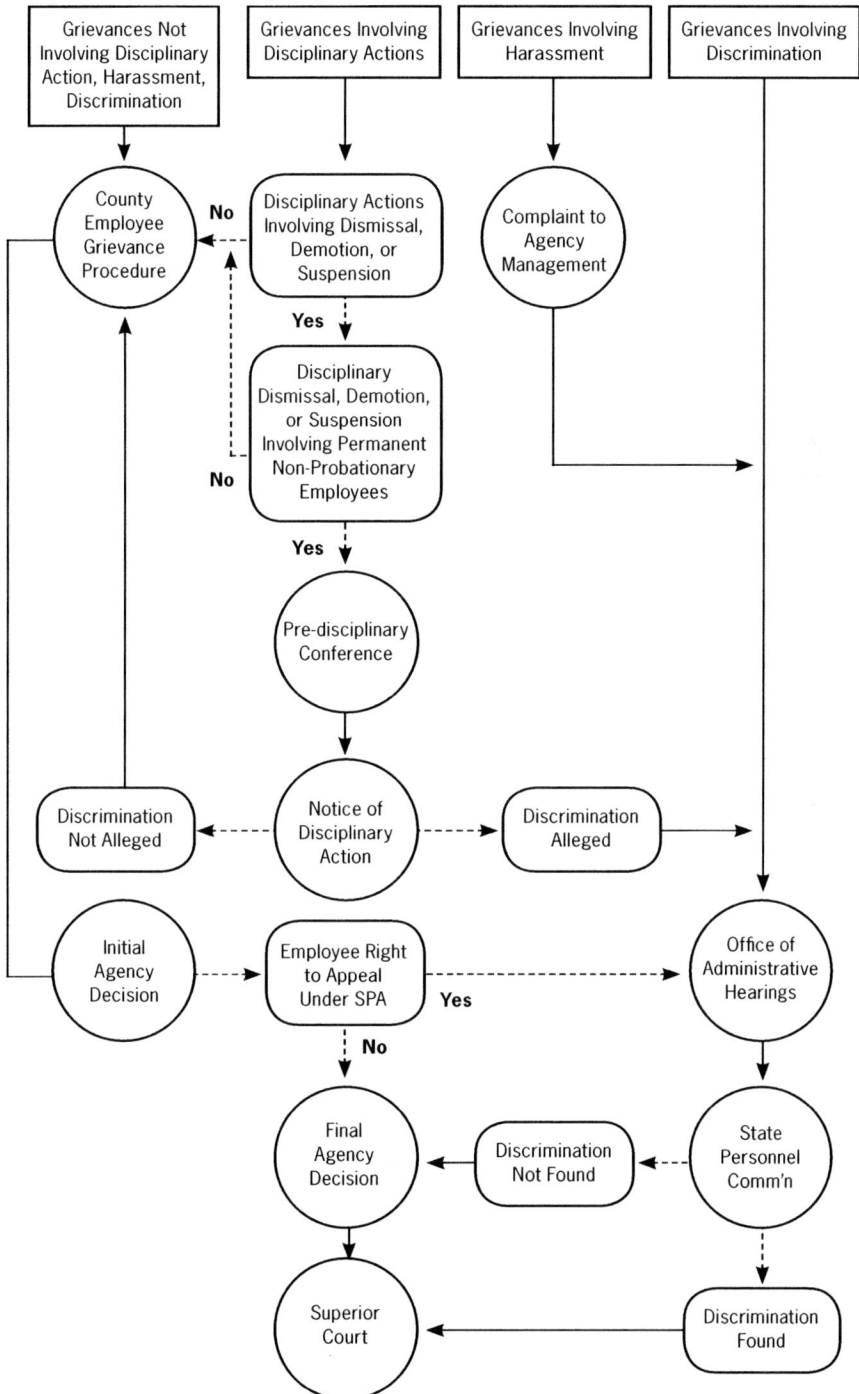

Grievances Not Involving Disciplinary Action, Harassment, Discrimination

Grievances Involving Disciplinary Actions

Grievances Involving Harassment

Grievances Involving Discrimination

County Employee Grievance Procedure

Disciplinary Actions Involving Dismissal, Demotion, or Suspension

Complaint to Agency Management

No

Yes

Disciplinary Dismissal, Demotion, or Suspension Involving Permanent Non-Probationary Employees

No

Yes

Pre-disciplinary Conference

Notice of Disciplinary Action

Discrimination Not Alleged

Discrimination Alleged

Initial Agency Decision

Employee Right to Appeal Under SPA

Office of Administrative Hearings

Yes

No

Final Agency Decision

Discrimination Not Found

State Personnel Comm'n

Superior Court

Discrimination Found

social services employee may appeal the director's decision by commencing a contested case pursuant to North Carolina's Administrative Procedure Act.[87] To do so, the employee must file a petition with the North Carolina Office of Administrative Hearings (OAH) within thirty days of receipt of the director's decision and serve a copy of the petition on the county social services director.[88]

After the petition is filed, OAH assigns an administrative law judge (ALJ) to hear the case.[89] The employee and the county social services director must be given at least fifteen days' notice of the hearing.[90] Hearings involving the suspension, demotion, or discharge of county social services employees generally are held in the county in which the employee lives.[91] Both the employee and the director have the right to be represented by legal counsel at the hearing, to call, examine, and cross-examine witnesses, to present evidence, and to make legal arguments to the ALJ.[92] At the hearing, the county social services director has the burden of proving, by a preponderance of the evidence, that the employee was suspended, demoted, or discharged for just cause.[93]

After the hearing, the ALJ issues a recommended decision to the State Personnel Commission and sends a copy of the recommended decision to the employee and the director.[94] The State Personnel Commission must adopt the ALJ's recommended decision as the commission's decision in the case unless it determines that the ALJ's decision is clearly contrary to the preponderance of admissible evidence in the

---

87. See G.S. 126-35(a); G.S. 150B-23.

88. See G.S. 150B-23(a). The county social services director must send notice of the employee's appeal to the county manager or the chair of the board of county commissioners by certified mail within fifteen days of the director's receipt of notice of the appeal. G.S. 126-37(c).

89. See G.S. 150B-32; G.S. 150B-33.

90. See G.S. 150B-23(b). The county may intervene in the administrative proceeding within thirty days of the date it receives notice of the employee's appeal. See G.S. 126-37(c).

91. See G.S. 150B-24.

92. See G.S. 150B-25; G.S. 150B-27 (subpoenas); G.S. 150B-28 (discovery); G.S. 150B-29 (rules of evidence).

93. See G.S. 126-35(d); G.S. 150B-34(a).

94. The recommended decision of the administrative law judge (ALJ) must contain findings of fact that are based on the evidence presented at the hearing and conclusions of law that address the legal issues raised by the employee and director. See G.S. 150B-34(a).

record of the hearing or erroneous as a matter of law.[95] A copy of the commission's decision must be served personally or by certified mail on the employee, the director, the county (if the county has intervened), the parties' attorneys, and the Office of Administrative Hearings.[96]

If the commission determines that the county social services director's suspension, demotion, or discharge of the employee unlawfully discriminated against the employee on the basis of the employee's race, religion, color, creed, national origin, sex, age, or handicapping condition, the commission may issue a final agency decision requiring that the employee be reinstated or promoted and paid the salary he or she otherwise would have received.[97]

In cases that do not involve findings of unlawful discrimination, the commission may issue an advisory decision recommending that the employee's suspension, demotion, or discharge be set aside if the commission determines that the director did not follow the proper legal procedures in suspending, demoting, or discharging the employee, that the director did not have just cause to suspend, demote, or discharge the employee, or that the director acted arbitrarily or capriciously in suspending, demoting, or discharging the employee.[98] In these cases, the county social services director must issue a written final decision that accepts, rejects, or modifies the commission's advisory decision within ninety days and serve the final decision on the employee, the employee's attorney, and the county (if the county intervened in the administrative proceeding).[99] If the director rejects or modifies the commission's advisory decision, the director must state his or her reasons for doing so.[100]

---

95. *See* G.S. 150B-36.

96. *See* G.S. 150B-36(b3). The commission generally is required to issue its decision within sixty days of the date it receives the record of the administrative hearing or within sixty days of the date of its last official meeting, whichever is longer. *See* G.S. 150B-44.

97. *See* G.S. 126-37. The commission's decisions in these cases are binding on the county social services director and the county but are, on petition by the county social services director or county, subject to judicial review under Article 4 of the Administrative Procedure Act.

98. *See* G.S. 126-37(b1).

99. *See id.*

100. *See id.* The director, however, is not required to make additional or alternate findings of fact or conclusions of law. *See* Cunningham v. Catawba County Dep't of Social Servs., 128 N.C. App. 70, 493 S.E.2d 82 (1997).

After the director or the State Personnel Commission issues a final decision, the employee who filed the appeal may seek judicial review of the decision by filing a petition in the superior court pursuant to Article 4 of the state Administrative Procedure Act.[101] A petition for judicial review must be filed within thirty days of service of the director's or commission's final decision and served on the county social services director.[102]

The superior court judge must reverse or remand the director's decision if the court determines that the director heard new evidence after receiving the advisory decision, or did not accept the advisory decision and failed to specify the reasons therefor.[103] If the director's final decision does not adopt the ALJ's recommended decision, the superior court judge is not bound by the director's findings of fact or conclusions of law and may grant relief to the employee if the judge determines, based on his or her *de novo* review of the record of the administrative hearing, that the director's decision was unlawful.[104] If the director's decision adopts the ALJ's recommended decision, the judge may reverse the director's decision if, using the "whole record" test for judicial review, the director's findings of fact are unsupported by substantial, admissible evidence in the record.[105] The superior court judge also may reverse the director's decision if the judge determines that the director's decision was unconstitutional, exceeded the director's statutory authority, was made upon unlawful procedure, was legally erroneous, or was arbitrary, capricious, or an abuse of discretion.[106]

---

101. *See* G.S. 126-37(b2); G.S. 150B-43. The petition may be filed in Wake County or in the county in which the employee resides. G.S. 150B-45.

102. *See* G.S. 150B-45. The county may intervene in the proceeding in superior court even if it failed to seek intervention in the administrative proceeding. *See* G.S. 126-37(c). The decision of the superior court, however, is binding on the county regardless of whether it intervenes.

103. *See* G.S. 150B-51(a).

104. *See* G.S. 150B-51(c).

105. *See* G.S. 150B-51(b)(5). *See also* Thompson v. Bd. of Educ., 292 N.C. 406, 233 S.E.2d 538 (1977); Lackey v. Dep't of Human Resources, 306 N.C. 231, 293 S.E. 2d 171 (1982); General Motors v. Kinlaw, 78 N.C. App. 521, 338 S.E.2d 114 (1985); Leiphart v. N.C. School of the Arts, 80 N.C. App. 339, 342 S.E.2d 914 (1986); ACT-UP Triangle v. Comm'n for Health Servs., 345 N.C. 699, 483 S.E.2d 388 (1997).

106. *See* G.S. 150B-51(b).

If the superior court judge affirms the director's decision to suspend, demote, or discharge a county social services employee, the employee may appeal the superior court decision to the North Carolina Court of Appeals.[107]

State law also gives county social services employees the right to file grievances and appeals regarding certain personnel actions and employment practices that do not involve disciplinary suspensions, demotions, or firings, including, but not limited to

- workplace harassment based on age, sex, race, color, national origin, religion, creed, or handicapping condition;
- denials of promotion, transfer, or training due to age, sex, race, color, national origin, religion, creed, political affiliation, or handicapping condition; and
- violations of the federal Fair Labor Standards Act, the federal Age Discrimination in Employment Act, the federal Family Medical Leave Act, and the federal Americans with Disabilities Act.[108]

## Independent Contractors

Although most of the functions of the county social services department are performed by employees of the department, county social services departments also may use independent contractors or "contract employees" to perform some of the work that otherwise might be performed by county social services employees.

Using independent contractors or "contract employees" instead of, or in addition to, "regular" employees may have several advantages from the perspective of the department or county, including increased

---

107. Conversely, the county social services director or the county may appeal a superior court judgment that reverses the director's decision.

108. See G.S. 126-34 and G.S. 126-34.1. The procedures for these grievances and appeals are similar, but not always identical, to the procedure for grievances and appeals involving disciplinary action. See G.S. 126-34; G.S. 126-34.1; G.S. 126-36; G.S. 126-36.2; 25. N.C. ADMIN. CODE 01I .2310(a); and 25 N.C. ADMIN. CODE 01I .2310(b). A person who has been denied employment with the county social services department in violation of the equal employment opportunity requirements of state law has the right to appeal the denial to the State Personnel Commission. See G.S. 126-34.1(b); G.S. 126-36.1. County social services employees may have additional grievance rights under county personnel ordinances and policies.

flexibility with respect to scheduling and workload and cost-savings with respect to fringe benefits.

"Independent contractor," however, "is a distinct legal status determined by factors that go beyond an employer and an employee's common desire to contract for work on that basis," and county social services departments must comply with federal and state rules in determining whether someone who works for the county social services department is an "independent contractor" or an employee.[109]

109. *See* Diane M. Juffras, "Determining Whether a Worker is an Independent Contractor or an Employee," *Popular Government* 72(1) (Fall 2006): 25; Diane M. Juffras, "Independent Contractor or Employee? The Legal Distinction and Its Consequences," *Public Employment Law Bulletin* No. 32 (Chapel Hill: School of Government, The University of North Carolina at Chapel Hill, 2005).

# Chapter 9

# Social Services Attorneys

The legal services provided by attorneys are an integral part of the work of county social services departments. Attorneys represent county social services departments in juvenile court proceedings involving abused, neglected, and dependent children. Lawyers also provide legal advice or representation to social services departments in paternity and child support proceedings, in guardianship proceedings, and other legal matters involving social services programs, clients, or employees.

Under North Carolina's "state-supervised and county-administered" social services system, each county is responsible for providing the county social services department with the legal services that are necessary to enable the department to properly administer state-mandated social services programs. State law, however, does not mandate the means by which the county must provide legal services for the county social services department. And in the absence of a statute expressly authorizing the county social services director to employ or retain an attorney, it is clear that the board of county commissioners has the ultimate legal authority and responsibility for determining how the county will provide legal services to the county social services department.[1]

---

1. In determining how to provide legal services for the county social services department, the board of county commissioners should consult with the county social services director regarding the department's legal needs. Similarly, a

Every county social services department, therefore, has some type of relationship with an attorney who represents the department in legal proceedings. But the nature and scope of that relationship varies from county to county.

Some counties use a "county attorney" model under which the social services department is represented by the attorney, firm, or office that has been designated by the board of county commissioners as the county attorney. Other counties use a "staff attorney" model under which the social services attorney is hired by the county social services director, is an employee of the social services department, and works under the director's supervision. And other counties use a "contract attorney" model under which an attorney is retained to represent the county social services department on a contractual or fee-for-service basis.

Each of these models has potential advantages and potential drawbacks. The "best" model of legal representation for the county social services department, therefore, must be determined on a county-by-county basis, based on the department's legal needs, available resources, and other relevant factors.

## County Attorneys

State law requires each board of county commissioners to appoint, retain, or employ an attorney to serve as the county attorney.[2]

Some counties employ an attorney to serve as the county attorney. Most county attorneys, however, are self-employed lawyers or members of law firms who are retained by the county on a contractual basis and whose legal practice is not limited to providing legal services to the county. In either case, the county attorney's salary or compensation is determined by the board of county commissioners and the county attorney serves at the board's pleasure.[3]

---

county social services director who has concerns about the quality, cost, or adequacy of the legal services that are provided for the department should raise those concerns with the county manager, the county attorney, or the board of county commissioners.

2. Section 153A-114 of the North Carolina General Statutes [hereinafter G.S.].
3. G.S. 153A-114.

State law provides that the county attorney is the legal adviser to the board of county commissioners.[4] The precise nature and scope of the county attorney's responsibilities and work, however, is determined by the board of county commissioners. In a few counties, the county attorney represents the county and all of its constituent departments, including the county social services department, in all or almost all of the legal proceedings and matters involving the county or county agencies.

State law, however, does not require that the county social services director or department be represented by the county attorney. And, in many counties, the county attorney does not advise or represent the county social services director and department.

## Special County Attorneys for Social Services

State law allows the board of county commissioners, with the approval of the county social services board, to appoint an attorney to serve as the "special county attorney for social services" or to designate the county attorney as the special county attorney for social services.[5]

If an attorney is appointed as the special county attorney for social services pursuant to Section 108A-16 of the North Carolina General Statutes [hereinafter G.S.], the attorney's duties include providing legal advice to the county social services director, the county social services board, and the board of county commissioners with respect to social services matters and performing any other duties that may be assigned by the county social services director, the county social services board, the board of county commissioners, or state law.[6]

A special county attorney for social services may be retained by the county on a contractual or fee-for-service basis or hired as a full- or part-time county employee (though not as an employee of the county social services department). The salary or compensation of a special county for social services is determined by the board of county commissioners.[7]

---

4. *Id.*
5. G.S. 108A-16.
6. G.S. 108A-18.
7. G.S. 108A-17.

In practice, few, if any, attorneys who provide legal services for county social services departments do so as special county attorneys for social services.

## Assistant County Attorneys

Some counties employ one or more assistant county attorneys to provide legal services to the county social services department. These attorneys generally are hired and supervised by the county attorney and are not employees of the county social services department.

## Social Services Staff Attorneys

An increasing number of counties provide legal representation for the county social services department through staff attorneys who are employees of the county social services department.

Like other county social services employees, social services staff attorneys are appointed and supervised by the county social services director. Like other county social services employees, social services staff attorneys who are in "career" status may be fired by the director only for "just cause."[8] And, as in the case of other county social services employees, the qualifications, classification, and compensation of social services staff attorneys are governed by the State Personnel Act, the rules adopted by the State Personnel Commission, and other state laws governing county social services employees.

Social services staff attorneys generally are employed on a full-time basis and work exclusively on social services matters. The precise nature and scope of their work is determined by the county social services director and is usually set forth in the written job descriptions for their positions.

## Contract Attorneys

Some counties contract with an attorney or law firm to provide legal services for the county social services department. Attorneys who provide legal services to the county social services department under a

---

8. The discipline and discharge of county social services employees is discussed in detail in Chapter 8.

contract with the county are independent contractors, not employees of the county or the county social services department. The nature and scope of their work and the amount and manner of their compensation are determined by the terms of their contracts.

Legal services contracts involving the county social services department must be approved by the board of county commissioners unless the board has expressly or implicitly delegated that authority to the county manager, the county attorney, the county social services director, or another county official, board, or office.[9]

Legal services contracts involving the county social services department must be preaudited by the county finance officer in accordance with the Local Government Budget and Fiscal Control Act (LGBFCA).[10] The state's competitive bidding requirements, however, do not apply to contracts between the county and an attorney to provide legal services to the county social services department.[11]

## The Attorney–Agency Relationship

Most attorneys who are employed or retained to provide legal services to the county social services department probably assume that the county social services department, rather than the county, the board of county commissioners, the county social services director, or the county social services board, is their client, and that their professional responsibilities as lawyers therefore are owed to the county social services department, acting through the social services director, rather than the county, the county commissioners, or the social services board. The North Carolina State Bar's Revised Rules of Professional Conduct, however, recognize that "defining precisely the identity of the client and prescribing the resulting obligations of . . . lawyers may be . . . difficult in the government context and is a matter [that cannot be determined

---

9. G.S. 153A-12. The fact that someone executes or signs a contract does not necessarily mean that he or she has the legal authority to approve or enter into the contract. *See* Frayda S. Bluestein, *A Legal Guide to Purchasing and Contracting for North Carolina Local Governments,* 2d ed. (Chapel Hill: School of Government, The University of North Carolina at Chapel Hill, 2004), 6–7, 15–16.

10. G.S. 159-28(d).

11. *See* G.S. 143-129. *See also* Bluestein, *A Legal Guide to Purchasing and Contracting for North Carolina Governments,* 23.

solely within] the scope of these Rules."[12] So there may be instances in which the county, rather than the county social services department or director, is the client of the attorney who provides legal services to the social services department or director—especially when legal services are provided under the county attorney model, the assistant county attorney model, or special county attorney for social services model.

Unlike some states, North Carolina does not have a statute or rule that determines who is a social services attorney's client. Therefore, regardless of which model a county uses to provide legal services to the county social services department, it is important that the social services attorney's job description, contract, or agreement clearly identify whether the attorney's client is the county social services department, the county social services director, the county social services board, the county, or some combination of these.

If an attorney is employed or retained to represent the county social services department, the department—as an organization, rather than the county social services director or individual employees of the department—is the attorney's client.[13] A government agency, corporation, or other organization, however, can act only through its officers, employees, and agents. And the county social services director and his or her designated representatives are the "duly authorized constituents" or agents of the social services department. So, a social services attorney must consult with the director and the director's staff regarding the means by which the department's objectives are pursued through legal representation, and generally must accept the director's or staff's decision regarding the objectives of the attorney's legal representation

---

12. 27 N.C. ADMIN. CODE 02 Rule 1.13, Comment 6.

13. 27 N.C. ADMIN. CODE 02 Rule 1.13(a). A social services attorney must advise the county social services director or a social services employee that the attorney represents the department and does not represent the director or employee if the attorney knows or reasonably should know that the department's interests are adverse to those of the director or employee. 27 N.C. ADMIN. CODE 02 Rule 1.13(d). The social services attorney may represent the county social services director or a social services employee if the department's written consent is given by an appropriate departmental official other than the individual who will be represented, the attorney reasonably believes that he or she will be able to provide competent and diligent legal representation to the department and to the director or employee, and the dual representation will not involve the assertion of a legal claim between the department and the director or employee. 27 N.C. ADMIN. CODE 02 Rule 1.13(e); 27 N.C. ADMIN. CODE 02 Rule 1.7.

of the department, the settlement of legal proceedings involving the department, and decisions regarding departmental policy and operations, even if the social services attorney doubts the prudence or utility of those decisions.[14]

## The Role and Responsibilities of Social Services Attorneys

The precise nature and scope of the work and responsibilities of social services attorneys varies from county to county and among social services attorneys within particular counties.

In some counties, a social services attorney is responsible for representing the county social services department in juvenile court proceedings and does not advise or represent the social services board, director, department, or staff in other legal matters. In other counties, a social services attorney may represent the agency in child support or guardianship proceedings but not in juvenile proceedings. And in some counties, a social services attorney may advise or represent the department in all, or almost all, legal matters involving the department.

In every instance, though, it is important for the agency and the attorney to have a clear understanding of the social services attorney's role and responsibilities. And to ensure that this is the case, the social services attorney's job description or contract should clearly specify the precise nature and scope of the attorney's relationship with the agency and the nature and scope of the attorney's work and responsibilities.

The professional responsibilities of social services attorneys, like those of other attorneys, are governed by the North Carolina State Bar's Revised Rules of Professional Conduct.[15] Among other things, these

---

14. 27 N.C. ADMIN. CODE 02 Rule 1.13, Comment 3; 27 N.C. ADMIN. CODE 02 Rule 1.2. A social services attorney, however, must proceed as is reasonably necessary in the department's best interest if he or she knows that the social services director or an employee of the social services department is acting, intends to act, or is refusing to act in violation of his or her legal obligation to the department or in violation of law which reasonably might be imputed to the department and that the director's or employee's action is likely to result in substantial injury to the department. 27 N.C. ADMIN. CODE 02 Rule 1.13(b).

15. The rules of professional responsibility and legal ethics that apply to attorneys in child welfare cases are discussed in detail in Jennifer L. Renne, *Legal Ethics in Child Welfare Cases* (Washington, DC: American Bar Association Center on Children and the Law, 2004). *See also* Mimi Laver, *Foundations for Success:*

rules require lawyers to provide competent representation of clients;[16] to act with reasonable diligence and promptness in representing clients;[17] to consult with clients about the means by which their legal objectives are to be accomplished;[18] to keep their clients reasonably informed about the status of legal matters;[19] to protect the confidentiality of information obtained in connection with legal representation of their clients;[20] to avoid conflicts of interest in representing clients;[21] to exercise independent, professional judgment and render candid advice to clients;[22] to refrain from asserting frivolous legal claims;[23] to refrain from making false statements to the court or offering evidence that they know to be false;[24] to refrain from engaging in unauthorized *ex parte* communications with judges;[25] to refrain from making false statements of law or fact to others when representing a client;[26] and to comply with other rules of legal ethics and professional responsibility.

## The North Carolina Department of Justice

The North Carolina Department of Justice is a state agency headed by the attorney general.[27] The attorney general and the deputy and assistant attorneys general employed by the Department of Justice provide

---

*Strengthening Your Agency Attorney Office* (Washington, DC: American Bar Association Center on Children and the Law, 1999).

16. 27 N.C. ADMIN. CODE 02 Rule 1.1.
17. 27 N.C. ADMIN. CODE 02 Rule 1.3.
18. 27 N.C. ADMIN. CODE 02 Rule 1.4(a)(2).
19. 27 N.C. ADMIN. CODE 02 Rule 1.4(a)(3).
20. 27 N.C. ADMIN. CODE 02 Rule 1.6. Although the social services attorney generally does not represent the county social services director or employees of the social services department, communications between the county social services director or employees and the social services attorney are protected by the attorney–client privilege and generally may not be disclosed unless the department consents, the disclosure is authorized by the Rules of Professional Conduct, or the disclosure is necessary in order to carry out the attorney's representation of the department.
21. 27 N.C. ADMIN. CODE 02 Rules 1.7 through 1.11.
22. 27 N.C. ADMIN. CODE 02 Rule 2.1.
23. 27 N.C. ADMIN. CODE 02 Rule 3.1.
24. 27 N.C. ADMIN. CODE 02 Rule 3.3.
25. 27 N.C. ADMIN. CODE 02 Rule 3.5(a)(3).
26. 27 N.C. ADMIN. CODE 02 Rule 4.1.
27. G.S. 114-1.

legal representation and advice to all state government departments, agencies and commissions.[28]

Attorneys who work in the Health and Public Assistance Section and other sections of the department's Administrative Division provide legal assistance for state social services agencies, including the Division of Social Services, the Division of Medical Assistance, and the Division of Aging and Adult Services in the North Carolina Department of Health and Human Services. The attorney general's staff also includes four regionally based child welfare attorneys.

## The North Carolina Association of Social Services Attorneys

The North Carolina Association of Social Services Attorneys is a voluntary, nongovernmental association of attorneys who represent state and county social services agencies.

In cooperation with the School of Government and the North Carolina Association of County Attorneys, the association sponsors two training conferences each year. Many of the association's members also participate on an e-mail listserv that provides a forum for asking questions and sharing knowledge regarding legal practice in the social services context.

---

28. G.S. 114-2(2).

# Chapter 10

# Nonprofit Organizations and Social Services

Business, nonprofit, civic, charitable, and religious organizations, as well as families, neighbors, and other individuals, have always played, and continue to play, a vital role in the provision of social services to individuals and families in North Carolina and the United States.

## Nonprofit Organizations and Social Services: A Brief Historical Overview

> In the colonial period, churches, voluntary organizations, neighbors, and relatives provided emergency or supplemental cash and in-kind assistance, counseling, and support for people in need. Few formal voluntary service agencies existed. But in the early 1800s . . . organizations and charitable societies to care for children, mothers, and the disadvantaged proliferated throughout the country.[1]

In 1812 North Carolina's General Assembly issued a corporate charter to the Newbern Female Charitable Society, authorizing the society to provide for the relief of the poor and the education of poor female

---

1. Steven Rathgeb Smith, "Social Services," in Lester M. Salamon, ed., *The State of Nonprofit America* (Washington, DC: Brookings Institution Press, 2002), 158.

children.[2] The Female Orphan Asylum Society of Fayetteville was incorporated the following year to provide for the care of orphans for whom the county wardens of the poor otherwise would be responsible.[3] And the Raleigh Female Benevolent Society was founded in 1820 to provide for "the relief of aged widows and other distressed females who may be considered fit objects of charity; to provide employment to such females as are able and willing to work, and who cannot meet with employers; to give articles of cloathing [sic] to orphans and other destitute children; to promote the education of poor children, and cause them to be instructed in some of the most useful domestic employments; to promote order and industry amongst the poorer classes of society, and to discourage idleness and vice as far as practicable."[4]

In 1872 the Grand Lodge of North Carolina's Masonic Fraternity established the Oxford Orphan Asylum (now known as the Masonic Home for Children at Oxford).[5] By 1926, seventeen of North Carolina's twenty-three orphanages were operated by religious or fraternal organizations.[6]

The Children's Home Society of North Carolina was established in 1902. Rather than establishing an orphanage, the society placed orphans and dependent children in foster homes. And almost from the beginning, the society's work was facilitated and supplemented by the state's nascent public social services system. During the 1920s, county superintendents of public welfare were, "for all practical purposes, agents of the society both in referring children to the society and in investigating prospective [foster] homes" and several boards of county commissioners appropriated public funds to support the society's work.[7]

Thus, while care for the needy was, from the beginning, a *public* responsibility, *private* citizens, acting individually and through voluntary associations, gradually became more and more involved in providing public assistance and social services for the poor, the disabled, and, especially, children so that, by the late nineteenth century, social

2. Roy M. Brown, *Public Poor Relief in North Carolina* (Chapel Hill: The University of North Carolina Press, 1928), 152.

3. Brown, *Public Poor Relief in North Carolina*, 152.

4. Raleigh Female Benevolent Society, "Revised Constitution and Bylaws" (Raleigh: J. Gales & Son, 1828).

5. Brown, *Public Poor Relief in North Carolina*, 152.

6. *Id.* at 153.

7. *Id.* at 155.

work "had become more of a private or voluntary matter than a public" responsibility.[8]

During the twentieth century, however, the pendulum swung in the other direction. The past seventy years have been marked, first, by a renewed sense of *public* or governmental responsibility for social services, as evidenced by the creation and expansion of federal and state public assistance and social services programs through the New Deal of the 1930s and the Great Society of the 1960s, and, second, by a renewed appreciation that responsibility for social welfare is *shared* by public and private social services agencies.

During the early twentieth century, it became increasingly clear that the work of private charitable organizations, while valuable, was insufficient to address the social and economic problems that confronted the nation.

> [The Great Depression] hit the nation with a jarring impact. Some thirteen to fifteen million workers lost their jobs. Banks were closed, some permanently. Many citizens lost their life's savings. Factories lay idle. Stores had few customers. Hundreds of thousands of farmers were forced off their land. Numerous others lost their homes. Huddled figures shuffling despondently in bread lines or at soup kitchens testified to destitution and suffering to an extent unknown in American history.
>
> The task of relieving the jobless and their families was first undertaken by private local agencies. It quickly became evident, however, that they were unprepared to meet the crisis. To begin with, they were ill suited to the task because the "services" they performed would not feed the hungry or shelter the homeless. Furthermore, the financial needs of so many people—not only the aged, the sick, the disabled, and other members of the lower classes but also the plain, ordinary, middle class people who had worked all their lives but who were not unemployed, penniless, and

---

8. William I. Trattner, *From Poor Law to Welfare State,* 6th ed. (New York: Free Press, 1999), 214.

hungry, the so-called new poor—were clearly beyond
their meager means. As one observer aptly remarked,
"Trying to turn back this tide of distress through private philanthropic contributions is about as useless as
trying to put out a forest fire with a garden hose." * * *
Voluntary charity simply could not cope with the situation; only public agencies could deal with the collapse
of the economy, mass unemployment, and widespread
destitution.[9]

The Great Depression, therefore, "answered, once and for all, the vexing
question of whether private or public agencies should be responsible"
for social welfare.[10] And the answer to that question was that responsibility for social welfare must be *shared* by government, business,
nonprofit, civic, fraternal, charitable, and religious organizations, individuals, families, neighbors, and communities.

The creation and expansion of the American "welfare state" since the
1930s not only increased the involvement and responsibility of government with respect to social welfare but also led to the emergence of a
vibrant private nonprofit sector and to a unique government–nonprofit
partnership in the area of social welfare.[11]

Increasingly in the 1960s, the federal government
turned over the delivery of service to private nonprofit organizations. * * * The private, nonprofit sector
became a major beneficiary of this system of services.
* * * By the 1980s, the federal government alone provided $40 billion in support to the private nonprofit
sector, while state and local governments provided
additional amounts from their own resources.

Federal demand enabled the nonprofit sector to
grow by leaps and bounds. Indeed, in 1940 there were
only 12,500 charitable, tax exempt organizations. By

9. Trattner, *From Poor Law to Welfare State*, 273.

10. *Id.* at 273–74.

11. Lester M. Salamon, *America's Nonprofit Sector*, 2d ed. (New York: The Foundation Center, 1999), 62–63; Donald T. Critchlow, "Implementing Family Planning Policy: Philanthropic Foundations and the Modern Welfare State," in Donald
T. Critchlow and Charles H. Parker, eds., *With Us Always: A History of Private Charity and Public Welfare* (Lanham, MD: Rowman and Littlefield, 1998), 212.

1990, there were over 700 thousand, with most of this growth taking place after the 1960s. * * *

The result of this new . . . welfare state . . . blended public and private action [and] . . . marked a creation unique to the United States, reflecting a deep-seated American tradition of associative enterprise that combines self-reliance and private voluntarism with communitarianism and government activity.[12]

It is clear, therefore, that government has, and always has had, an important role with respect to the social welfare of our nation and its citizens—a role that can "never be replaced by charities."[13] There is, however, "room for public welfare *and* private charity . . . and the best results [can be achieved] by the two working in harmony rather than by one outdoing or assuming superiority over the other."[14]

Government has a solemn responsibility to help meet the needs of poor Americans and distressed neighborhoods, but it does not have a monopoly on compassion. America is richly blessed by the diversity and vigor of neighborhood healers: civic, social, charitable, and religious groups . . . [that] lift people's lives in ways that are beyond government's know-how, usually on shoestring budgets, and they heal our nation's ills one heart and one act of kindness at a time. [Government, therefore, should encourage the] indispensable and transforming work of faith-based and other charitable service groups [and] . . . work in fruitful partnership with community-serving and faith-based organizations—whether run by Methodists, Muslims, Mormons, or good people of no faith at all.[15]

---

12. Critchlow, "Implementing Family Planning Policy," 212.

13. President George W. Bush, "Commencement Address at the University of Notre Dame" (May 20, 2001), available at www.whitehouse.gov/news/releases/2001/05/20010521-1.html (last visited April 14, 2008).

14. Trattner, *From Poor Law to Welfare State*, 214.

15. President George W. Bush, "Foreword" to *Rallying the Armies of Compassion* (January 2001), available at www.whitehouse.gov/news/reports/faithbased.pdf (last visited April 14, 2008).

## Nonprofit Social Services Agencies in the United States and North Carolina

There are approximately 100,000 nonprofit social services agencies in the United States, and approximately 800 to 1,200 nonprofit social services agencies in North Carolina.[16]

Today, nonprofit social services agencies "have a more central role in society's response to social problems than ever before."[17]

> Nonprofit organizations are important providers of
> social services that deal with problems such as drug
> addiction, alcoholism, child abuse, schizophrenia,
> AIDS, teenage pregnancy, child care, family counseling,
> and homelessness.[18]

Nonprofit social services agencies, however, "vary greatly in scale, character, and [organizational structure and] formality" as well as with respect to the types of services they provide and how they are funded.[19]

Many nonprofit social services agencies are "informal, community-based groups and associations."[20] In addition, many churches or religious congregations provide some sort of social service to the community but do so through "programs that do not exist as formal organizational entities apart from the church" or congregation.[21]

---

16. Smith, "Social Services," 155. The figure for North Carolina nonprofit social services agencies is a very rough estimate based on national and state data contained in Salamon, *America's Nonprofit Sector*, 34, and Gita Gulati-Partee, "A Primer on Nonprofit Organizations," *Popular Government* 66(4) (Summer 2001): 31–36.

17. Smith, "Social Services," 150. Nonprofit social services agencies, however, also face "profound challenges" including increased competition, increased public demand for services, increased government regulation, and limited fiscal and personnel resources.

18. Evan M. Berman and Jonathan P. West, "Public-Private Leadership and the Role of Nonprofit Organizations in Local Government: The Case of Social Services," *Policy Studies Review* 14(1-2) (1995): 235–251.

19. Smith, "Social Services," 153. *See also* Lester M. Salamon, *America's Non-profit Sector*, 2d ed. (New York: The Foundation Center, 1999), 109–122.

20. Smith, "Social Services," 153.

21. *Id.* A 1998 survey of a nationally representative sample of *local* religious congregations found that almost 60 percent provided or supported the provision of one or more social services. Mark Chaves and William Tsitsos, "Congregations and Social Services: What They Do, How They Do It, and with Whom" (Washington, D.C.: Aspen Inst., 2001), available at www.nonprofitresearch.org/usr_doc/

> Classic examples of such informal associations [include] self-help groups such as Alcoholics Anonymous . . . [,] support groups for survivors of . . . [cancer and other diseases, and] . . . soup kitchens and shelters (especially those . . . affiliated with churches) . . . .[22]

These groups typically

> lack legal status and depend on small cash and in-kind donations to support their activities. * * * These informal groups usually accept no external grant funds and depend completely on volunteers, although they may receive periodic support from more formal institutions and may collaborate with established public and nonprofit institutions.[23]

There are, however, a number of large, national, nonprofit social services agencies, such as the American Red Cross, Catholic Charities USA, Lutheran Services in America, and Jewish Family Services. These agencies generally are incorporated as tax-exempt charitable organizations under section 501(c)(3) of the federal Internal Revenue Code, provide social services to millions of people, and receive billions of dollars in public and private funding.

And in the middle of the continuum are thousands of other nonprofit social service organizations that often have a formal associational or corporate structure, a small professional or semi-professional staff,

---

Tsitsos%20Report.pdf (last visited April 14, 2008). Of these congregations, most provided short-term and emergency services (food, shelter, and clothing). Services generally were provided by small groups of volunteers; only 6 percent of the congregations employed at least one person more than quarter-time to coordinate or provide social services and only 3 percent received public funding for social services. Mark Chaves, "Religious Congregations and Welfare Reform: Who Will Take Advantage of 'Charitable Choice'?" (Washington, D.C.: Aspen Inst., 1999), available at www.nonprofitresearch.org/usr_doc/19966.pdf (last visited April 14, 2008).

22. Smith, "Social Services," 153.

23. *Id.*

affiliations with the United Way,[24] and a small to moderate but often diversified base of private, and sometimes public, funding.[25]

The diversity of North Carolina's nonprofit social services agencies is reflected in the list and descriptions of agencies and organizations that follow:[26]

- The Alliance of AIDS Services—Carolina is one of several regional nonprofit agencies that provide social services, transportation, housing, and other services to people with HIV/AIDS.
- Another Choice for Black Children, Inc., is a Charlotte-based nonprofit agency that provides adoption and family services.
- The Asheville-Buncombe Community Christian Ministry is one of dozens of local interfaith or religious social services agencies in North Carolina. Others include Interfaith Social Services in Chapel Hill, Orange Congregations in Mission in Hillsborough, and Urban Ministries programs in Durham, Fayetteville, Greensboro, and Raleigh.
- Catholic Social Services of the Diocese of Charlotte, North Carolina, Inc. (CSS) provides adoption services, pregnancy support services, counseling, immigration services, refugee resettlement services, and other social services to persons living in western North Carolina. A sister agency provides similar services to persons living in eastern North Carolina. CSS has ten offices, a staff of almost 100, almost 500 volunteers, and an annual budget of over $5 million (including about $1.8 million in federal and state funding). It serves about 18,000 persons each year.

---

24. The United Way is not a single organization but rather a group of independent, but affiliated, state, regional, and local organizations that provide services to a wide variety of nonprofit and community agencies and provide a means for coordinated fundraising efforts for those agencies. Additional information about United Way of North Carolina (UWNC) and its affiliated United Way organizations is available on the UWNC website at www.nc211.org (last visited April 14, 2008).

25. Smith, "Social Services," 153. *See also* Gulati-Partee, "A Primer on Nonprofit Organizations."

26. Business corporations and other "for-profit" entities also play an important role in providing social services. *See* Smith, "Social Services," 155–158; Salamon, *America's Nonprofit Sector*, 115. This chapter, however, focuses almost exclusively on the role of *nonprofit* organizations in providing social services and the relationships between state and local governments and these nonprofit social services agencies.

- The Children's Home Society of North Carolina, Inc., (CHS) provides pregnancy counseling, family and therapeutic foster care, and adoption services through eight regional offices across the state. CHS is funded through private contributions, government-funded performance-based contracts, churches, foundations, and the United Way. It is one of approximately forty licensed child-placing agencies in the state.
- Crisis Assistance Ministry, a nonprofit organization in Charlotte, contracts with Mecklenburg County, the city of Charlotte, and the N.C. Office of Economic Opportunity to administer several federal, state, and local assistance programs that provide emergency assistance to low-income families. Government funding and in-kind assistance constitutes more than half of the agency's $12 million annual budget.
- The Durham Rescue Mission (DRM) is a faith-based, nonprofit organization that provides food, shelter, and other assistance to homeless and needy persons in Durham. DRM relies upon gifts from individuals, churches, businesses, civic groups, organizations, and foundations, and operates without any government funding.
- The Food Bank of Central and Eastern North Carolina is one of seven America's Second Harvest affiliates in North Carolina. It distributes about $50 million in donated food each year to thousands of North Carolinians who are at risk of hunger.
- With an annual budget of more than $20 million, Lutheran Family Services in the Carolinas provides adoption, foster care, and residential services for children, refugee and immigration services, counseling, and other social services to more than 10,000 North Carolinians through three regional offices.
- Founded in 1899, the Methodist Home for Children in Raleigh provides residential care, foster care, adoption, and substance abuse services for children and families. Residential services for children also are provided by the Masonic Home for Children at Oxford, the Baptist Children's Homes of North Carolina, and other nonprofit organizations.
- The North Carolina Partnership for Children is a public–private partnership that administers North Carolina's "Smart Start" early childhood development program. The purposes of the Smart Start program are to improve the quality of child care, make child care more affordable and accessible, provide access to health services,

and offer family support. The partnership consists of a state-created, publicly funded, nonprofit agency (the North Carolina Partnership for Children, Inc.) and a statewide network of local, nonprofit Smart Start agencies.

- The Salvation Army is a Christian denomination that operates thrift stores and provides food, financial assistance, and social services to needy persons.
- Senior Services, Inc. of Winston-Salem is one of dozens of nonprofit organizations that provide social services to North Carolina's senior citizens.
- Telamon Corp. is a nonprofit corporation that provides literacy and early childhood education, job training, emergency services, housing, and other human services to farm workers, children, low-income families, and special needs populations in twelve states, including North Carolina.
- The Welfare Reform Liaison Project in Greensboro is a faith-based social services organization that was founded in 1998 by Mt. Zion Baptist Church. The project has received funding from the North Carolina Department of Commerce and the state's Division of Social Services to provide job training for welfare recipients.

## Relationships between Government and Nonprofit Social Services Agencies

In recent years, state and "local governments all across the United States have increased their involvement with nonprofit organizations."[27] This trend is especially evident in the context of public-private partnerships in the area of social services.[28]

---

27. Gordon P. Whitaker and James C. Drennan, "Local Government and Nonprofit Organizations, Article 11 in *County and Municipal Government in North Carolina*" (Chapel Hill: School of Government, The University of North Carolina at Chapel Hill, 2007), available at www.sog.unc.edu/pubs/cmg/cmg11.pdf.

28. *See* Steven Rathgeb Smith and Michael Lipsky, *Nonprofits for Hire: The Welfare State in the Age of Contracting* (Cambridge, MA: Harvard University Press, 1993); Richard P. Nathan, "The 'Nonprofitization Movement' as a Form of Devolution" in Dwight F. Burlingame et al., eds., *Capacity for Change? The Nonprofit World in the Age of Devolution* (Indianapolis: Indiana University Center on Philanthropy, 1996), 23–55; Mark Carl Rom, "From Welfare State to Opportunity, Inc.: Public-Private Partnerships in Welfare Reform," *American Behavioral Scientist* 43(1): 155–176 (1999).

In some instances, government agencies cooperate or collaborate with nonprofit and community organizations "to plan ways to address community needs, to coordinate delivery of . . . services, and to operate programs together."[29] In other instances, government agencies purchase public services from nonprofits, rather than providing these services directly.[30] And state and local governments also "provide both in-kind and financial grants to help nonprofits produce public services."[31]

### COLLABORATION AND COOPERATION BETWEEN GOVERNMENT AND NONPROFIT AGENCIES

> By working together to identify problems that require public attention and to develop ways to address those problems, local governments and nonprofits can share expertise and information, gain the insights of diverse perspectives, and explore new ways of solving problems. Discussions among government officials and staff, non-profit leaders, and other concerned citizens can produce both a fuller understanding of public problems and more creative and effective ways to deal with them.[32]

The decision to enter into a collaborative or cooperative partnership is "usually a mutual decision" that can be initiated by a government agency or official or by a nonprofit organization.[33]

> Regardless of who initiates the partnership, however, government officials and nonprofit leaders must each see that they can meet their own organizational goals better by working together than by working alone.[34]

Collaborative "partnerships" between local governments and non-profits are common but not universal in North Carolina.[35]

---

29. Whitaker and Drennan, "Local Government and Nonprofit Organizations."
30. *Id.*
31. *Id.*
32. *Id.*
33. *Id.*
34. *Id.*
35. Whitaker and Drennan, "Local Government and Nonprofit Organizations;" Gordon P. Whitaker and Rosalind Day, "How Local Governments Work with Non-profit Organizations in North Carolina," *Popular Government* 66(2) (Winter 2001): 25-32.

A 1999 survey of North Carolina cities and counties found that almost a third of responding cities and almost half of responding counties were involved with nonprofit organizations in coordinating the delivery of public services to the community.[36] In this type of partnership, local government agencies, such as the county social services department, and nonprofit agencies "each carry out their own activities in ways that fit with or depend upon the work of the others."[37] For example, since nonprofit social services agencies sometimes provide services that complement or supplement the social services provided by public social services agencies and sometimes provide services that are not offered by existing government social services programs, a county social worker might "refer clients to a mix of nonprofit and government services" or coordinate the social services department's delivery of assistance to a client with nonprofit social services agencies in the community.[38]

Local governments also partner with nonprofit organizations by cooperatively planning the services that each will provide and by collaborating in joint service programs.[39]

The work of faith and community coordinators in several county departments of social services is one example of partnership, cooperation, and collaboration between counties and nonprofit social services agencies. About nineteen North Carolina counties provide public funding for these coordinators, who act as liaisons between the county and local churches and community social services agencies, recruit community and faith-based organizations to provide mentoring and other services to clients of the county social services department, and encourage involvement of community and faith-based organizations in providing social services to the community.[40]

---

36. Whitaker and Day, "How Local Governments Work with Nonprofit Organizations in North Carolina," 26–27.

37. Whitaker and Drennan, "Local Government and Nonprofit Organizations."

38. *Id.*

39. *Id.* A 1999 survey of North Carolina cities and counties found that almost a third of the responding cities and almost half of the responding counties cooperated with nonprofit organizations with respect to service planning and that about a third of the responding cities and counties collaborated with nonprofit organizations in providing joint service programs. Whitaker and Day, "How Local Governments Work with Nonprofit Organizations in North Carolina," 26–27.

40. *See* John L. Saxon, "Faith-Based Social Services: What Are They? Do They Work? Are They Legal? What's Happening in North Carolina?" *Popular Government* 70(1) (Fall 2004): 4–5, 10.

## GOVERNMENT FUNDING AND SUPPORT OF NONPROFIT SOCIAL SERVICES AGENCIES

Nationally, nonprofit social services agencies depend on government funding for more than one-third of their financial support and government provides approximately $20 billion in funding to nonprofit social services agencies each year.[41]

In some instances, government support of nonprofit social services agencies takes the form of in-kind support or financial grants. In other instances, government funding for nonprofit social services is provided through performance contracts involving the provision of social services by nonprofit agencies.

The Institute of Government's 1999 survey of North Carolina cities and counties found that local governments provided almost $75 million in financial support to nonprofit organizations in the 1998 fiscal year.[42] More than 60 percent of responding cities and counties reported providing in-kind support for nonprofit organizations, while almost 80 percent of responding cities and 95 percent of responding counties reported budgeting public funding for nonprofit organizations.[43]

Statewide, 35 percent of the nonprofits that received funding from cities and 40 percent of the nonprofits that received funding from counties were nonprofit human services agencies.[44] In larger counties, almost 70 percent of the nonprofits that received funding were nonprofit human services agencies.[45]

Public funding of nonprofit organizations, however, raises a number of important issues of public policy and law.[46] First, North Carolina law

---

41. Salamon, *America's Nonprofit Sector*, 113–114.

42. Whitaker and Day, "How Local Governments Work with Nonprofit Organizations in North Carolina," 27. Unless otherwise noted, the survey data refer to financial support for *all* types of nonprofit organizations for *all* types of services, not just nonprofit human services agencies or providers.

43. *Id.* at 26.

44. *Id.* at 28.

45. *Id.* at 20.

46. "As a general rule, a nonprofit's receipt of public funds does not make it subject to the rules that govern public agencies, such as those pertaining to bidding, public personnel, public records, and open meetings." Frayda S. Bluestein and Anita R. Brown-Graham, "Local Government Contracts with Nonprofit Organizations: Questions and Answers," *Popular Government* 67(1) (Fall 2001): 32, 39. Federal and state law, however, may impose specific requirements on nonprofit organizations that receive federal or state funding. G.S. 143-6.2, for example, requires nongovernmental entities that receive state or federal pass-through

provides that public funds may be spent only for "public purposes."[47] All public funding for nonprofit social services agencies, therefore, must be for a valid *public* purpose. And even when there is no question that public funding of nonprofits is *legal*, state and local government officials still must determine what services or programs will be supported, which nonprofits will be funded, how much funding will be provided, how funding decisions will be made, and how nonprofits will be held accountable for their use of public funding.[48]

### GOVERNMENT FUNDING OF FAITH-BASED SOCIAL SERVICES PROGRAMS

Faith-based social services programs and agencies constitute a particular subset of nonprofit social services agencies. Government funding of faith-based social services programs and agencies, therefore, involves some of the same issues that arise in connection with government

---

grant funds from a state agency to adopt a conflict-of-interest policy and file that policy with the grantor agency.

47. N.C. CONST. art. V, §§ 2(1) and 2(7). *See also* G.S. 153A-449; G.S. 160A-20.1; G.S. 160A-279; G.S. 153A-255; G.S. 160A-492; G.S. 160A-494; G.S. 160A-497; Hughey v. Cloninger, 297 N.C. 86, 95, 253 S.E.2d 898, 903–04 (1979); David M. Lawrence, *Local Government Finance in North Carolina*, 2d ed. (Chapel Hill: Institute of Government, The University of North Carolina at Chapel Hill, 1990), 1–14; Bluestein and Brown-Graham, "Local Government Contracts with Nonprofit Organizations," 32–33.

48. These questions are discussed in detail in Margaret Henderson et al., "Deciding to Fund Nonprofits: Key Questions," *Popular Government* 67(4) (Summer 2002): 33–39 and Margaret Henderson et al., "Establishing Mutual Accountability in Nonprofit-Government Relationships," *Popular Government* 69(1) (Fall 2003): 18–29. State law requires nonprofit organizations that receive more than $1,000 in state funds to submit to an audit if requested by the state auditor. G.S. 159-40(b). State law also allows a city or county to require a nonprofit to conduct an audit and file a copy of the audit with the city or county if the nonprofit receives more than $1,000 in grants or appropriations from the city or county in any fiscal year. G.S. 159-40(a). All nongovernmental entities that receive state or federal pass-through grant funds from a state agency are required to file a certification with the agency and the state auditor stating that the grant funds were used for the purposes specified in the grant. G.S. 143-6.2; 9 N.C. ADMIN. CODE 03M .0205. Grantees that receive less than $500,000 must file an accounting of state funds received, used, or expended. Grantees that receive more than $500,000 must conduct a "yellow book" audit. Nonprofit social services agencies that receive more than $500,000 per year in grants or cost-reimbursement contracts directly from *federal* agencies generally are required to file a "yellow book" compliance audit under the federal Single Audit Act of 1984, as amended. 31 U.S.C. §§ 7501 through 7507.

funding of nonprofit social services agencies generally. There are, however, additional legal and policy issues with respect to public funding of faith-based social services programs and agencies.[49]

As noted above, many churches and other religious organizations offer social services to the community but do so without establishing a formal entity separate and apart from the church or organization. In other instances, faith-based social services organizations are structurally and operationally independent of individual churches, denominations, or other religious organizations. And in some cases, faith-based social services programs or agencies are affiliated, either loosely or closely, with related religious organizations.

More importantly, some faith-based social services programs and agencies are more religious in character while others operate in a more secular manner. Some faith-based social services programs and agencies explicitly and consciously integrate religious activities, prayer, worship, or "spiritual technologies" into the social services they provide. But some do not and, although "imbued with strong religious motivations" or affiliated with religious organizations, "follow the same norms and procedures . . . as 'secular' social service organizations."[50]

State and local governments have a long history of funding the provision of social services through religiously affiliated social services agencies.[51] During the past decade, however, a series of "charitable choice" and "faith-based and community organization" initiatives by the federal government have placed more emphasis on faith-based social services than they have received at any time in American history and have "pushed the envelope" with respect to government funding of faith-based social services.[52]

---

49. Some of these issues are discussed in more detail in Saxon, "Faith-Based Social Services," and Bluestein and Brown-Graham, "Local Government Contracts with Nonprofit Organizations."

50. Andrew Walsh, ed., *Can Charitable Choice Work?* (Hartford, CT: Trinity College, 2001), 2. *See also* Saxon, "Faith-Based Social Services," 6.

51. *See* Saxon, "Faith-Based Social Services," 6.

52. Federal charitable choice and faith-based initiatives, the assumptions underlying these initiatives, their implementation, and issues regarding their legality are discussed in Saxon, "Faith-Based Social Services." *See also* Bluestein and Brown-Graham, "Local Government Contracts with Nonprofit Organizations" (discussing constitutional limitations regarding public funding of faith-based organizations).

Many people *assume* that faith-based social services are effective, and there is *some* anecdotal and statistical evidence that supports this assumption. However, "policy makers should not assume that the 'faith factor' alone can make [a faith-based organization] effective in carrying out its mission[, and g]overnment support of [faith-based organizations] should be performance-based and contingent on the achievement of demonstrable results.[53]

In addition, policymakers need to be aware of the potential constitutional problems involved in funding faith-based social services programs—especially when direct financial assistance is provided to pervasively religious institutions and faith-saturated social services programs. It is clear that state and local governments in North Carolina are not prohibited from funding or contracting with faith-based social services programs or agencies. In-kind or financial assistance provided by a state or local government to a faith-based social services program appears to be constitutionally permissible as long as the assistance (1) is not given for, or diverted to, activities that promote religious indoctrination, (2) does not constitute government endorsement of religion, and (3) does not entangle government with religion.[54]

### GOVERNMENT CONTRACTS WITH NONPROFIT SOCIAL SERVICES AGENCIES
In addition to collaborating with and providing grants to nonprofit social services agencies, state and local governments sometimes enter into contracts with nonprofit organizations for the "purchase" of social

53. Lewis D. Solomon and Matthew J. Vlissides Jr., "In God We Trust?: Assessing the Potential of Faith-Based Social Services" (Washington, DC: Progressive Policy Institute, 2001) at 1–2, available at www.ppionline.org/documents/FBOs_v2.pdf) (last visited April 14, 2008).

54. *See* Saxon, "Faith-Based Social Services," 8–9. *See also* Anita R. Brown-Graham, "Contracts with Faith-Based Organizations" in Bluestein and Brown-Graham, "Local Government Contracts with Nonprofit Organizations," 40–41. *Cf.* Americans United for Separation of Church and State v. Prison Fellowship Ministries, 432 F. Supp. 2d 862 (S.D.Iowa 2006). Public funding that is provided *indirectly* (for example, through the use of vouchers that individuals can use to obtain services from an array of public or private providers) to faith-based social services agencies (even those that thoroughly integrate religious activities into their services) appears to be constitutionally permissible as long as (1) the government is neutral between religious and secular social services providers and (2) the people who receive services have a "genuine and independent choice" among religious and secular social services providers. Saxon, "Faith-Based Social Services," 8–9.

services on behalf of the public or a government agency.[55] These "purchase of service" contracts typically specify what services the nonprofit organization will provide in return for government funding, who will receive services, how many clients will be served, how services will be delivered, how the nonprofit organization will be paid for the services it provides, how the organization's provision of services will be measured or evaluated, and how the organization will be held accountable for its performance.[56]

The Institute of Government's 1999 survey of North Carolina cities and counties found that almost 40 percent of responding cities and 60 percent of responding counties entered into "purchase of service" contracts with nonprofit organizations, but did not indicate what percentage of these contracts involved social services.[57]

State law does not require state or county social services agencies to use a "competitive bidding" procedure for "purchase of service" contracts with nonprofit organizations.[58] The procedure for deciding which nonprofits will receive public funding and for entering into grants or contracts with nonprofit social services agencies, therefore, varies widely across the state.[59] Local governments, however, are required to

---

55. Whitaker and Drennan, "Local Government and Nonprofit Organizations."

56. *See* Whitaker and Drennan, "Local Government and Nonprofit Organizations"; Whitaker and Day, "How Local Governments Work with Nonprofits in North Carolina," 30.

57. Whitaker and Day, "How Local Governments Work with Nonprofits in North Carolina," 30.

58. G.S. 143-129; G.S. 143-131. *See* Bluestein and Brown-Graham, "Local Government Contracts with Nonprofit Organizations," 37–38. State policy, local ordinances, or federal law, however, may require state or county social services agencies to use a "competitive bidding" procedure for procurement or "purchase of service" contracts with nonprofit organizations in certain circumstances. *See*, for example, 45 C.F.R. §§ 92.36 and 92.37 requiring state and local governments that receive federal grants to follow specified procedures in connection with subgrants to or procurement contracts with nonprofit organizations. The requirements of 45 C.F.R. §§ 92.36 and 92.37, however, do not apply to subgrants and contracts under the federal Social Services Block Grant. 45 C.F.R. § 92.4(a)(2).

59. Although a grant is a type of contract, the process for awarding grants usually is different from the process of awarding contracts. "Competition is typically structured differently, and in many cases a grant may describe the required performance in less detail than other contracts." Bluestein and Brown-Graham, "Local Government Contracts with Nonprofit Organizations," 35.

comply with certain state laws when contracting with nonprofit social services agencies.[60]

## BUILDING EFFECTIVE GOVERNMENT–NONPROFIT RELATIONSHIPS

Government social services agencies and nonprofit social services agencies can and do work together to meet the social and economic needs of North Carolinians. "The challenge for the two sectors is to find ways to work together that permit them to fulfill their unique responsibilities while complementing each other's work."[61]

There is, of course, "no one *right* relationship between governments and nonprofit organizations."[62] Governments and nonprofit organizations, however, can strengthen their relationships through frequent and accurate communication; discussing their differing perceptions of problems, issues, organizations, and relationships; increasing their understanding of each other's work, strengths, resources, and limitations; developing clear and mutual expectations; engaging in mutual problem-solving; providing constructive feedback to each other; being mutually accountable to each other; and addressing issues regarding imbalance of power in their relationships.[63]

60. Some of these requirements are summarized in Bluestein and Brown-Graham, "Local Government Contracts with Nonprofit Organizations."

61. Lydian Altman-Sauer et al., "Strengthening Relationships between Local Governments and Nonprofits," *Popular Government* 66(2) (Winter 2001): 33, 34.

62. Altman-Sauer et al., "Strengthening Relationships between Local Governments and Nonprofits," 35.

63. *See* Altman-Sauer et al., "Strengthening Relationships between Local Governments and Nonprofits" and Henderson et al., "Establishing Mutual Accountability in Nonprofit-Government Relationships."

# Chapter 11

# Social Services Programs

State and county social services agencies in North Carolina administer dozens of social services programs that provide a wide range of assistance and services to North Carolinians.[1]

## Overview of Public Assistance and Social Services Programs

Public assistance and social services programs address a variety of social and economic problems—poverty, hunger and malnutrition, lack of medical care, homelessness, child abuse and neglect, elder abuse and neglect, teen-aged pregnancy, out-of-wedlock births, unemployment, and more—that impair the well-being of children, families, the poor, disabled persons, and senior citizens. To address these problems, some social services programs provide financial assistance, food assistance, or health care. Others provide services that protect vulnerable children or adults from abuse or neglect, that collect child support from absent parents, or that assist individuals or families to become more self-sufficient.

The term "social services" can be used to refer collectively to all of the programs administered by state and county social services agencies. Often, however, these programs are divided into two broad, and somewhat imprecise, categories: *public assistance* programs and *social services* programs. Public assistance programs generally provide financial assistance (either direct cash payments to recipients or payments to persons who provide goods or services to recipients) to certain categories of the poor and are *means tested* (that is, a person is not eligible for assistance unless his or her income and assets are less than the specified financial eligibility standard for the program). The Work First, Food and Nutrition Services, Medicaid, and State–County Special Assistance programs are some examples of public assistance programs. By contrast, social services programs generally provide in-kind benefits or services to recipients and generally are not means tested. Examples of social services programs include child protective services, adult protective

---

1. Approximately two million North Carolinians (more than 20 percent of the state's population) receive some type of assistance or service each year through the state Department of Health and Human Services (DHHS) or county departments of social services. [Source: Author's estimate based on statistics obtained from several DHHS sources.]

services, guardianship services, adoption placement services, and child support enforcement services.

Public assistance and social services programs primarily serve children, families, the poor, disabled persons, and senior citizens. Some social services programs provide assistance only for children and families. Others serve only elderly or disabled persons. In a broader sense, though, social services programs serve the entire community and state.

Each particular social services program has its own rules about who may receive assistance or services.[2] An individual or family, therefore, might be eligible for assistance or services under one program, but ineligible for assistance or services under another. Some social services programs are means tested and provide assistance only to persons whose incomes and assets are low enough to be considered poor. Other social services are not means tested and may be provided to individuals regardless of their financial status. As a general rule, individuals and families who are eligible for public assistance or social services are not required to pay for the services they receive or reimburse the state for the assistance they have been provided.[3]

Most social services programs are created by federal or state laws enacted by the U.S. Congress or North Carolina's General Assembly. Social services programs that are created by federal law are called federal social services programs, or federal–state social services programs if they are funded by the federal government and administered by state or local social services agencies. The Medicaid, Food and Nutrition Services, and child support enforcement programs are examples of federal–state social services programs. Social services programs that are created pursuant to state, rather than federal, law are called state social

---

2. This aspect of eligibility for social services sometimes is referred to as a "silo" configuration.

3. Families who apply for child support enforcement services, however, may be required to pay an application fee of $10 or $25. *See* Section 110-130.1(a) of the North Carolina General Statutes [hereinafter G.S.]. The state Medicaid program also requires eligible recipients to make copayments with respect to some services, and, in some instances, may recover the cost of medical assistance from the estates of deceased Medicaid recipients. *See* G.S. 108A-70.5. And rules adopted by the state Social Services Commission require client contributions for adult day care services, adult day health services, some housing and home improvement services, in-home aide services, personal and family counseling services, and meal preparation and delivery services provided through the Social Services Block Grant. *See* 10A N.C. ADMIN. CODE 71S .0201.

services programs. The State–County Special Assistance program and State Foster Care Assistance program are examples of state social services programs. Social services programs, however, also may be created at the county level through action by the board of county commissioners, the board of social services, or the county social services director if there is federal, state, county, or private funding available to pay the cost of the program, and these programs are called county social services programs.

Some federal and state laws create a legal right or entitlement with respect to particular public assistance or social services programs.[4] This means that an individual or family has a legally enforceable right to receive assistance or services under the program if the individual or family meets all of the eligibility requirements for the program, and that the state (or county) must provide assistance or services under the program to all eligible individuals or families regardless of how many people are eligible for assistance or how much it costs to provide assistance to eligible recipients.[5] If a social services agency refuses to provide assistance or services to which an individual or family is legally entitled, the individual or family may sue the agency and seek a court order requiring the agency to provide the assistance or services. The existence and scope of this legal entitlement to assistance, however, is based on the law that governs the social services program and may be abolished or changed by legislative action.

## Administration of Public Assistance and Social Services Programs

Under North Carolina's county-administered and state-supervised social services system, county departments of social services are primarily responsible for administering federal–state and state public assistance

---

4. The Medicaid and Food and Nutrition Services programs are two examples of entitlements. By contrast, state law (G.S. 108A-27.15) expressly provides that Work First assistance is not an entitlement and that the state Work First laws do not create any property right with respect to assistance under the Work First program.

5. When federal or state laws do not create an entitlement to public assistance or social services, an individual generally has the right to apply for assistance, to be treated fairly and equally with respect to his or her application, and to receive assistance if he or she is eligible for assistance and the agency has sufficient money or resources to provide the requested assistance or services.

and social services programs under the supervision of the state Department of Health and Human Services (DHHS).

In the case of public assistance programs, the counties' administrative responsibilities generally include processing applications for assistance, determining eligibility for assistance, reviewing continued eligibility for assistance, and investigating potential fraud and abuse. State, rather than county, social services agencies generally are responsible for making assistance payments to or on behalf of eligible individuals and families and for making final agency decisions in administrative appeals regarding eligibility.

In the case of social services programs, county social services departments generally are responsible for investigating reports regarding the abuse, neglect, or dependency of juveniles, investigating reports regarding the abuse, neglect, or exploitation of disabled adults, processing applications for services, determining eligibility for services, and providing services directly or through other public or private entities.

Title VI of the federal Civil Rights Act of 1964 prohibits state and county social services agencies from discriminating against persons on the basis of race, color, or national origin in the provision of public assistance and social services and requires state and county social services agencies to take reasonable steps to ensure that persons with limited English proficiency have meaningful access to the programs, services, and information that these agencies provide.[6]

### APPLYING FOR ASSISTANCE AND SERVICES

County departments of social services generally provide public assistance and social services to an individual or family only in response to a request for assistance from the individual or family.[7] A request for assistance or services generally must be made by completing a written application for assistance or services and filing the application with the department. Rules for some social services programs recognize an

---

6. *See* 42 U.S.C. § 2000d.

7. The county social services department is required to provide adult protective services, child protective services, and guardianship services regardless of whether an individual or family applies for services. Child protective services, for example, must be provided if the department determines, in response to a report from the family, a relative, friend, neighbor, teacher, doctor, or other source, that a child may be abused, neglected, or dependent and needs protection.

individual's right to file an application for assistance or services on the same day he or she first contacts the social services department.

When an individual or family applies for assistance or services, a county social services employee generally interviews the applicant, reviews the application, requests additional information needed to determine the applicant's eligibility, determines whether the applicant meets the eligibility requirements for assistance or services, and sends a written notice to the applicant stating whether he or she is eligible for assistance and services.

In some instances, the county social services department must determine an applicant's eligibility within a specific period of time after the applicant submits an application for assistance. For example, under the Food and Nutrition Services program, the social services department generally must determine a household's eligibility within thirty days from the date the household applies for assistance or within five days in emergency situations.

### ELIGIBILITY FOR ASSISTANCE AND SERVICES

As noted above, each particular social services program has its own detailed requirements regarding who is eligible for assistance or services. In most instances, therefore, the fact that an individual or family meets all of the eligibility requirements for one social services program does not necessarily mean that the individual or family is eligible for assistance or services under another social services program.[8]

Eligibility requirements for social services programs generally are found in federal statutes and regulations, in state statutes and rules, or in both, depending on whether the program in question is federally funded. For example, the eligibility requirements for the Food and Nutrition Services program are found almost entirely in the federal Food Stamp Act and in regulations promulgated by the U.S. Department of Agriculture. Eligibility for the State–County Special Assistance program, by contrast, is governed by state statutes and rules, not federal law. And eligibility for the state Medicaid program is governed by both federal and state law.

Eligibility rules for social services programs are contained and explained in a series of eligibility, policy, and procedure manuals that

---

8. There are exceptions to this rule. A person who is receiving Work First Family Assistance, for example, generally is automatically eligible for Medicaid.

are published by the state Department of Health and Human Services (DHHS) and used by county social services employees.[9] These manuals, however, do not, in and of themselves, have the force and effect of law and they may not establish eligibility requirements that are in addition to or inconsistent with those stated in federal and state law.[10]

Eligibility requirements for social services programs fall into two broad categories:

- financial eligibility requirements, and
- non-financial or personal eligibility requirements.

When a social services program includes both financial and non-financial eligibility requirements, an individual or family must meet both the financial and non-financial eligibility requirements in order to receive assistance or services under that program.

### FINANCIAL ELIGIBILITY REQUIREMENTS

Some, but not all, social services programs impose financial eligibility requirements with respect to the amount of an individual's or family's income and assets.[11]

When a social services program includes rules regarding financial eligibility, these rules usually require individuals and families to meet two distinct financial eligibility standards:

- one based on the amount of the individual's, family's, or household's income, and
- a second based on the value of the assets or property owned by the individual, family, or household.

---

9. Many of these eligibility manuals are accessible online at info.dhhs.state .nc.us/olm/manuals/default.aspx (last visited April 16, 2008).

10. See Surgeon v. N.C. Div. of Social Servs., 86 N.C. App. 252, 264, 357 S.E.2d 388, 394 (1987); Dillingham v. N.C. Dep't of Human Resources, 132 N.C. App. 704, 710, 513 S.E.2d 823, 827 (1999); Duke Univ. Med. Ctr. v. Bruton, 134 N.C. App. 39, 51–52, 516 S.E.2d 633, 640–41 (1999). Cf. Okale v. N.C. Dep't of Health and Human Servs., 153 N.C. App. 475, 477–79; 570 S.E.2d 741, 743 (2002).

11. An otherwise eligible individual may receive the following social services without regard to his or her income: child protective services, adult protective services, adoption services, adult placement services, delinquency prevention services, individual and family adjustment services, problem pregnancy services, and other specified services provided under the Social Services Block Grant. See 10A N.C. ADMIN. CODE 71R .0506.

*Income Eligibility Rules*

When a social services program includes rules regarding financial eligibility, these rules generally require that an individual's, family's, or household's net "countable" income not exceed the income eligibility limit for that program.

Countable income generally is defined as gross income minus excluded income. The eligibility rules for some programs exclude certain types of income from consideration in determining financial eligibility.[12] Net countable income means countable income minus any deductions from countable income allowed under the income eligibility rules of a program.[13] In some programs, net countable income is used to determine both eligibility and the amount of assistance that will be provided.

Income eligibility limits vary from program to program. Programs that are not means tested do not have income eligibility limits. The income eligibility limit for some means tested programs is equal to the federal poverty level (FPL) or a multiple—125 percent, 130 percent, 185 percent, or 200 percent—of the FPL.[14] But the income eligibility limit for some means tested programs is much lower than the federal poverty level.[15] So some individuals and families who are poor according to the federal poverty level are not poor enough to receive some types

---

12. For example, the Food and Nutrition Services program excludes earned income tax credit payments and HUD utility allowance payments from countable income.

13. For example, the eligibility rules for the Food and Nutrition Services program include several deductions from a household's countable income, including a "standard" deduction (currently $134 per month for households of fewer than four members) plus 20 percent of the household's earned income.

14. Households are not eligible for food and nutrition assistance if their net monthly incomes exceed the federal poverty level (FPL). Children under the age of six are financially eligible for Medicaid if their family incomes are less than twice the FPL. The FPL is established by the U.S. Department of Health and Human Services; is adjusted each year; varies based on the number of persons in the household; and attempts to provide a rough measure of the amount of income a family needs in order to obtain adequate housing, food, and other basic necessities. In 2007 the FPL for a family of three living in North Carolina was $17,170 per year (or about $1,431 per month).

15. The income eligibility limit for Work First Family Assistance as of September 1, 2007, is $544 per month for a family of three (approximately 37 percent of the FPL). As of September 1, 2007, the current medically needy income limit for Medicaid for a single, elderly or disabled person is $242 per month (approximately 28 percent of the FPL).

of means tested public assistance, while other individuals and families who are not poor, using the federal poverty level as the standard, are needy enough to receive other types of public assistance.

*Resource Eligibility Rules*

Most public assistance programs that have income eligibility limits also have resource eligibility rules.[16] These rules provide that an otherwise eligible individual or family is not eligible for assistance if the value of his or her countable assets exceeds the program's resource eligibility limit.[17] But certain types of property or assets are not countable assets and, therefore, are not considered in determining whether an individual meets a program's resource eligibility requirements.[18] And resource eligibility limits, like income eligibility limits, vary from program to program.[19]

Three public assistance programs—the Medicaid, Food and Nutrition Services, and State–County Special Assistance programs—limit the eligibility of individuals who transfer assets for less than fair market value in order to qualify for assistance.[20]

## NON-FINANCIAL OR PERSONAL ELIGIBILITY REQUIREMENTS

All social services programs have at least one non-financial or personal eligibility requirement that is usually based on an individual's personal status—for example, as a disabled adult, a dependent child, or an abused or neglected juvenile—or on his or her non-financial need for assistance or services. These types of personal eligibility requirements sometimes are referred to as categorical eligibility requirements,

---

16. There is no resource eligibility limit for Medicaid eligibility for some categories of children and pregnant women who meet Medicaid's income eligibility requirements.

17. Resource eligibility rules also determine how the value of an asset or other property is calculated.

18. In the Food and Nutrition Services program, for example, one motor vehicle per adult household member is excluded in determining a household's eligibility.

19. Under the Food and Nutrition Services program, the resource eligibility limit for most households is $2,000. The Medicaid resource eligibility limits for elderly and disabled persons range from $2,000 to $6,000.

20. *See* G.S. 108A-58.1 and 42 U.S.C. § 1396p (Medicaid); 7 U.S.C. § 2015(h) (Food and Nutrition Services); G.S. 108A-46.1 (State–County Special Assistance).

meaning that assistance is provided only to certain categories of needy individuals or families.

Many social services programs impose additional non-financial eligibility requirements regarding citizenship and immigration status, residency, and other factors.

### Citizenship and Immigration Status

Federal law restricts the eligibility of non-citizens—aliens (non-citizens) who are living in the U.S. legally as well as illegal or undocumented aliens—to receive Food and Nutrition Services, Medicaid, Work First, and other federal, state, or local public benefits.[21]

A noncitizen's eligibility for public benefits depends, in part, on whether he or she is a "nonqualified alien" or a "qualified alien." A qualified alien is a noncitizen who

- is a lawful permanent resident alien;
- has been lawfully admitted to the U.S. as a refugee;
- has been granted asylum;
- has been "paroled" into the U.S. for at least a year;
- has been granted withholding of deportation;
- was granted conditional entry into the U.S. before April 1, 1980;
- was admitted to the U.S. as a Cuban or Haitian "entrant"; or
- is a battered spouse or child who meets certain criteria specified in federal law.[22]

By contrast, a non-citizen is a "nonqualified alien" if he or she is

- a nonimmigrant, *or*
- an illegal or undocumented alien, *or*
- a *legal* immigrant who is not a "qualified alien."

---

21. The eligibility of non-citizens to receive publicly funded benefits and services is discussed in detail in Jill Moore, "Are Immigrants Eligible for Publicly Funded Benefits and Services?" *Local Government Law Bulletin* No. 110 (Chapel Hill: School of Government, The University of North Carolina at Chapel Hill, 2007). The terms "alien" and "non-citizen" are synonymous. *Immigrants* are aliens who are living in the U.S. with the intent to remain here indefinitely. *Legal immigrants* are immigrants who are living in the U.S. with legal permission. *Illegal* or *undocumented immigrants* are immigrants who do not have legal permission to live in the U.S. *Non-immigrants* are aliens who are present in the U.S. on a temporary basis as tourists, students, and so forth.

22. *See* 8 U.S.C. § 1641.

Nonqualified aliens generally are ineligible to receive any public benefit that is provided or funded by the federal government, a state government, or a local government, including

- Medicaid (other than emergency services);
- food and nutrition services;
- Work First Family Assistance payments;
- low-income home energy assistance;
- adoption and foster care assistance payments;
- subsidized child day care assistance;
- refugee assistance;
- Supplemental Security Income (SSI) payments;
- any other retirement, welfare, health, disability, or unemployment benefit, food assistance, public or subsidized housing assistance, postsecondary education, or similar benefit that is provided to individuals, families, or households and is funded by federal, state, or local government appropriations or provided by a federal, state, or local government agency;
- any professional or commercial license that is issued by a federal, state, or local government agency;
- any publicly funded grant, contract, or loan.[23]

Federal law, however, allows nonqualified aliens to receive the following types of government benefits, services, and assistance:

- Medicaid benefits for emergency services (other than organ transplants);
- social services provided under the Social Services Block Grant or other public social services programs, child protective services, adult protective services, domestic violence services, mental health and substance abuse services, crisis counseling and intervention services, short-term shelter and housing assistance for homeless persons, victims of domestic violence or other crimes, and runaway, abused, or abandoned children, food and nutrition services provided by soup kitchens, community food banks, and community or senior nutrition programs, and other services *if* those services are necessary for the protection of life or safety, are not dependent on an individual's income or financial resources,

---

23. 8 U.S.C. §§ 1611(c)(1) and 1621; 63 Fed. Reg. 41657 (Aug. 4, 1998).

and are provided through the delivery of in-kind services at the community level;
- short-term, non-cash emergency disaster relief, immunizations, benefits under the federal school lunch and breakfast programs, and food assistance under the WIC (women, infants, and children) program; and
- public police, fire, ambulance, transportation, and sanitation services.[24]

Although "qualified aliens" generally are not disqualified from receiving government services or public benefits, federal law does impose a number of restrictions with respect to their eligibility for SSI benefits, food and nutrition services, and federal means-tested public benefit programs (including the Medicaid, Temporary Assistance for Needy Families, and State Children's Health Insurance programs).[25] For example, many, but not all, qualified aliens are subject to a five-year waiting period under the Food and Nutrition Services program.[26] And most qualified aliens who acquired the status of qualified alien after August 22, 1996, are subject to a five-year waiting period with respect to eligibility for Medicaid (other than emergency services), Work First (Temporary Assistance to Needy Families), and Health Choice (State Children's Health Insurance).[27]

Federal law also allows states to limit the eligibility of some qualified aliens for state public benefits and for assistance and services provided under the Medicaid, Temporary Assistance to Needy Families, and Social Services Block Grant programs, but North Carolina has not done so.[28]

---

24. 8 U.S.C. §§ 1611(b), 1615(a), 1615(b)(1)(C); 66 Fed. Reg. 3613 (Jan. 16, 2001).

25. 8 U.S.C. §§ 1612 and 1613. These restrictions are discussed in more detail in Moore, "Are Immigrants Eligible for Publicly Funded Benefits and Services?"

26. 8 U.S.C. § 1612(a). The waiting period does not apply to certain aliens with military connections; elderly persons who were residing lawfully in the U.S. on August 22, 1996; children under the age of eighteen; refugees, Cuban or Haitian entrants, Amerasian immigrants, and other qualified aliens specified by federal law.

27. 8 U.S.C. § 1613. The waiting period does not apply to certain aliens with military connections, refugees, Cuban or Haitian entrants, Amerasian immigrants, and other qualified aliens specified by federal law.

28. 8 U.S.C. §§ 1612(b), 1622, and 1623.

Citizenship or immigration status, therefore, is relevant in determining an individual's eligibility for some, but not all, public assistance and social services programs administered by county social services departments. When citizenship or immigration status is relevant to an individual's eligibility for public assistance or social services, the county social services department usually must receive satisfactory documentary evidence to verify the individual's citizenship or immigration status.[29] But the authority of public social services agencies to inquire about an individual's citizenship or immigration status may be limited if citizenship or immigration status is not an eligibility requirement for assistance or services or relevant to the provision of assistance or services.[30]

### Residency

Most, if not all, public assistance programs administered by county social services departments require that a person be a resident of the state in order to receive assistance. Under the rules for these programs, a person generally is considered to be a resident of North Carolina if he or she lives in the state and intends to remain in the state permanently or indefinitely, as opposed to temporarily.[31] A state, however, generally may not require that applicants for public assistance or social services live in the state for some minimum period of time (for example, thirty

---

29. Rules for the Food and Nutrition Services program, for example, do not require a county department of social services to verify an applicant's statement that he or she is a U.S. citizen unless the statement is questionable but require the agency to verify an applicant's statement regarding immigration status. N.C. Food and Nutrition Services Policy Manual §§ 225.03 and 225.04, available at info.dhhs.state.nc.us/olm/manuals/dss/ei-30/man/FSs225.htm#P12_90 (last visited April 16, 2008). The U.S. Department of Justice and the former Immigration and Naturalization Service have published proposed guidelines for verifying citizenship and immigration status with respect to eligibility determinations for federal public benefits. See 62 Fed. Reg. 61,344 (Nov. 17, 1997); 63 Fed. Reg. 41,662 (Aug. 4, 1998). See also Alison Brown, "When Should Agencies Inquire About Immigration Status?" Popular Government 65(1) (Fall 1999): 29–34.

30. See 62 Fed. Reg. 61,360 (Nov. 17, 1997).

31. See 42 C.F.R. § 435.403(i)(1), 10A N.C. ADMIN. CODE 21B .0303, and Okale v. N.C. Dep't of Health and Human Servs., 153 N.C. App. 475, 570 S.E.2d 741 (2002) (Medicaid residency requirement).

days, ninety days, or twelve months) in order to be considered state residents.[32]

There are also some instances in which a county department of social services may or must provide assistance or services to an individual or family even if the individual or family does not live in the county. For example, a county social services department generally must investigate a report of suspected child abuse that occurred in the county even if the child normally resides in another county or in another state. A county also may provide assistance or services to families who encounter some crisis or emergency while they are passing through the county.

### Employment

The Work First and Food and Nutrition Services programs require some recipients to look for work, to participate in job training or work experience activities, or to accept or maintain employment as a condition of receiving assistance.

### Substance Abuse

Individuals who have been convicted of a felony (other than a Class H or Class I felony under North Carolina law) involving the possession, use, or distribution of a controlled substance are permanently disqualified from receiving assistance under the Food and Nutrition Services and Temporary Assistance for Needy Families (Work First) programs. Individuals who have been convicted of a Class H or Class I controlled substance felony in North Carolina may receive assistance under the Food and Nutrition Services and Work First programs if they are otherwise eligible for assistance, have been released from custody for at least six months, have not committed a controlled substance offense within six months of conviction or release, and are actively participating in or have successfully completed a required substance abuse treatment program.[33]

County social services departments must use two written questionnaires to screen all adults who apply for Work First assistance for alco-

---

32. *See* Shapiro v. Thompson, 394 U.S. 618 (1969) and Saenz v. Roe, 526 U.S. 489 (1999) (holding that twelve-month state residency requirements with respect to public assistance programs were unconstitutional). These U.S. Supreme Court decisions may throw into question the validity of North Carolina's ninety-day state residency requirement for State–County Special Assistance (G.S. 108A-41(b)(3)).

33. G.S. 108A-25.2.

hol and drug abuse and to refer a Work First applicant to a qualified substance abuse professional for further evaluation if the screening indicates alcohol or drug abuse. If a qualified substance abuse professional determines that a Work First applicant is addicted to alcohol or drugs and needs professional substance abuse treatment services, the applicant must participate in an appropriate treatment program, if one is available, and submit to random testing for alcohol or drug use as a condition of receiving assistance.[34]

### HEARINGS AND APPEALS

When a county social services department denies an individual's application for assistance or services or reduces or terminates the assistance or services provided to an individual, the department must provide the individual with a written notice that clearly states the action that is being taken, the facts upon which the department's decision is based, the law or rules upon which the decision is based, and the manner in which the individual may appeal the department's decision.[35]

If an individual who has applied for or received public assistance or social services is dissatisfied with a decision by the county department of social services granting, denying, terminating, or modifying assistance or services, he or she may appeal the department's decision by requesting, orally or in writing, an administrative "fair hearing" within sixty days of the date of the department's decision.[36]

In some instances, the first step in the appeals process is a "local" hearing before the county social services director or the director's designee.[37] In other instances, and in cases in which an applicant or recipient is dissatisfied with the department's decision following a local hearing, the fair hearing is conducted by a hearing officer employed by the state Division of Social Services.[38] In both instances, the person who appeals

---

34. G.S. 108A-29.1.

35. G.S. 108A-79(c); King v. N.C. Dep't of Human Resources, 93 N.C. App. 89, 376 S.E.2d 245 (1989).

36. G.S. 108A-79; G.S. 108A-73. *See also* Yates v. N.C. Dep't of Human Resources, 98 N.C. App. 402, 390 S.E.2d 761 (1990). An applicant or recipient may appeal decisions regarding Food and Nutrition Services eligibility within ninety days from the date of notice of the decision.

37. G.S. 108A-79(d).

38. G.S. 108A-79(i). Different appeal procedures apply to appeals regarding Work First eligibility in "electing" counties. *See* G.S. 108A-27.3(a)(14); 1999 Op. N.C. Att'y Gen. 12.

the department's decision has the right to examine his or her case record and all documents that the department intends to use at the hearing; to be represented, at his or her own expense, by a lawyer or other person; to testify and to present evidence; to cross-examine witnesses; and to present arguments to the hearing officer.[39]

After a hearing before a state DSS hearing officer and within ninety days of the date the appeal was first filed, the state DSS must issue a written final decision based on the evidence presented and the applicable law and send the final decision to the appellant and the county social services department by certified mail.[40] An applicant or recipient who is dissatisfied with the final decision may file a petition seeking judicial review of the decision with the superior court in the county in which the case arose within thirty days of his or her receipt of notice of the final decision.[41]

## FRAUD AND ABUSE

Fraud and abuse exist in every public assistance and social services program. Fraud in public assistance and social services programs, though, may not be as widespread as some people think. In state fiscal year 1996–97, for example, suspected recipient fraud accounted for about 0.5 percent of the total amount of assistance paid under the Aid to Families with Dependent Children program. During the same period, county departments of social services found recipient fraud in 1,615 Food Stamp cases, but the amount of fraudulently received Food Stamp benefits was less than 0.2 percent of the total value of Food Stamp coupons issued. In addition, it is important to note that improper overpayments (and underpayments) of public assistance may result from errors by

---

39. G.S. 108A-79(e); G.S. 108A-79(i). With some exceptions, the rules of evidence that apply in civil proceedings in trial courts apply in hearings before state DSS hearing officers. G.S. 108A-79(i); G.S. 150B-29. Hearings before state DSS hearing officers must be recorded. G.S. 108A-79(i).

40. G.S. 108A-79(j).

41. G.S. 108A-79(k). It is not entirely clear whether a county department of social services may seek judicial review of a final decision by the state DSS. *See* Forsyth County Board of Social Servs. v. N.C. Dept. of Human Resources, 317 N.C. 689, 346 S.E.2d 414 (1986). *Cf.* 1987 N.C. Sess. Laws ch. 599, § 3 (amending G.S. 108A-79(k)); G.S. Ch. 150B, Art. 4.

county social services staff or nonfraudulent mistakes by individuals or families who receive assistance, as well as fraud.[42]

*Obtaining Public Assistance and Social Services through Fraud*
Fraud, in the context of public assistance and social services programs, may be defined generally as the willful, knowing, and intentionally deceptive making of a false statement or withholding of material information for the purpose of obtaining assistance or services to which an individual is not entitled.[43]

Although public attention often focuses on alleged fraud by individuals who have applied for or are receiving public assistance, public assistance fraud laws also apply to fraud committed by persons, agencies, or institutions that provide assistance or services to the poor, including employees of social services agencies; grocers who participate in the Food and Nutrition Services program; and doctors, pharmacists, and hospitals that participate in the Medicaid program.[44]

When a county department of social services determines that an individual may have committed fraud in connection with a public assistance or social services program, the department generally may pursue one or more of the following options:

- request that the district attorney prosecute the individual for criminal fraud;
- initiate an administrative proceeding to determine whether the individual has committed fraud and, if so, to disqualify the individual from receiving further assistance;[45]

---

42. Under some public assistance programs, individuals or families may be required to repay the state or county for overpayments of public assistance even when those overpayments were caused by agency error or an inadvertent mistake by the recipient rather than fraud. *See* 7 C.F.R. § 273.18 (Food and Nutrition Services).

43. A person who makes a false statement to a county social services department may be found guilty of fraud even if the department and its staff were not actually deceived by the person's statement. *See* State v. Bass, 53 N.C. App. 70, 280 S.E.2d 7 (1981).

44. *See* G.S. 108A-39; G.S. 108A-53(a); G.S. 108A-53(d); G.S. 108A-63; State v. Bass, 53 N.C. App. 40, 280 S.E.2d 7 (1981). G.S. 108A-70.10 through G.S. 108A-70.16 establish additional civil remedies for false claims by health care providers under the state Medicaid program.

45. This option is available only with respect to suspected fraud by a person who has applied for or received assistance under the Work First, Food and

- recover the overpayment of assistance by accepting voluntary payments from the responsible individual;[46]
- recover the overpayment by reducing the assistance to which the responsible individual otherwise would be entitled;[47]
- recover the overpayment by attaching the responsible individual's state income tax refund;[48]
- file a civil lawsuit for fraud seeking a money judgment against the responsible individual;
- file a civil action in district court seeking an order garnishing up to 20 percent of the responsible individual's disposable wages or earnings to recoup a public assistance overpayment resulting from fraud.[49]

### Criminal Fraud Statutes

Several state statutes make it a crime to obtain, or to attempt to obtain, public assistance through fraud.[50] G.S. 108A-39, for example,

---

Nutrition Services, or subsidized child day care programs. Administrative hearings involving suspected fraud by applicants or recipients in the Work First and Food and Nutrition Services programs are conducted by county social services departments or the state Division of Social Services. Administrative hearings involving suspected fraud by applicants or recipients in the subsidized child day care program are conducted by the state Division of Child Development. Applicants or recipients who have committed fraud in these programs may be disqualified from receiving further assistance under these programs for a period of at least twelve months and, under some circumstances, may be permanently disqualified from receiving further assistance.

46. Some public assistance rules provide that all adult members of an individual's household or family assistance unit are jointly and severally liable for overpayments resulting from an individual's fraudulent misrepresentation or withholding of information and, in these instances, they, as well as the individual who committed fraud, may be subject to some administrative or civil remedies.

47. This option is not available with respect to claims against Medicaid recipients or claims against recipients of State–County Special Assistance who do not have noncountable income or resources.

48. See G.S. Ch. 105A.

49. G.S. 108A-25.3. This option may not be used if the county social services department has failed to exhaust available administrative remedies to recoup the overpayment, if the responsible individual has been ordered to pay restitution for the overpayment in a criminal proceeding, or if garnishing the individual's earnings would jeopardize his or her ability to become or remain financially self-sufficient.

50. Fraud in connection with public assistance and social services programs also may be punishable under general criminal statutes, such as G.S. 14-100

provides that a person who makes a fraudulent misrepresentation in order to obtain public assistance may be found guilty of a Class I felony if the amount of assistance exceeds \$400 or a Class 1 misdemeanor if the amount of assistance does not exceed \$400. Other statutes impose criminal penalties for fraud in connection with particular public assistance programs, including the Food and Nutrition Services, Medicaid, Health Choice, and subsidized child day care programs.[51]

If a person is convicted of obtaining public assistance through fraud, the court may require him or her to make restitution by paying the state or county the amount of assistance that was fraudulently received.[52] A person who is convicted of fraud in connection with the Food and Nutrition Services program is automatically disqualified from receiving food and nutrition assistance for a period of at least twelve months.[53]

## Mandated and Optional Social Services Programs

State law requires county social services departments to administer some public assistance and social services programs and allows them to provide additional social services. Because counties have some flexibility with respect to the social services programs they provide, the exact number and type of social services provided by county social services departments varies, at least somewhat, from county to county.

In North Carolina, county social services departments are required to administer a number of public assistance programs and to provide

---

(obtaining property by false pretenses).

51. G.S. 108A-53; G.S. 180A-53.1; G.S. 108A-63; G.S. 108A-64; G.S. 108A-70.28; G.S. 110-107.

52. *See* G.S. 15A-1340.34 through G.S. 15A-1340.38; State v. Freeman, 47 N.C. App. 171, 266 S.E.2d 723 (1980).

53. The disqualification period is twenty-four months following a second conviction for fraud or for a first conviction for using or receiving food and nutrition benefits in a transaction involving the sale of a controlled substance and ten years following a first or second conviction for misrepresenting one's identity or residence in order to receive or attempt to receive multiple food and nutrition benefits. A person may be permanently disqualified from receiving food and nutrition benefits following a third conviction for Food and Nutrition Services fraud, a second conviction for using or receiving food and nutrition benefits in a transaction involving the sale of a controlled substance, or a first conviction involving the use of food and nutrition benefits to purchase firearms or explosives.

a variety of mandated human and social services. These programs and services include the following:

1. the Work First program (Temporary Assistance for Needy Families)[54]
2. the Food and Nutrition Services program[55]
3. the Medicaid program[56]
4. the Health Choice (children's health insurance) program[57]
5. the Low-Income Energy Assistance program[58]
6. the State–County Special Assistance program[59]
7. the Special Assistance to the Blind program[60]
8. the child support enforcement (IV-D) program[61]
9. child day care services (Social Services Block Grant (SSBG))[62]
10. child protective services[63]
11. child welfare, foster care placement prevention, family reunification, and permanency planning services[64]
12. foster care placement for abused, neglected, or dependent children[65]
13. the State Foster Care Assistance program[66]
14. the federal foster care and adoption assistance programs[67]

---

54. G.S. 108A-27(g). In counties that are designated as "electing" counties, the Work First program may be administered by the county social services department or another public or private agency designated by the board of county commissioners. G.S. 108A-27(f).

55. G.S. 108A-51.

56. 10A N.C. Admin. Code 21A .0101.

57. G.S. 108A-70.26(a).

58. G.S. 108A-25(a)(5).

59. G.S. 108A-40.

60. This program may be administered locally by the county social services department or by the board of county commissioners. See G.S. 111-35.

61. This mandate does not apply in approximately thirty counties in which the child support enforcement program is administered by the state Division of Social Services. Counties that are required to administer the child support enforcement program may do so through the county social services department or through another public or private agency designated by the board of county commissioners. See G.S. 110-129(5); G.S. 110-141.

62. 10A N.C. Admin. Code 71R .0103(a).

63. G.S. 108A-14(a)(11); G.S. Ch. 7B, Subchapter 1.

64. G.S. Ch. 7B, Subchapter 1.

65. G.S. 108A-14(a)(12).

66. G.S. 108A-49.

67. Id.

15. foster care services for children (SSBG)[68]
16. foster home licensure services[69]
17. adoption services[70]
18. adult protective services[71]
19. guardianship services[72]
20. adult care home inspection, monitoring, and supervision[73]
21. adult placement services (SSBG)[74]
22. foster care services for adults (SSBG)[75]
23. in-home aide services[76]
24. adult care home case management services[77]
25. resident evaluation services for certain adult care home residents[78]
26. adult day care inspection, monitoring, and supervision[79]
27. adult day care assistance[80]
28. family planning services (SSBG)[81]
29. health support services (SSBG)[82]
30. individual and family adjustment services (SSBG)[83]
31. adjustment services for blind or visually impaired persons (SSBG)[84]
32. youth employment certification[85]
33. disposition of unclaimed bodies.[86]

---

68. 10A N.C. ADMIN. CODE 71R .0103(a).
69. 10A N.C. ADMIN. CODE 70E .0101.
70. G.S. 108A-14(a)(6); G.S. 108A-14(a)(13).
71. G.S. 108A-14(a)(14); G.S. 108A-103.
72. G.S. 108A-15.
73. G.S. 108A-14(a)(8); G.S. 131D-2(b)(1a); G.S. 131D-26.
74. 10A N.C. ADMIN. CODE 71R .0103(a).
75. Id.
76. 10A N.C. ADMIN. CODE 06U .0103; 10A N.C. ADMIN. CODE 71R .0103(a).
77. 10A N.C. ADMIN. CODE 71D .0101.
78. 10A N.C. ADMIN. CODE 71E .0102.
79. 10A N.C. ADMIN. CODE 06P .0402.
80. 10A N.C. ADMIN. CODE 06T .0203.
81. 10A N.C. ADMIN. CODE 71R .0103(a).
82. Id.
83. Id.
84. Id.
85. G.S. 108A-14(a)(7).
86. G.S. 130A-415(c).

Counties have some administrative responsibilities with respect to all mandated social services programs. With respect to some, they also have some fiscal responsibilities. The precise nature, scope, and extent of the counties' obligation to provide mandated social services, however, varies from program to program and service to service. In some instances, the counties' obligation is relatively open-ended. In other instances, its scope is not clearly defined or is limited by available funding, staffing, or other resources. In some instances, mandated social services may be provided by the county social services department or by other public or private entities under contracts or agreements with the county social services department.

All county social services departments in North Carolina provide a number of social services beyond those mandated by the state. These programs are usually referred to as "nonmandated" or "optional" services despite the fact that they provide assistance that may be essential to the well-being of individuals, children, and families. These optional social services may include

1. transportation services
2. general assistance programs
3. the community alternatives program (Medicaid)
4. the State–County Special Assistance program for certain disabled adults
5. employment and training support services
6. family preservation services
7. problem pregnancy services
8. adolescent parenting services
9. early childhood intervention services
10. residential and day treatment services for emotionally disturbed children
11. delinquency prevention services
12. personal and family counseling services
13. housing and home improvement services
14. respite care services
15. community living services
16. surplus food and commodity distribution.

## Overview of Major Public Assistance and Social Services Programs

### MEDICAID

Medicaid is the largest, most costly, and most complex public assistance program administered by the state Department of Health and Human Services and county departments of social services.[87]

Although people often confuse the Medicaid and Medicare programs, Medicaid is distinct and different from Medicare, which is a federal health-insurance program administered by the federal Social Security Administration. Some elderly or disabled persons, however, are eligible for and covered by both Medicaid and Medicare.

Medicaid is a categorical, needs-based, federal–state public assistance program that provides medical care for the poor. Eligibility requirements for the Medicaid program are established by state law within broad parameters set by the federal Medicaid law.

Federal law generally requires state Medicaid programs to cover approximately twenty-one specific categories of low-income individuals, including elderly and disabled persons who receive federal Supplemental Security Income (SSI) benefits, children and families who receive Temporary Assistance to Needy Families, pregnant women and infants with incomes below 150 percent of the federal poverty level (FPL), and children whose family incomes are below (or, in some instances, below 133 percent of) the FPL. Federal law also gives state Medicaid programs the option of covering other specified categories of pregnant women, children, and elderly or disabled persons, including elderly and disabled persons with incomes below the FPL, elderly or disabled adult care home residents who receive State–County Special Assistance but not SSI, and children and elderly or disabled persons who are considered medically needy because of high medical care costs.

North Carolina's Medicaid program covers approximately 1.6 million persons (approximately 18.5 percent of the state's population). Children

---

87. More detailed information about North Carolina's Medicaid program is contained in annual reports published by the state DHHS Division of Medical Assistance, available online at www.dhhs.state.nc.us/dma (last visited April 16, 2008). Unless otherwise noted, the information and statistics regarding North Carolina's Medicaid program included in this section are derived from the state's annual Medicaid report for state fiscal year (SFY) 2006 at www.dhhs.state.nc.us/dma/2006report/2006report.pdf (last visited April 16, 2008).

and pregnant women constitute approximately 70 percent of Medicaid recipients in North Carolina; elderly and disabled persons constitute approximately 30 percent of North Carolina Medicaid recipients.

Federal law requires state Medicaid programs to provide certain types of medical care for eligible Medicaid recipients and allows them to provide other specified types of medical care. North Carolina's Medicaid program covers a comprehensive array of medical services; including inpatient and outpatient hospital services; nursing home care; physicians' services; laboratory and X-ray services; prescription drugs; payment of Medicare premiums, deductibles, and copayments for certain Medicare beneficiaries; durable medical equipment; dental care and dentures; chiropractic care; home health care; personal care; mental health care; physical and occupational therapy; community alternatives; hospice; family planning; early periodic screening, diagnosis, and treatment services for individuals under the age of twenty-one; and necessary transportation related to medical care and services.[88]

State Medicaid programs are allowed, within federally established parameters and limitations, to determine the amount, scope, and duration of covered Medicaid services, to require nominal copayments for certain services, and to set the payment rates for participating health care providers.[89]

Eligible Medicaid recipients receive a Medicaid identification card, which they can use to obtain medical care from approximately 57,000 hospitals, nursing homes, doctors, dentists, and other health care providers that participate in the state Medicaid program.[90]

---

88. Medicaid services for elderly and disabled Medicaid recipients accounted for approximately 70 percent of Medicaid spending in SFY 2006. Payments for approximately 43,000 Medicaid-eligible nursing home patients and other long-term care services accounted for approximately one-third of Medicaid spending in SFY 2006. The state Division of Medical Assistance estimates that almost half of all Medicaid payments are for optional services provided to mandatory eligibles and for services provided to optional eligibles.

89. Health care providers that participate in the Medicaid program are required to accept Medicaid payment as payment in full for services provided to Medicaid recipients except to the extent that federal and state law impose copayment or cost sharing requirements on Medicaid recipients. *See* 42 U.S.C. §§ 1396a(a)(25) and 1320a-7b(d).

90. Most Medicaid recipients in North Carolina are enrolled in a managed care program, in which a primary care provider acts as a "gatekeeper" controlling recipients' access to medical care. North Carolina's Medicaid program also requires prior approval for coverage of some Medicaid services.

North Carolina's Medicaid program was implemented on January 1, 1970. The Medicaid program is administered at the state level by the DHHS Division of Medical Assistance (DMA). A private company, Electronic Data Systems Corporation, contracts with the DMA to process and pay Medicaid claims. County departments of social services are primarily responsible for determining whether persons who apply for Medicaid meet Medicaid's eligibility requirements.[91]

North Carolina's Medicaid program costs approximately $9 billion per year. The federal government pays almost 65 percent of the cost of Medicaid services and half of the cost of administering North Carolina's Medicaid program. Prior to October 1, 2007, counties were required to pay 15 percent of the non-federal share of the cost of Medicaid services for county residents (about 5.5 percent of the total cost) and the non-federal share of local administrative costs for the Medicaid program.[92] In 2007, however, the General Assembly enacted legislation phasing-out the counties' fiscal responsibility for Medicaid services provided to county residents and shifting that responsibility to the state.[93]

## FOOD AND NUTRITION SERVICES
The Food and Nutrition Services program is a means tested, federal–state public assistance program that helps individuals and households with limited incomes buy the food they need for a nutritionally adequate diet.[94]

---

91. The DHHS Division of Vocational Rehabilitation Services determines whether individuals are eligible for Medicaid based on disability.

92. North Carolina was one of only a handful of states that required counties to pay part of the cost of Medicaid services provided to county residents. According to the North Carolina Association of County Commissioners, North Carolina's 100 counties spent more than $425 million in county funds for Medicaid services for county residents in SFY 2007 and county spending for Medicaid consumed more than 20 percent of county property tax revenues in twenty-four counties (www.ncacc.org/documents/medicaidestimates_2007-08.xls) (last visited April 16, 2008). *See also* John L. Saxon, "The Fiscal Impact of Medicaid on North Carolina Counties," *Popular Government* 67(4) (Summer 2002): 14–22.

93. SL 2007-323.

94. The Food and Nutrition Services program served approximately 870,000 North Carolinians in March 2007. "North Carolina Food Stamp Participation Report" (Raleigh: N.C. Division of Social Services, 2007), available at www.dhhs.state.nc.us/dss/stats/docs/FS_Participation_FFY2007_Q2.pdf (last visited April 16, 2008).

Individuals and households who apply for food and nutrition services and are determined to be eligible for benefits receive an electronic benefit transfer (EBT) card that they can use to purchase food at grocery stores that participate in the food and nutrition services program. Food and nutrition assistance may not be used to purchase tobacco, pet food, paper products, soap products, or alcoholic beverages. The maximum food and nutrition services benefit is $155 per month for a one-person household, $284 per month for a two-person household, $408 per month for a three-person household, and $518 per month for a four-person household.[95]

Financial and nonfinancial eligibility requirements for the Food and Nutrition Services program are established by federal law.[96] Able-bodied adults between the ages of eighteen and forty-nine years who do not have any dependent children may receive food and nutrition assistance for only three months in a thirty-six month period unless they are working or participating in a workfare or employment and training program other than job search.[97]

The Food and Nutrition Services (Food Stamp) program is administered at the federal level by the U.S. Department of Agriculture's Food and Nutrition Service and is administered at the state level by the state DHHS Division of Social Services. Boards of county commissioners, acting through county departments of social services, are responsible for local administration and operation of the Food and Nutrition Services program in North Carolina.[98]

The federal government pays the full cost of food and nutrition assistance (approximately $1.1 billion in North Carolina in SFY 2008)

---

95. The maximum food and nutrition benefit increases with household size. The actual amount of a household's food and nutrition benefits is based on the amount of the household's net countable income and generally is less than the maximum food and nutrition benefit.

96. The income limit for Food and Nutrition Services eligibility is based on 100 percent of the federal poverty level. The U.S. Department of Agriculture provides an online eligibility screening tool for food and nutrition benefits at http://65.216.150.143/fns/ (last visited April 16, 2008).

97. Other eligible persons who live in the household with an able-bodied adult between the ages of eighteen and forty-nine years may receive food and nutrition benefits even if that adult is not eligible for food and nutrition benefits. The Food and Nutrition Services employment requirement for able-bodied adults does not apply in certain economically distressed counties in the state.

98. G.S. 108A-51.

and half of the cost of administering the Food and Nutrition Services program.[99]

### WORK FIRST (TANF)

Work First—North Carolina's program of Temporary Assistance for Needy Families (TANF)—is a means tested, federal–state public assistance and social services program that provides temporary financial assistance, employment services, and other social services for low-income families with dependent children.

In 1996 Congress enacted federal welfare reform legislation that replaced the Aid to Families with Dependent Children (AFDC) program with a new Temporary Assistance for Needy Families program, which was intended to "end welfare as we know it."[100] North Carolina implemented the TANF program administratively in October 1996 and statutorily in 1997, creating the Work First program.[101]

North Carolina's Work First program

> is based on the premise that parents have a responsibility to support themselves and their children. Through Work First, parents can get short-term training and other services to help them become employed and self-sufficient, but the responsibility is theirs, and most families have two years to move off Work First Family Assistance.[102]

---

99. "[Public Assistance and Social Services] Budget Estimates" (Raleigh: N.C. Division of Social Services, 2007), available at www.dhhs.state.nc.us/dss/budget/docs/rptStateTotals2007-2008.pdf (last visited April 16, 2008). North Carolina counties are required to pay the non-federal share of local administrative costs for the Food and Nutrition Services program.

100. Pub. Law 104-193 (August 22, 1996). The 1996 federal welfare reform legislation is discussed in more detail in John L. Saxon, "Welfare Reform: What Will It Mean for North Carolina?" *Popular Government* 62(4) (Summer 1997): 15–27.

101. SL 1997-443, §§ 12.5–12.6; G.S. 108A-27 through G.S. 108A-39. North Carolina's Work First program is described in more detail in John L. Saxon, "Welfare Reform: Legislation Enacted by the 1997 General Assembly," *Social Services Law Bulletin* No. 26 (Chapel Hill: Institute of Government, The University of North Carolina at Chapel Hill, 1997). North Carolina's current Work First program is described in the TANF State Plan for FFY 2006–2007 [hereinafter "North Carolina Work First Plan"], available at www.dhhs.state.nc.us/dss/workfirst/docs/TANF_StatePlan_0607.pdf (last visited April 16, 2008).

102. North Carolina Work First Plan, 1.

To achieve the goal of self-sufficiency for families, Work First emphasizes three strategies:

1. diversion (keeping families off welfare by helping them cope with
   unexpected emergencies or setbacks);
2. work and time limits (shortening the length of time that families
   receive welfare assistance by making work mandatory and
   limiting the time a family can receive assistance); and
3. retention (helping families stay off public assistance by
   encouraging them to save and helping to make sure that they
   really are better off working than on welfare).[103]

Eligibility for Work First assistance and services is governed primarily by requirements set forth in the North Carolina Work First Plan,
which is developed by DHHS and reviewed and approved biennially by
the North Carolina General Assembly.[104]

The Work First program is administered at the state level by the
state DHHS Division of Social Services and locally by county departments of social services (or, in counties that are designated as "electing" counties, by the county department of social services or another
public agency or private entity designated by the board of county
commissioners).[105] Counties have the option of administering the
standard Work First program or requesting designation as an electing
county that is given additional authority and flexibility to establish and
operate a county Work First program.[106]

Funding for North Carolina's Work First program is provided
through the federal TANF Block Grant and state and county tax revenues. State law imposes a fiscal "maintenance of effort" requirement on
counties with respect to county funding for Work First, child welfare,
and related services.[107]

---

103. North Carolina Work First Plan, 1.

104. *See* G.S. 108A-27.9 and G.S. 108A-27.10.

105. *See* G.S. 108A-27(g) and G.S. 108A-37(f).

106. *See* G.S. 108A-27(d), G.S. 108A-27(e), and G.S. 108A-27.3. The following
eight counties currently are designated as electing counties: Beaufort, Caldwell,
Catawba, Iredell, Lenoir, Lincoln, Macon, and Wilson.

107. *See* G.S. 108A-27.12(c) and G.S. 108A-27.12(d). The county Work First
maintenance of effort requirement is tied to the county budgeted funding for
emergency assistance and administration under the former AFDC program and
employment and training under the former JOBS program. The Work First main-

*Work First Family Assistance (WFFA)*

The Work First program provides monthly cash assistance payments through Work First Family Assistance (WFFA) to eligible families.[108]

The maximum amount of WFFA payable for one child in a "child only" case under the standard Work First program is $181 per month; the maximum WFFA payment for a parent and two children is $272 per month.[109] In order to discourage out-of-wedlock births, North Carolina's Work First program includes a family cap under which WFFA is not paid with respect to a child who is born ten months after a month in which the child's family received WFFA.[110]

Financial and non-financial eligibility requirements for Work First Family Assistance under the standard Work First program are set forth in North Carolina's Work First State Plan. Eligibility requirements for Work First Family Assistance in an electing county are set forth in the county's Work First plan, which is adopted by the board of county commissioners, incorporated in a separate section of the Work First State Plan, and approved by the General Assembly.[111]

---

tenance of effort requirement for electing counties is less than that for standard counties.

108. Statistical reports prepared by the Jordan Institute for Families at the School of Social Work at The University of North Carolina at Chapel Hill indicate that about 50,000 individuals (children and, in some cases, their parent or parents) received Work First Family Assistance (WFFA) payments in May 2007 (sasweb.unc.edu/cgi-bin/broker?_service=default&_program=wrkfirst.idemog .sas&county=North%20Carolina&label=&fn=x) (last visited April 16, 2008). Most cases involving Work First Family Assistance (WFFA) are "child only" cases—that is, cases in which a dependent child lives with a relative other than his or her parent or step-parent. About 90 percent of WFFA cases involve families with fewer than three children.

109. In May 2007, the median, statewide WFFA payment to families was $181.00 and the total amount of WFFA payments to families was approximately $6 million (sasweb.unc.edu/cgi-bin/broker?_service=default&_program=wrkfirst .idemog.sas&county=North%20Carolina&label=&fn=x) (last visited April 16, 2008). Most families that receive WFFA payments are also eligible for Medicaid and food and nutrition benefits. The amount of WFFA paid to eligible families in an electing county is governed by the provisions of the county's Work First plan and may be more or less than the WFFA payment schedule under the standard Work First program. *See* G.S. 108A-27.4(e)(4).

110. North Carolina Work First Plan, 19.

111. *See* G.S. 108A-27.4(e)(4), G.S. 108A-27.3(a)(2), G.S. 108A-27.3(d), G.S. 108A-27.9(d), and G.S. 108A-27.10. Eligibility requirements for Work First

In order to receive WFFA, a non-disabled parent generally is required
to register with the Employment Security Commission under the First
Stop Employment Assistance program and, unless he or she is a single
parent with a child under the age of six and necessary child care is
unavailable, participate in up to thirty-five hours per week in work or
work-related activities.

State law also requires the parent of a dependent child to sign a
"mutual responsibility agreement" as a condition of receiving WFFA
under the standard Work First program.[112] Under this agreement,
a child's parent must look for work, accept and retain any suitable
employment, conduct himself or herself suitably on the job, and
ensure that the child attends school regularly.[113] The agreement also
may require a parent to cooperate with the child support enforcement
program; participate in financial management and life skills classes;
participate in substance abuse screening, assessment, and treatment;
participate in work activities; attend family violence counseling; and
ensure that the child is properly immunized and receives regular medical care.

Because the Work First program provides *temporary* assistance to
needy families, state law provides that a family that includes a parent who is subject to the WFFA work requirements generally may not
receive WFFA for more than twenty-four months.[114] And federal law

Family Assistance in electing counties may be more restrictive or more liberal
than those under the standard Work First program.

112. *See* G.S. 108A-27.6(a)(3); North Carolina Work First Plan, 14.

113. The agreement also establishes employment goals for a parent, describes
the plan for the parent's participation in work and work-related activities, and
describes the case management and supportive services that will be provided to
help the family become self-sufficient.

114. G.S. 108A-27.1. The twenty-four-month time limit is cumulative, not
consecutive, and does not apply to "child only" cases. This time limit is suspended for up to three years for Work First recipients who are enrolled at least
part-time in a post-secondary education program and maintain a grade point
average of at least 2.5. G.S. 108A-27.2(2). The North Carolina Work First Plan
also allows the county social services board, or its designee, to extend a family's
time limit under certain circumstances. When a family reaches its time limit, it
is ineligible for WFFA for a period of thirty-six months. In 2006 approximately
575 families lost WFFA due to the twenty-four-month time limit (sasweb.unc
.edu/cgi-bin/broker?_service=default&_program=wrkfirst.idemog.sas&county=
North%20Carolina&label=&clock=24) (last visited April 16, 2008). Electing
counties are authorized to establish different WFFA time limits as long as

generally imposes a nationwide, lifetime limit of sixty months on the provision of assistance using federal TANF funding.[115]

### Work First Diversion Assistance
The Work First Diversion Assistance program is designed to help low-income families avoid going on welfare by providing them with financial and other assistance they need to get or keep a job or access other financial assistance that will help meet their needs.[116] An eligible family of three may receive a lump sum, cash payment of up to $816 once in a twelve-month period.[117] Receipt of diversion assistance does not count against the WFFA time limit.

### Work First Emergency Assistance
Standard and electing counties are required to provide assistance to low-income families with dependent children to respond to emergencies, such as evictions or utility terminations.[118] Receipt of emergency assistance does not count against the WFFA time limit. Eligibility requirements for emergency assistance are specified in each county's Work First plan.[119]

---

they are not inconsistent with the federal sixty-month TANF time limit. *See* G.S. 108A-27.1(b).

115. 42 U.S.C. § 608(a)(7). This time limit does not apply to "child only" cases. Federal law and the North Carolina Work First Plan authorize the county social services board, or its designee, to grant hardship exemptions from the federal time limit. In 2006, 341 families who were receiving WFFA reached the sixty-month time limit, but extensions were granted to 185 of those families (sasweb.unc.edu/cgi-bin/broker?_service=default&_program=wrkfirst.idemog.sas&county=North%20Carolina&label=&clock=60) (last visited April 16, 2008).

116. Under the standard Work First program, diversion assistance may be provided to families with incomes of up to twice the federal poverty level. Electing counties are authorized to establish different eligibility requirements for diversion assistance.

117. Families that receive diversion assistance are also eligible for Medicaid for a limited period of time and may be eligible for food and nutrition assistance, subsidized child care, and other assistance and services.

118. G.S. 108A-27.7(d) and G.S. 108A-27.4(h).

119. Emergency assistance may not be provided to families with incomes that exceed twice the federal poverty level.

*Work First Services*
Standard and electing counties are required to serve low-income families who need child care, employment services, transportation, substance abuse services, and other social services that will help families become and remain self-sufficient.[120] Eligibility requirements for Work First services and the amount and scope of services provided to eligible families are specified in each county's Work First plan.[121]

*First Stop Employment Assistance*
The First Stop Employment Assistance program provides job search, job training, community service experience, and job placement services to adults who receive WFFA and are not exempt from the Work First work requirements.[122] The program is administered by the state Employment Security Commission with the participation of and in cooperation with county social services departments, community colleges, and other public agencies.

## STATE–COUNTY SPECIAL ASSISTANCE
The State–County Special Assistance program is a means-tested, state–county public assistance program that provides financial assistance to elderly or disabled persons who need to live in an adult care home and are unable to afford the cost of their care.[123]

The State–County Special Assistance program is administered locally by county social services departments under the supervision of the state DHHS Division of Aging and Adult Services. Counties are responsible for paying half (approximately $75 million per year) of the cost of special assistance payments plus local administrative costs (approximately $5 million per year).

---

120. G.S. 108A-27.7(c) and G.S. 108A-27.4(e)(2).
121. Work First services may not be provided to families with incomes that exceed twice the federal poverty level. Employment services may be provided to the noncustodial parents of children who receive WFFA.
122. G.S. 108A-29.
123. G.S. 108A-41. This program also provides financial assistance for a limited number of elderly and disabled persons who are at risk of admission to an adult care facility but would prefer to continue living in their own homes with additional assistance and services. *See* SL 2005-276, § 10.39.

## Adult Protective Services

State law requires county social services departments to respond to reports involving the abuse, neglect, or exploitation of disabled adults.[124] If a department finds that a disabled adult needs protective services, it must provide or arrange for essential medical, social, or legal services if the disabled adult consents.[125] If the individual lacks the capacity to consent, the department may seek a court order authorizing it to provide protective services.[126]

## Child Support Enforcement (IV-D)

The federal–state child support enforcement program is often referred to as the "IV-D" program because it was created through the enactment of Title IV-D of the federal Social Security Act.

The child support enforcement (IV-D) program provides financial and medical support for children by locating absent parents who are responsible for supporting their children, establishing or seeking court orders to establish the paternity of children who are born out-of-wedlock, obtaining voluntary support agreements or seeking court orders requiring parents to pay child support, enforcing or seeking judicial enforcement of child support orders, obtaining modifications of child support orders, and collecting and distributing child support payments to families.[127]

State and county child support enforcement agencies are required to provide child support enforcement services on behalf of any child who receives Work First Family Assistance or foster care assistance, and on behalf of any child when the child's parent or custodian applies for child support enforcement services and pays a modest application fee.[128]

North Carolina's child support enforcement program is administered by the state DHHS Division of Social Services and by county child support enforcement agencies.[129] DHHS provides child support enforcement services in 30 of the state's 100 counties through seventeen regional offices.

---

124. G.S. 108A-103.
125. G.S. 108A-104.
126. G.S. 108A-105.
127. In SFY 2006, North Carolina's IV-D program was responsible for over 400,000 child support cases and collected more than $630 million in child support.
128. *See* 42 U.S.C. § 654(4)(A)(i), (ii); 45 C.F.R. § 302.22; G.S. 110-130.1(a), (c).
129. G.S. 110-141.

County agencies (such as the county social services department, the county attorney, or a separate county IV-D office) or private contractors that are designated by boards of county commissioners provide child support services in seventy counties.[130]

### Subsidized Child Day Care

The subsidized child day care program is a federal–state assistance program that pays all or part of the cost of child day care for low-income families and children who need child day care because the child's parent or parents are working or looking for work, because the child's parent or parents are in school or participating in job training, because the child is receiving protective services and needs care in order to remain in his or her home, because the child's family is experiencing a crisis and is unable to care for the child, because care is needed to prevent foster care placement, to reunify a foster child with his or her family, or to support the provision of child welfare services, or because the child is developmentally delayed or at risk of developmental delay.[131]

Subsidized child day care is available without regard to income when care is needed in connection with the provision of child protective services, child welfare services, or foster care services. In other instances, a family is not eligible for subsidized child day care unless its gross monthly income is less than the maximum income limit set by the General Assembly. If a family is eligible for subsidized child day care because the family's income is less than the maximum income limit, the family is responsible for paying 8 to 10 percent of its monthly countable income for the child's care.

A family that is found eligible for subsidized child day care is given a voucher that indicates the hours that care is needed and the amount, if any, that the family must pay for the cost of the child's care. The family may use the voucher to obtain child day care from any authorized child day care provider, including licensed child day care centers, licensed child day care homes, unlicensed church day care programs, and informal child day care arrangements, as long as the provider signs a pro-

---

130. *See* G.S. 110-129(5), G.S. 110-130, and G.S. 110-141.

131. The subsidized child day care program serves approximately 100,000 children. Subsidized child day care generally will not be provided for a child between the ages of thirteen and eighteen years unless the teenager has a special or developmental need, is receiving child protective services or foster care services, or is under court-ordered supervision.

vider agreement with the local purchasing agency, is operating legally, and meets certain health and safety requirements. The maximum reimbursement rates for the subsidized child day care program are established by state law but vary from county to county and are based on the type of provider and, in the case of a licensed child care center, the center's "star rating."

The subsidized child day care program is administered at the state level by the state DHHS Division of Child Development. It is administered locally by county social services departments or other local purchasing agencies.

The state uses a combination of state and federal funding, including federal funding received under the Child Care and Development Block Grant, the Temporary Assistance for Needy Families Block Grant, and the Social Services Block Grant, to provide more than $360 million per year for subsidized child day care.[132] Each county receives an annual allocation of federal and state funding for subsidized child day care based on the amount of funds available and the need for subsidized child day care in the county. Because funding for the subsidized child day care program is not sufficient to provide assistance to all eligible families and eligible families do not have a legal entitlement to subsidized child day care assistance, county social services departments and other local purchasing agencies that administer the program establish priorities for serving eligible families, and eligible families who cannot be served usually are placed on waiting lists until funding becomes available.[133]

## HEALTH CHOICE

North Carolina's Health Choice (State Child Health Insurance) program is a means-tested, federal–state, nonentitlement assistance program that provides health insurance coverage for over 100,000 uninsured

---

132. Federal funding pays approximately 65 percent of the cost of subsidized child day care. State funding for subsidized child day care is provided through the Smart Start program as well as the subsidized child day care program. Counties are authorized, but not required, to appropriate county funding for subsidized child day care.

133. As of April 2007, there were approximately 15,000 children on the waiting list for subsidized child day care. "Monthly Statistical Summary" (Raleigh: N.C. Division of Child Development, 2007), available at ncchildcare.dhhs.state .nc.us/pdf_forms/april_2007_statistical_report.pdf (last visited April 16, 2008).

children in families whose incomes are less than twice the federal poverty level and are not eligible for Medicaid.[134]

The Health Choice program is administered at the state level by the state DHHS Division of Medical Assistance and the North Carolina Teachers' and State Employees' State Health Plan. County departments of social services are responsible for processing applications and determining eligibility for Health Choice.

Federal funding pays approximately 75 percent of the annual $200 million cost of the Health Choice program. State funding pays the remaining cost of the program.

## CHILD WELFARE SERVICES

The term "child welfare services" refers to a broad array of programs and services that county social services departments provide for abused, neglected, and dependent children and their families. These services include

- investigating and assessing reports regarding suspected child abuse, neglect, or dependency;
- providing in-home counseling and supportive services to help abused, neglected, or dependent children stay at home with their families when they may safely remain in their homes;
- petitioning the juvenile court for orders adjudicating juveniles as abused, neglected, or dependent and, when necessary, removing abused, neglected, or dependent juveniles from their homes;
- placing abused, neglected, or dependent juveniles in licensed foster homes and providing financial assistance for their care;
- working to ensure safe, permanent, and nurturing families for abused, neglected, and dependent children;
- finding suitable adoptive families, guardians, or legal custodians for abused, neglected, or dependent children who cannot be reunited with their parents or families;

---

134. See G.S. 108A-70.18 through G.S. 108A-70.28. North Carolina's Health Choice program was established in 1998 in response to Congress' enactment of Title XXI of the federal Social Security Act (the State Child Health Insurance Program). Families with incomes that exceed 150 percent of the federal poverty level are required to pay an enrollment fee and nominal copayments. See G.S. 108A-70.21(c), (d), (e).

- providing independent living skills for foster children who cannot be reunited with their parents or families or adopted;
- preventing child abuse and neglect by providing public information, coordinating agency and community services for families, improving parenting skills, strengthening social support networks for families, and providing other family support services.

Child welfare services are provided by county social services departments under the supervision of the state DHHS Division of Social Services and are financed by a combination of federal, state, and county funding.

### Child Protective Services

State law requires that cases of suspected child abuse, neglect, or dependency be reported to the county department of social services.[135] When a county department of social services receives a report regarding suspected child abuse, neglect, or dependency, it must conduct a prompt and thorough assessment of the child's situation, determine whether the child is abused, neglected, dependent, or needs protective services, ascertain the risk of harm to the child, and, if necessary, take appropriate action to protect the child.[136]

---

135. G.S. 7B-301. This statute also requires an individual or institution to contact the county social services department when there is cause to believe that a child has died as the result of maltreatment. North Carolina's mandatory reporting requirements with respect to child abuse, neglect, and dependency are discussed in detail in Janet Mason, *Reporting Child Abuse and Neglect in North Carolina*, 2d ed. (Chapel Hill: School of Government, The University of North Carolina at Chapel Hill, 2003), available at www.sog.unc.edu/pubs/electronicversions/rca/rca.htm (last visited April 16, 2008). In SFY 2006, county social services departments received almost 70,000 reports involving the suspected abuse, neglect, or dependency of almost 120,000 children. "N.C. Division of Social Services Child Welfare Statistics," available at sasweb.unc.edu/cgi-bin/broker?_service=default&_program=cwweb.icanscr.sas&county=North%20Carolina&label= (last visited April 16, 2008).

136. G.S. 7B-302. In SFY 2006, county social services departments determined that approximately 25 percent of the children who were the subjects of reported abuse, neglect, or dependency had been abused or neglected, were dependent, or needed protective services, and provided protective services or recommended that protective services be provided to approximately 40 percent of the children who were the subjects of reports. "N.C. Division of Social Services Child Welfare Statistics" (sasweb.unc.edu/cgi-bin/broker?_service=default&county=North+Carolina&label=&_program=cwweb.report.sas&fn=ALL&cnty=N&type=CHILD) (last visited April 16, 2008).

Because North Carolina's Juvenile Code seeks to protect children by means that respect the right of family autonomy as well as children's needs for safety, continuity, and permanence, county social services departments provide a wide range of in-home treatment and supportive services to abused, neglected, dependent, and at-risk children and their families and seek to keep families intact in cases in which the risk of harm to a child does not require the child's removal from the home.

State law, however, authorizes the county social services director to file a petition asking the juvenile court to enter an order to protect an abused, neglected, or dependent child by removing the child from his or her home and placing him or her in the custody of the county social services department or authorizing the provision of other protective services.[137]

*Foster Care Placement and Assistance*

Foster care placement is the placement, usually temporary, of an abused, neglected, dependent, or delinquent child by the county social services department in a state-licensed foster home or group home.[138] Children may be placed in foster care through a voluntary agreement between the child's parent, custodian, or guardian and the county social services department or pursuant to a juvenile court order.

Financial assistance for children placed in foster homes and facilities is provided through a combination of federal, state, and county funding, including funding provided through the federal Temporary Assis-

---

137. G.S. 7B-302(d); G.S. 7B-403; G.S. 7B-903. In SFY 2003, county social services departments filed juvenile court petitions regarding approximately 5,800 abused, neglected, or dependent children. "North Carolina Child Protective Services Data, 2002–03" (Raleigh: N.C. Child Advocacy Institute, 2005), available at www.ncchild.org/images/stories/cpscard2.pdf (last visited April 16, 2008).

138. As of September 30, 2005, 5,314 children who had been placed in the legal custody of county social services departments lived with nonrelatives in licensed foster care homes or group homes. "Federal Child and Family Service Review" (Raleigh: N.C. Division of Social Services, 2007), available at www.dhhs.state.nc.us/dss/stats/docs/child%20welfare%20docs/nc_statewide_assessment_final.pdf (last visited April 16, 2008). In a broader sense, the term "foster care" is sometimes used to refer to all children who are placed in the legal custody of county social services departments, including those who live in their own homes, with relatives in kinship placements, in pre-adoptive placements, or in institutions. As of September 30, 2005, county social services departments had legal custody of 10,773 "foster" children.

tance for Needy Families Block Grant, the federal Title IV-E foster care assistance program, and the State Foster Care Benefits Program.[139]

*Family Preservation and Permanency Planning Services*
Because unnecessary or unduly long foster care placements are financially costly and adversely affect the well-being of children, federal and state child welfare policies emphasize the importance of preventing the removal of children from their homes in cases in which removal is not required to protect children from harm, the reunification of children with their families in cases in which children can be returned safely to their homes, and the placement of abused, neglected, and dependent children in safe and permanent homes within a reasonable period of time when they cannot be reunited with their families. County social services departments, therefore, are required to "provide preventive services to help families deal with their problems so that children can remain in their own homes, as well as reunification services aimed at reuniting children with their families as soon as possible when removal is necessary."[140]

When a child is placed in the custody of a county social services department, North Carolina's Juvenile Code generally requires the juvenile court to hold periodic hearings to review the child's continued placement with the department and, when custody has been removed from a parent, guardian, custodian, or caretaker and the child cannot return home, whether the child can be placed in a safe and permanent living arrangement.[141] When a child has been placed in the legal custody of a county social services department, reunification is not possible or in the child's best interest, and adoption has been determined to be the best plan for the child, the department may file a petition in juvenile court seeking termination of the parents' rights with respect to the child.[142]

---

139. The State Foster Care Benefits Program is authorized by G.S. 108A-48.

140. Janet Mason, "Social Services," in David M. Lawrence, ed., *County and Municipal Government in North Carolina* (Chapel Hill: School of Government, The University of North Carolina at Chapel Hill, 2007), available at www.sog.unc.edu/pubs/cmg/cmg42.pdf (last visited April 16, 2008).

141. *See* G.S. 7B-906 through G.S. 7B-911.

142. G.S. 7B-1103.

*Independent Living Services (LINKS)*

The Independent Living Services (LINKS) program is North Carolina's independent living services program for foster children. Services provided through the LINKS program are designed to help foster children make a successful transition from foster care to independent living as young adults:

> Older youth and young adults who have experienced extended time in foster care are at increased risk of negative consequences once they leave care, such as dropping out of school, unplanned parenthood, high rates of untreated illness, homelessness, criminal activity, depression and suicide. In order to help these youth and young adults have better outcomes, the NC LINKS program provides services and resources to all youth in foster care age 16 to 18 and to those young adults who are between the ages of 18 and 21 and are participating in a CARS agreement, as well as to young adults who aged out of foster care at age 18 and are not participating in a CARS agreement. * * * County Departments of Social Services are required to offer LINKS services to these two populations if they have eligible youth or young adults who are or were in their custody. Counties are strongly encouraged to provide services to youth in foster care ages 13 through 15 and to youth and young adults who were discharged from their custody as teens but prior to their 18th birthday.[143]

*Adoption Placement Services and Adoption Assistance*

Adoption placement services are designed to find safe and permanent homes for children whose parents have relinquished them for adoption or had their parental rights terminated and to provide support for the families who want to adopt those children.

In North Carolina, adoption placement services are provided by county social services departments and licensed private adoption agencies. These services include accepting children for adoptive placement, recruiting and screening adoptive parents, and arranging

---

143. N.C. Division of Social Services website at www.dhhs.state.nc.us/dss/links/index.html (last visited July 10, 2008).

and supervising placements. State law generally requires that a "county department of social services or a licensed child-placing agency conduct a pre-placement assessment of every prospective adoptive home and a report to the court on every adoptive placement."[144]

Adoption assistance payments are available for certain adopted children with special needs. Funding for adoption assistance payments is provided through a combination of federal, state, and county funding, including funding provided under Title IV-E of the federal Social Security Act, Title IV-B of the federal Social Security Act, the State Adoption Fund, and the state Special Needs Adoptions Incentive Fund.[145]

---

144. Mason, "Social Services." See G.S. 48-1-109.

145. The State Adoption Fund and the state Special Needs Adoptions Incentive Fund are authorized by G.S. 108A-50 and G.S. 108A-50.1.

# Chapter 12

# Social Services Funding, Budgets, and Spending

## Social Services Funding

More than any other area of local government finance, social services financing is complicated by intricate patterns of federal, state, and county funding.[1]

Financing of public assistance and social services programs in North Carolina is a shared responsibility of the federal government, the state, and the counties. Inevitably this sharing of financial responsibility raises questions, and sometimes controversies, regarding how much each level of government should pay for public assistance and social services programs.

Since the 1930s, the federal government has assumed a major role in financing social services programs. Federal funding for social services, however, also requires the expenditure of substantial county and state funds.

---

1. This chapter incorporates, revises, and expands excerpts from Janet Mason, "Social Services," Article 42, in David M. Lawrence, ed., *County and Municipal Government in North Carolina* (Chapel Hill: School of Government, The University of North Carolina at Chapel Hill, 2007), available online at www.sog.unc.edu/pubs/cmg/cmg42.pdf, and Janet Mason and John Saxon, "Social Services," Chapter 12, in Charles D. Liner, ed., *State and Local Government Relations in North Carolina: Their Evolution and Current Status*, 2d ed. (Chapel Hill: Institute of Government, The University of North Carolina at Chapel Hill, 1995), 199–222.

Moreover, North Carolina's system of county administration and state supervision of social services programs generates complex practices and issues regarding the division of financial responsibility between the state and counties. Some county expenditures are required by the General Assembly's assignment of responsibility to the counties for a portion of the non-federal cost of certain programs. Some are required as a condition of receiving other federal and state funds for social services. Others are required in order to provide needed, and sometimes mandated, services and programs for which state and federal funds are either unavailable or insufficient.

In both state and county government, many concerns about social services relate to cost containment and to lack of control. These issues are reflected in a special sensitivity when legislative, regulatory, policy, or judicial mandates are received unaccompanied by the funds to implement them, whether those mandates are directed from the federal government to the state or from the state to the counties.

### FEDERAL FUNDING OF PUBLIC ASSISTANCE AND SOCIAL SERVICES PROGRAMS

The federal government provides significant funding to North Carolina and other states for certain public assistance and social services programs, including Medicaid, food and nutrition assistance, and temporary assistance for needy families.[2] In state fiscal year (SFY) 2006–07, North Carolina received more than $8.25 billion in federal funding for public assistance and social services programs, and federal funding covered approximately 65 percent of the total spending for all state and county public assistance and social services programs in North Carolina.

Federal funding for social services and the requirements attached to that funding vary from program to program, creating what some people call a series of "silos" that segregate federal funding for different social services programs and establish separate federal requirements with respect to each program.

At the federal level, Congress is primarily responsible for enacting the laws that create federally funded public assistance and social ser-

---

2. Some public assistance and social services programs administered by county social services departments are supported entirely by state funding, county funding, or state and county funding and do not receive any federal financial assistance.

vices programs and appropriating federal funding for those programs.[3] Federal laws, including the Social Security Act, the Food Stamp Act, and annual federal budget and appropriations acts, determine

- how much money the federal government will provide for each federally funded public assistance or social services program,
- how the money will be distributed among the states,
- the purposes for which the federal funds may be used,
- the conditions with which the states must comply to receive the federal funding, and
- whether the states will be required to pay part of the costs of the program.

Federal funding for social services programs is distributed by the U.S. Department of Health and Human Services and other federal agencies to North Carolina and other states through federal grants to the states, which then allocate federal funding to state agencies or "pass through" federal funding to subgrantees, including, in North Carolina, county social services departments.[4]

Almost all federal social services grants to states are categorical, program grants. These grants fund ongoing social services programs, rather than one-time or short-term projects, and may be used only for specified purposes or programs and in accordance with the federal requirements or conditions that are attached to them. In order to receive this type of grant, a state generally must submit a state plan or application to the federal agency that is responsible for administering the grant, receive federal approval of its plan or application, and comply with additional "administrative and reporting requirements that help ensure both financial and programmatic accountability."[5] Federal grants

---

3. Funding for social services programs comes from general tax revenues received by the federal government and is appropriated pursuant to Congress' authority to tax and spend for the general welfare under Article III, Section 8, of of the United States Constitution.

4. In North Carolina, the General Assembly allocates federal social services funding received under the Temporary Assistance for Needy Families Block Grant, the Social Services Block Grant, the Low-Income Energy Assistance Block Grant, and the Child Care and Development Block Grant as part of the state budget and appropriations acts.

5. Ben Canada, "Federal Grants to State and Local Governments: Overview and Characteristics" (Washington, DC: Congressional Research Service, 2000), 3.

to states for state Medicaid and child support enforcement programs are two examples of categorical grants.

Some federal social services funding is provided to states through federal "block grants," including the Social Services Block Grant (SSBG), the Temporary Assistance for Needy Families Block Grant, the Low-Income Energy Assistance Block Grant, and the Child Care and Development Block Grant. A block grant is a type of categorical, program grant that allows federal funding to be used for a broad range of activities, services, or programs.[6] Block grants usually give recipient states more discretion and flexibility in identifying problems and designing programs to address them.[7] States, for example, are

> given wide discretion to determine the services [that
> will be provided with federal funding under the Social
> Services Block Grant] . . . and the groups that may be
> eligible for services . . . . * * * In addition to support-
> ing social services [aimed at achieving or maintaining
> economic self-support to prevent, reduce, or eliminate
> dependency; achieving or maintaining self-sufficiency,
> including reduction or prevention of dependency; pre-
> venting or remedying neglect, abuse, or exploitation of
> children and adults unable to protect their own inter-
> ests, or preserving, rehabilitating or reuniting families;
> and preventing or reducing inappropriate institutional
> care by providing for community-based care, home-
> based care, or other forms of less intensive care, states
> are allowed to use SSBG funding] for staff training,
> administration, planning, evaluation, and purchasing

---

Unlike project grants, program grants generally are not awarded on a competitive basis.

6. Canada, "Federal Grants to State and Local Governments," 3. Some block grants are created by consolidating "a number of existing categorical programs into one" grant. Canada, "Federal Grants to State and Local Governments," 3.

7. Researchers who have examined the recent history of federal block grants, however, have found that the flexibility given to states sometimes "erodes as Congress responds to patterns of state implementation." Kenneth Finegold et al., "Block Grants: Historical Overview and Lessons Learned," *New Federalism Series No. A-63* (Washington, DC: Urban Institute, 2004), 6, available online at www.urban.org/UploadedPDF/310991_A-63.pdf (last visited April 16, 2008).

technical assistance in developing, implementing, or
administering the State social service program.[8]

Federal block grants also typically minimize administrative and reporting requirements, and, in some instances, limit or "cap" the federal government's fiscal responsibility.[9]

Both categorical and block grants to states for social services programs generally allocate federal funding to states according to a distribution formula prescribed by federal law and, therefore, are sometimes
referred to as formula grants. Distribution formulas may be based on
one or more variables, including state population, per capita income,
prior program expenditures, program performance, caseloads, and so
forth.

Federal funding pays the entire cost of assistance provided to individuals and families under some public assistance programs, including
the Food and Nutrition Services and Low-Income Energy Assistance
programs. In most instances, though, federally funded public assistance
and social services programs require states to pay part of the cost of
administering those programs or part of the cost of providing assistance or services under those programs. In those programs, the portion
of program costs paid with federal funds is called the federal share,
while the portion paid by state (or state or local) funding is referred to
as the non-federal share.

In some cases, the federal share is based on a federal financial participation (FFP) rate specified in federal law. Federal funding usually
covers at least half of the total cost of assistance or services provided
under these programs and half of the cost of administering these programs.[10] In the Medicaid program, for example, the federal government

8. House of Representatives Ways and Means Committee, *Background Material
and Data on the Programs within the Jurisdiction of the Committee on Ways and Means*
(Washington, DC: Government Printing Office, 2004), 10-6. *See also* 42 U.S.C.
§ 1397. Some federal social services block grants, including the Temporary Assistance for Needy Families Block Grant, allow states to transfer a specified portion
of their federal block grant funding to other block grants.

9. "Researchers have found that over time, the real value of block grant funding gradually declines . . . ." Finegold et al., "Block Grants," 6.

10. Administrative costs generally include the salaries and related personnel
costs of county social services employees and reasonable and necessary operating
expenses (for example, telephones and supplies) related to the administration of
public assistance and social services programs.

pays approximately half of the cost of administering state Medicaid programs and approximately 50 to 75 percent of the cost of providing medical assistance to eligible Medicaid recipients, using an FFP formula that is based, in part, on each state's per capita income.

Federal social services grants that use an FFP formula require states to provide state funding to pay the non-federal share of program costs. This type of requirement generally is referred to as the state–federal "match." Match requirements are specified by federal law and might require states to provide $1 in state funding for every $1 of federal funding, $1 in state funding for every $3 of federal funding, or some other amount. Federal funding for child support enforcement programs, for example, generally requires a match of $1 for every $2 of federal funding.

Other federal social services grants, including the Temporary Assistance for Needy Families Block Grant, include a "maintenance of effort" provision that requires states to maintain a specified level of financial effort with respect to a particular program or activity and ensures that federal funding only supplements, and does not supplant, state funding. By contrast, some federal social services grants, including the Social Services Block Grant, do not require states to match or supplement federal funding.

Some federally funded public assistance programs, such as the Food and Nutrition Services and Medicaid programs, are called "entitlement" programs because all persons who meet the programs' eligibility requirements are entitled to receive assistance or services. The federal government's financial obligation with respect to entitlement programs is open-ended because federal law obligates Congress to appropriate a sufficient amount of funding to pay the federal share of benefits for everyone who is entitled to assistance.[11]

In other programs, such as Temporary Assistance for Needy Families, the Low-Income Energy Assistance program, and the Social Services Block Grant, the federal government's financial obligation is "capped." Congress appropriates a fixed amount of federal funding for the program. If federal funding for the program is insufficient to provide assistance or services to everyone who is eligible, the state must limit the

---

11. When federal law requires North Carolina to pay a portion of the non-federal cost of a federal entitlement program, the state's (or the state's and counties') financial obligation for the program also is open-ended.

number of people served by the program, limit the amount of benefits or the level of services provided to eligible persons, or provide additional state funding for the program.

As noted above, all federal social services grants come with certain conditions or "strings" attached to the receipt of federal funding. These conditions generally are referred to as federal "mandates," though, strictly speaking, states may avoid them by declining to accept federal funding for a particular program.[12] Some of the conditions attached to federal social services grants include requirements that

- social services programs be administered by or under the supervision of a single state agency;
- social services programs be administered in all political subdivisions in the state; and
- state or local government employees who administer social services programs be employed under a merit-based personnel system.

Federal social services "mandates" also may specify who is eligible or ineligible for assistance under federally funded social services programs, what types of assistance and services may be provided, how much assistance may be provided, how long assistance may be provided, and how much states (or, in North Carolina, state and local governments) must contribute to the cost of these programs.

### STATE AND COUNTY FUNDING FOR SOCIAL SERVICES

In North Carolina, the state, counties, or the state and counties are responsible for paying

- the entire cost of state or county public assistance and social services programs that are not established pursuant to federal law or do not receive federal funding; and

---

12. Federal mandates, therefore, constitute a "carrot" rather than a "stick." Federal and state social services mandates are discussed in greater detail in John L. Saxon, "Mandates, Money, and Welfare: Financing Social Services Programs," *Popular Government* 60(1) (Summer 1994): 2–15. The United States Supreme Court has decided at least two cases that address the constitutionality of federal mandates that are imposed on states as conditions of federal funding. *See* South Dakota v. Dole, 483 U.S. 203 (1987) and New York v. United States, 488 U.S. 1041 (1992).

• the non-federal share of the cost of federally funded public assistance and social services programs.[13]

In SFY 2006–07, North Carolina's General Assembly appropriated approximately $3.5 billion in state tax revenues for public assistance and social services programs, and state funding comprised more than one-fourth of total spending for these programs. North Carolina counties provided almost $1 billion in county funding for social services programs—or approximately 8 percent of total spending for social services.[14] Legislation enacted by North Carolina's General Assembly in 2007, however, will reduce the amount and percentage of county funding for social services programs and increase the amount and percentage of state funding for social services by phasing out the counties' fiscal responsibility for Medicaid services provided to county residents.[15]

In most states the non-federal share of the cost of federally funded public assistance and social services programs and the entire cost of other state social services program are paid entirely by the state government from state tax revenues. By contrast, under North Carolina's county-administered, state-supervised system, the non-federal share of social services costs and the cost of other state social services programs are divided between the state government and the counties.[16]

Counties are political subdivisions of the state.[17] Their duties and responsibilities, as well as their powers, are derived from and specified by statutes enacted by the General Assembly.[18] And, as discussed in

---

13. The state and counties also may supplement federal funding for social services programs beyond the amount required by federal match or maintenance of effort requirements.

14. Although counties historically have been responsible for less than one-tenth of the total cost of social services programs, county officials and taxpayers often feel that social services programs are an ever-increasing share of and an undue burden on county budgets. See Saxon, "Money, Mandates, and Welfare," and John L. Saxon, "The Fiscal Impact of Medicaid on North Carolina Counties," *Popular Government* 67(4) (Summer 2002): 14–22.

15. SL 2007-323.

16. North Carolina has been one of only a few states that require local governments to pay part of the non-federal share of the cost of the Medicaid program and some or all of the cost of other federally funded social services programs.

17. See McCormac v. Robeson County, 90 N.C. 441 (1884); Bell v. Johnston County, 127 N.C. 85, 37 S.E. 136 (1900).

18. See N.C. CONST. art. VII, § 1; Ch. 153A of the North Carolina General Statutes [hereinafter G.S.]; White v. Chowan County, 90 N.C. 437 (1884); State *ex*

Chapter 3, the state generally may delegate to counties all or part of its responsibility to administer or fund public assistance or social services programs.[19]

A number of state statutes address the responsibility of North Carolina counties to fund, as well as administer, public assistance and social services programs. For example, Section 108A-87 of the North Carolina General Statutes [hereinafter G.S.] gives North Carolina's General Assembly the authority to decide whether and how to divide the non-federal share of costs for social services programs between the state and counties.[20] Acting pursuant to this statute, the General Assembly historically required North Carolina counties to pay 15 percent of the nonfederal share of the cost of Medicaid services provided to county residents.[21] Legislation enacted by North Carolina's General Assembly in 2007, however, "phased out" the counties' fiscal responsibility for Medicaid services provided to county residents.[22]

State law also requires counties to pay the non-federal share of local administrative costs for the Food and Nutrition Services, Medicaid, and child support enforcement programs, the local administrative costs of the State–County Special Assistance program, half of the cost of assistance provided under the State–County Special Assistance program and the State Foster Care Assistance program, half of the non-federal share of most adoption and foster care assistance provided under Title IV-E of the Social Security Act, and much of the cost of providing child protective services for abused, neglected, and dependent juveniles. And state law requires counties to meet specified maintenance of effort requirements with respect to North Carolina's Work First program for needy families.[23]

---

rel. Tate v. Haywood County, 122 N.C. 812, 30 S.E. 352 (1898); Jones v. Madison County, 137 N.C. 579, 50 S.E. 291 (1905); O'Neal v. Wake County, 196 N.C. 184, 145 S.E. 28 (1928).

19. See Martin v. Wake County, 208 N.C. 354, 180 S.E. 777 (1935).

20. G.S. 108A-87(b) provides that the state, rather than counties, will pay the non-federal share of providing public assistance and social services to Native Americans who live on reservations that are held in trust by the United States.

21. The state Medicaid funding requirement for counties was not codified but, instead, was included as a provision in the biennial state budget and appropriations act. See, for example, SL 2005-276, § 10.11(b).

22. SL 2007-323.

23. G.S. 108A-27.12.

State law also governs the allocation of fiscal responsibility for public assistance and social services among North Carolina counties. G.S. 153A-257 provides that a needy person's legal residence, as defined by that section, in a county determines which county is responsible for paying the county share of public assistance or social services provided to the person.

And state law expressly authorizes counties to tax and spend to provide public assistance and social services for individuals and families. G.S. 153A-149(b)(8) authorizes counties to "levy property taxes without restriction as to rate or amount" in order to pay their share of the cost of mandated public assistance programs.[24] G.S. 153A-149(c)(30) authorizes counties to levy property taxes to pay the cost of "optional" or nonmandated public assistance and social services programs. Similarly, G.S. 153A-255 requires counties to provide mandated social services and authorizes counties to "undertake, sponsor, organize, engage in, and support other social service programs intended to further the health, welfare, education, employment, safety comfort, and convenience of its citizens."[25]

G.S. 108A-90 expressly requires each board of county commissioners to levy and collect taxes sufficient to meet the county's share of the cost of mandated public assistance and social services program. If a county does not pay or arrange for payment of its full share of these costs, G.S. 108A-93 authorizes the governor to withhold from the county any state appropriations for public assistance and related administrative costs or to direct the secretary of revenue and the state controller to withhold sales tax revenues that have been collected by the state on behalf of the county.[26] If a county's actual expenditures for public assistance (not including related administrative costs) exceed the amount

---

24. In state fiscal year (SFY) 2000–01, median county Medicaid funding per $100 of adjusted assessed property value was 8.4 cents. *See* Saxon, "The Fiscal Impact of Medicaid on North Carolina Counties," 18. County funding for Medicaid exceeded 12 cents per $100 of adjusted assessed property value in twenty-five of North Carolina's counties and was less than 6 cents per $100 of adjusted assessed property value in twenty-seven counties.

25. Although the county property tax is expressly designated by state law as a revenue source for public assistance and social services programs, counties may use any unrestricted tax or non-tax revenues to provide or pay for social services.

26. Before withholding funds, the governor must notify the chair of the board of commissioners of the proposed action. G.S. 108A-93. In the early 1990s, several North Carolina counties unsuccessfully attempted to withhold county

that was estimated by the state and budgeted by the county, state law allows the county to borrow money from the state, without interest, to pay the additional cost of public assistance.[27]

## The State Budget and Appropriations Act

North Carolina's state government operates on a fiscal year that runs from July 1 through June 30. During regular legislative sessions in odd-numbered years, the General Assembly adopts a state budget and makes appropriations for each of the following two fiscal years. The General Assembly returns for a "short" legislative session in even-numbered years to make adjustments to the state budget for the second year of the biennium.

The biennial state budget process begins with the formulation of budget recommendations by the governor, who by virtue of the Executive Budget Act is director of the budget, and presentation of those recommendations to the General Assembly.[28] State law requires the General Assembly to enact a current operations appropriations act by June 15 in odd-numbered years and by June 30 in even-numbered years in which a current operations appropriations act is enacted.[29]

The appropriations act includes specific appropriations for state departments and agencies, local governments, and nongovernmental entities from the General Fund, the Highway Fund, the Highway Trust Fund, and federal block grants (including the Temporary Assistance for Needy Families Block Grant, the Social Services Block Grant, the Low-Income Energy Assistance Block Grant, and the Child Care and Development Block Grant), and generally governs the expenditure of all money by the state, including federal funding received by the state, state tax and non-tax revenues, and receipts by state agencies.[30] In SFY 2005–06, the General Assembly appropriated approximately $3 billion of the

---

funding for the state Medicaid program. *See* Saxon, "Mandates, Money, and Welfare," 2.

27. G.S. 108A-89. The loan must be repaid within the next two fiscal years.

28. G.S. 143-11 and G.S. 143-12.

29. G.S. 143-15 and G.S. 143-15.1(a). The appropriations act is subject to gubernatorial approval before it becomes law. *See* N.C. Const. art. II, § 22.

30. *See* G.S. 143-16, G.S. 143-16.1, G.S. 143-16.3, G.S. 143-23, and G.S. 143-28.

state's $17 billion General Fund budget for public assistance and social services programs.[31]

## County Budgets, Appropriations, and Expenditures

The Local Government Budget and Fiscal Control Act (LGBFCA) governs the budgeting, expenditure, and accounting of all moneys received or spent by local government agencies, including county social services departments.[32] Under the LGBFCA, "units of local government" and "public authorities," as defined in G.S. 159-7, are responsible for their own budgeting, disbursing, and accounting. Local government agencies that are not units of local government or public authorities must have their budgeting, disbursing, and accounting done for them by the unit of local government of which they are a part.

Counties are units of local government under the LGBFCA. County departments of social services, however, are not units of local government or public authorities under the LGBFCA. This means that the budget for the county department of social services is part of the county budget and that the expenditure of money by the county social services department is subject to oversight by the county.

Nonetheless, the state Department of Health and Human Services (DHHS), the county social services board, and the county social services director, as well as the county manager and the board of county commissioners, play important roles with respect to the county social services budget.

To assist counties in planning their social services budgets, G.S. 108A-88 requires the state DHHS, by February 15 of each year, to notify each county social services director, county manager, and board of county commissioners of

  · the amount of state and federal funds estimated to be available to the counties for public assistance and social services programs and related administrative costs for the next fiscal year; and

---

31. SL 2005-276, §2.1. The appropriations act also appropriated approximately $735 million in federal funding under four federal social services block grants.

32. G.S. 159-8(a). The Local Government Budget and Fiscal Control Act (LGBFCA) is discussed in more detail in David M. Lawrence, *Local Government Finance in North Carolina*, 2d ed. (Chapel Hill: Institute of Government, The University of North Carolina at Chapel Hill, 1990).

- the percentage of county financial participation that is expected to be required for each program.[33]

Every county's proposed social services budget, however, contains more than the amounts indicated in the state's estimates for mandated programs. In the areas of child welfare and child protective services, for example, federal and state funds available to the county, along with any county match required to receive those funds, generally are insufficient to carry out the county's legal responsibilities with respect to abused, neglected, and dependent juveniles and, therefore, must be supplemented with additional county funding. Similarly, some state mandates, such as the requirement that a county social services director serve as guardian for incompetent adults when appointed by the court to do so, do not include designated sources of state funding and must be paid from county funds if other federal or state funding is not available. In addition, county social services departments sometimes provide nonmandated assistance and services to meet local needs and these "optional" services must be supported by county funding to the extent that other federal or state funding is unavailable.

The county social services director is responsible, with the assistance of the county social services board, for planning the proposed budget for the county social services department.[34] Under the LGBFCA, the county social services director must submit the department's proposed budget to the county budget officer by April 30.[35] The department's proposed budget must include the department's request for appropriations for the coming fiscal year, an estimate of departmental revenues for the coming year (including federal, state, and nonpublic funding), actual and estimated expenditures for each category of expenditure included in

---

33. In providing estimates to the counties in odd-numbered years, the state must include notification of any changes in public assistance funding levels, formulas, or programs that the governor has proposed to the General Assembly under the Executive Budget Act. Counties also must be notified of changes in the proposed budget of the governor and the Advisory Budget Commission that result from action by the General Assembly or Congress subsequent to the February 15 estimates. The initial estimates that counties receive usually are revised several times. DHHS budget estimates are posted on the Division of Social Services website at www.dhhs.state.nc.us/dss/budget/county.htm (last visited April 16, 2008).

34. G.S. 108A-9(3).

35. G.S. 159-10. If a county has a county manager, the county manager is the county budget officer. G.S. 159-9.

the county budget ordinance for the current and immediately preceding fiscal years, actual and estimated amounts realized for each source of revenue for the current and immediately preceding fiscal years, and any additional information requested by the budget officer.

The LGBFCA requires county budget officers to prepare a proposed budget for the county (including the county department of social services) and submit it to the board of county commissioners by June 1.[36] The law, however, "is silent as to the procedures the budget officer is to follow in developing the [proposed] budget."[37] It seems clear, though, that the county budget officer has the legal authority to revise the proposed budget request submitted by the county social services director with or without the consent of the director or the county social services board.

After the proposed county budget is submitted to the board of county commissioners, the board must hold a public hearing on the proposed budget and adopt a budget ordinance by July 1.[38] Except as otherwise provided by law, the board of county commissioners

> enjoys complete discretion over the content of the [budget] ordinance and the fiscal policy it represents. The budget officer's recommendations are simply that—recommendations. The board may accept them modify them, or reject them.[39]

The county budget ordinance must

- make appropriations of county revenues for specified purposes, functions, activities, or objectives;[40]

---

36. G.S. 159-11. *See also* G.S. 108A-9(4), which requires the county social services board to transmit or present the proposed social services budget to the board of county commissioners. The county budget prepared by the county budget officer must be filed with the clerk for the board of county commissioners and is available for public inspection. G.S. 159-12.

37. Lawrence, *Local Government Finance in North Carolina*, 143.

38. G.S. 159-12(b) and G.S. 159-13.

39. Lawrence, *Local Government Finance in North Carolina*, 150.

40. G.S. 159-7(b)(2). Appropriations may be made for specified object classes within each county department or agency, as a lump sum for each department or agency, or for broad programs that include two or more departments or agencies. Most county budget ordinances make appropriations on a departmental basis. A county budget ordinance, however, may require a county department to spend its

- appropriate sufficient funds to pay the county's share of mandated public assistance and social services programs;[41]
- levy the county property tax for the coming fiscal year;[42]
- include a statement of the county's estimated revenues for the coming fiscal year; and
- be balanced.[43]

In most instances, the unexpended and unencumbered funds appropriated to a county department are included in the fund balance remaining at the end of the fiscal year and may be appropriated by the board of county commissioners for other purposes as part of the county budget ordinance for the following fiscal year. By contrast, unexpended county appropriations for public assistance programs do not lapse or revert and remain available for expenditure by the county social services department.[44] The board of county commissioners, however, may consider these unexpended funds in determining the amount of further appropriations to the department.

All expenditures from revenues received by the county or county departments, other than those for capital or grant projects and those accounted for in internal service or trust or agency funds, must be authorized by the county budget ordinance. County budget ordinances, therefore, include appropriations from federal and state funds received by the county for public assistance and social services programs as well as appropriations for these programs from county tax revenues.[45] In fact, about half of the total amount budgeted for social services by all North Carolina counties is paid from federal and state funding and only half of it is funded by county tax revenues.[46]

For those programs for which the Division of Social Services allocates specific amounts to counties, each county is provided with

---

appropriation for the purposes specified in the more detailed budget upon which the budget ordinance was based.

41. G.S. 108A-90.

42. G.S. 159-7(b)(2) and G.S. 159-13(c).

43. G.S. 159-8(a). "A budget ordinance is balanced when the sum of estimated net revenues and appropriated fund balances is equal to appropriations." G.S. 159-8(a).

44. G.S. 108A-91.

45. They do not include public assistance payments made by the state directly to or on behalf of county residents.

46. *See* Saxon, "Mandates, Money, and Welfare."

funding authorizations for disbursements up to those amounts. By accepting these authorizations, a county certifies that the required local matching funds are available in its current budget. State and federal funds for other social services programs flow to the county in the form of reimbursements for program expenditures. The Division of Social Services provides budget forms for counties to use in allocating administrative costs among programs.

Under state law, the county social services director is responsible for administering "funds provided by the board of [county] commissioners for the care of indigent persons in the county . . . ."[47] State law, however, also requires that the expenditures by the county social services department be made in accordance with the LGBFCA.

The LGBFCA prohibits the expenditure of funds by county agencies unless the expenditure has been authorized under the county budget ordinance, requires that all county revenues and expenditures be accounted for through the establishment of an accounting system that uses generally accepted accounting principles, requires the "preauditing" of all financial obligations, requires the review and approval of all disbursements by county agencies, and establishes requirements regarding financial reporting and audits.[48]

Under the LGBFCA, the county finance officer is legally responsible for establishing and maintaining the county's accounting system, for preauditing obligations, reviewing and approving disbursements, managing cash and other assets, and preparing financial reports.[49] The finance officer's responsibilities with respect to the county social services budget, however, may be delegated to and exercised by the county social services director or a special deputy county finance officer employed by the county social services department.

47. G.S. 108A-14(a)(4).
48. These provisions of the LGBFCA are discussed in more detail in Lawrence, *Local Government Finance in North Carolina.*
49. G.S. 159-24.

# Chapter 13

# Confidentiality and Social Services

State and county social services agencies collect and use a significant amount of information in connection with the programs they administer, the services they provide, and the functions they perform. Most of this information is recorded and maintained in some form—in written documents, photographs, audio recordings, magnetic tapes, computer files, or electronic data bases. Many of the records maintained by a social services agency contain information regarding the individuals and families who apply for or receive public assistance and social services from the agency. Some contain information regarding the agency's employees. And others contain information about the agency's operation, administration, and budget.

All records maintained by state or county social services agencies are subject to North Carolina's Public Records Law (Chapter 132 of

the North Carolina General Statutes [hereinafter G.S.]).[1] Information
contained in social services records, however, is exempt from public
disclosure under the state Public Records Law *if* an applicable federal
or state statute provides that it is "confidential" or may not be publicly
disclosed.[2] And dozens of federal and state statutes and regulations provide that much of the information obtained or maintained by state and
county social services agencies is confidential and not subject to public
disclosure.[3]

State and county social services agencies, therefore, often encounter
situations in which they need to determine whether information is
confidential, and, if it is, whether they are prohibited from disclosing it,
whether and how they are allowed to use or disclose it, or whether they
are required to disclose it to particular individuals or agencies.

---

1. The application of North Carolina's Public Records Law to local governments
is discussed in detail in David M. Lawrence, *Public Records Law for North Carolina
Local Governments* (Chapel Hill: Institute of Government, The University of North
Carolina at Chapel Hill, 1997).

2. *See* News & Observer Publishing Co. Inc. v. Poole, 330 N.C. 465, 486, 412
S.E.2d 7, 19 (1992).

3. The right to informational privacy and confidentiality issues affecting state
and county social services agencies are discussed in more detail in John L. Saxon,
"Privacy and the Law," *Popular Government* 67(3) (Spring 2002): 6–12; John L.
Saxon, "What is Confidentiality?" *Social Services Law Bulletin* No. 30 (Chapel Hill:
Institute of Government, The University of North Carolina at Chapel Hill, 2001);
John L. Saxon, "Where Do Confidentiality Rules Come From?" *Social Services Law
Bulletin* No. 31 (Chapel Hill: Institute of Government, The University of North
Carolina at Chapel Hill, 2001); John L. Saxon, "A Process for Analyzing Issues
Involving Confidentiality," *Social Services Law Bulletin* No. 35 (Chapel Hill: Insti-
tute of Government, The University of North Carolina at Chapel Hill, 2002); John
L. Saxon, "An Annotated Index of Federal and State Confidentiality Laws," *Social
Services Law Bulletin* No. 37 (Chapel Hill: Institute of Government, The University
of North Carolina at Chapel Hill, 2002); John L. Saxon, "The HIPAA Privacy Rule
and County Social Services Agencies," *Social Services Law Bulletin* No. 39 (Chapel
Hill: Institute of Government, The University of North Carolina at Chapel Hill,
2003); and John L. Saxon, "Collection, Use, and Disclosure of Social Security
Numbers, *Social Services Law Bulletin* No. 40 (Chapel Hill: School of Government,
The University of North Carolina at Chapel Hill, 2005).

## Understanding Confidentiality

### WHAT IS CONFIDENTIALITY?

Confidentiality "has both a common, everyday meaning and a more precise legal definition."[4] Under the common understanding of confidentiality, information is confidential if it is communicated with the expectation or understanding that it will not be disclosed to others unless the person from whom it was received or the person to whom it pertains consents to its disclosure. By contrast, the law generally considers information to be confidential if, and only if, it is designated as confidential under an applicable law that prohibits or restricts its use or disclosure.

### WHY IS CONFIDENTIALITY IMPORTANT?

Confidentiality protects individuals from personal, social, and economic injury, harm, and discrimination that may result from the public disclosure of sensitive, embarrassing, or private information and allows individuals to establish and maintain important personal, social, and professional relationships.

Confidentiality, however, also serves important social or public purposes that are unrelated to, or go beyond, the protection of individuals' interests with respect to informational privacy. For example, federal rules regarding the confidentiality of alcohol and substance abuse treatment records protect patients from the stigma or harm they might suffer as a result of public disclosure of their alcohol or substance abuse. But they also serve an important social or public purpose: decreasing the social impact of alcohol and substance abuse by encouraging patients to seek treatment without fear of public scrutiny and protecting the confidential, professional relationship that is necessary for successful treatment.

### IS CONFIDENTIALITY ABSOLUTE?

The short answer is "no." Confidentiality does not mean that confidential information may never be used or disclosed under any circumstances. Instead, confidentiality is always subject, implicitly or explicitly, to one or more exceptions.

---

4. Donald T. Dickson, *Confidentiality and Privacy in Social Work* (New York: Free Press, 1998), 28.

For example, all, or almost all, confidentiality rules allow confidential information to be disclosed with the consent of the person to whom the information pertains.

And while informational privacy is an important individual and social value, it is not the only value that individuals, society, public policy, and the law must or should take into consideration.[5] Many confidentiality rules, therefore, allow otherwise confidential information to be disclosed when an individual's right to informational privacy is outweighed by competing personal, social, or governmental needs.[6] For example, the efficient administration of government functions and delivery of public services requires the collection, use, and disclosure of information that many people might consider to be personal, private, or confidential, and the public's interest in the effective and efficient administration of government functions may outweigh individual interests with respect to informational privacy.[7] Similarly, society's general interest in protecting individuals from serious harm, injury, or death may allow or require social workers, psychologists, physicians, attorneys, or others to disclose otherwise confidential information when the disclosure is necessary to prevent serious harm.[8] And a criminal defendant's constitutional right to a fair trial may outweigh another individual's right to informational privacy if otherwise confidential information is potentially exculpatory.[9]

## Confidentiality, Social Work, and Social Services

No principle of social work . . . is more elementary than that of confidentiality. * * * The concern in social work for confidentiality derives [first] from the basic concept of the dignity and human rights of individuals. * * * . . . [Because] respect for the integrity of . . .

5. *See* Amitai Etzioni, *The Limits of Privacy* (New York: Basic Books, 1999), 4.

6. *See* Etzioni, *The Limits of Privacy* at 4; David M. O'Brien, *Privacy, Law, and Public Policy* (New York: Praeger, 1979), 20, 27.

7. *See* Whalen v. Roe, 429 U.S. 589, 605–06 (1977); *In re* Albemarle Mental Health Center, 42 N.C. App. 292, 256 S.E.2d 818 (1979).

8. *See* Tarasoff v. Regents of the Univ. of California, 551 P.2d 334 (Cal. 1976); Dickson, *Confidentiality and Privacy in Social Work*, 147–169.

9. *See* Pennsylvania v. Ritchie, 480 U.S. 39 (1987); State v. McGill, 141 N.C. App. 98, 539 S.E.2d 351 (2000).

[individuals who need] help [is a fundamental principle of social work, the social work profession has
long recognized the] . . . right [of clients] not only to
determine the direction . . . [their lives] will take but
also to retain control . . . [over their lives, including
some control with respect to decisions regarding] what
information will be obtained from . . . [them] or given
to others . . . .[10]

Confidentiality in the fields of social work and social services, however, also is viewed as vital to the effective provision of social services
to clients. Confidentiality generally is considered as essential in establishing and maintaining

. . . the relationship of . . . [a] social worker [or social
services agency] with a person [or family] needing
help. * * * The giving of information by . . . . [a] client
to . . . [a] caseworker, as the . . . representative [of a
social services agency], and the receiving and obtaining
of information by the agency from the client and other
appropriate sources is inherent in the casework process
and in the confidential relationship established.[11]

Confidentiality in social work and social services is also considered
to be essential in protecting individuals and families who receive social
services from embarrassment, stigma, and harm.

In a culture that attaches particular importance to
independence and personal adequacy, any form of
need may be accompanied by some loss of prestige or
a change in personal status. This fact emphasizes the
importance of privacy in the helping process.[12]

And confidentiality also serves the public interest by encouraging people who need assistance and services to utilize available social

---

10. National Social Welfare Assembly Inc., *Confidentiality in Social Services to
Individuals* (New York: John B. Watkins Company, 1958), 5, 13, 13–14.
11. *Id.* at 5.
12. *Id.* at 14.

services, thereby promoting the general public welfare as well as their own.[13]

Recognizing that "the confidential nature of communications between social workers and their clients has been a cardinal principle of social work from the earliest years of the profession,"[14] the National Association of Social Workers (NASW) Code of Ethics requires social workers to treat all personal information about clients as confidential and to protect the confidentiality of all personal information obtained in the course of providing professional social work services.[15] The NASW Code also includes approximately two dozen additional standards regarding confidentiality and privacy in the provision of clinical social work services, including provisions

- requiring social workers to discuss with clients the nature of confidentiality and limitations of clients' right to confidentiality and to review with their clients the circumstances in which confidential information may be requested and in which disclosure of confidential information may be legally required;
- allowing social workers to disclose confidential information about clients when the disclosure is appropriate and the client (or a person legally authorized to consent on behalf of the client) has provided valid, informed consent to the disclosure
- allowing social workers to disclose confidential information about clients when disclosure is necessary to prevent serious, foreseeable, and imminent harm to a client or another identifiable person;
- requiring, when disclosure of confidential information is required or allowed, social workers to disclose only information that is directly relevant to the purpose for which the disclosure is made and to disclose the least amount of confidential information necessary to achieve the desired purpose;

---

13. *Id.* at 15.

14. Suanna J. Wilson, *Confidentiality in Social Work* (New York: Free Press, 1978), 215.

15. National Association of Social Workers (NASW), "Code of Ethics," available online at www.socialworkers.org/pubs/code/code.asp (last visited April 16, 2008). Although the NASW Code of Ethics does not have the force of federal or state law and is not binding on public social services agencies or employees who are not NASW members, it does provide a set of generally accepted principles governing the collection, use, and disclosure of information in the provision of social work and social services to individuals and families.

- prohibiting social workers from discussing confidential information in public or in semi-public areas or any other setting unless privacy can be ensured;
- requiring social workers to take reasonable steps to ensure that clients' records are stored in a secure location and that clients' records are not available to others who are not authorized to have access;
- addressing confidentiality and privacy considerations in serving families;
- addressing the confidentiality of information regarding deceased clients;
- governing the disclosure of information to third party payors, courts, and the media; and
- ensuring the confidentiality of information contained in electronic records, e-mails, faxes, and computer files.

## Confidentiality and the Law

As noted above, information is confidential as a matter of law if, and only if, an applicable law designates it as confidential and limits its use or disclosure under some circumstances.[16] Social workers and other social services employees, therefore, need "to know when information is protected by confidentiality and privacy laws, under what conditions, and to what extent—and when it is not."[17]

The law, however, does not provide one general or universal definition of confidentiality or establish general rules for determining whether information is confidential or determining the scope or extent of confidentiality. Instead, the precise meaning, nature, and scope of confidentiality may be determined only by examining the specific language of particular laws or legal rules that govern the acquisition, use, protection, and disclosure of specific types of information in particular situations.

---

16. Although one may have a moral or ethical obligation to refrain from disclosing confidential information, that obligation generally will not be recognized or protected by law.

17. Dickson, *Confidentiality and Privacy in Social Work*, 9.

### Confidentiality, Privacy, and Privilege

Confidentiality, privacy, and privilege "are related, overlapping concepts in the law."[18]

Privacy is the broadest of the three, encompassing an individual's rights to

- decisional privacy (the right to hold personal beliefs and make personal decisions without government coercion or interference);[19]
- personal privacy (the right to be free from unreasonable intrusion into one's private affairs and from unreasonable governmental surveillance, eavesdropping, and searches with respect to their persons, communications, and private property);[20] and
- informational privacy (the right to be free from unreasonable public disclosure of personal information and from the unnecessary collection, use, and disclosure of personal information by government agencies).[21]

Confidentiality is an aspect of, but not synonymous with and also broader than, the right to informational privacy.

Privilege is one particular aspect of confidentiality. Privileged communications generally refer to communications that are made by patients, clients, or other specified individuals to doctors, psychologists, social workers, attorneys, or other specified professionals or individuals within the scope of a personal or professional relationship.[22] Strictly

---

18. Dickson, *Confidentiality and Privacy in Social Work*, 51.

19. *See* Olmstead v. United States, 277 U.S. 438, 478 (1928); Griswold v. Connecticut, 381 U.S. 479 (1965); Loving v. Virginia, 388 U.S. 1 (1967); Roe v. Wade, 410 U.S. 113 (1973); Cruzan v. Missouri Dep't of Health, 497 U.S. 261 (1990); and Lawrence v. Texas, 539 U.S. 588 (2003).

20. *See* Smith v. Jack Eckerd Corp., 101 N.C. App. 566, 568, 400 S.E.2d 99, 100 (1991), and Katz v. United States, 389 U.S. 347 (1967).

21. *See* Hall v. Post, 323 N.C. 259, 264, 312 S.E.2d 711, 714 (1988), and Whalen v. Roe, 429 U.S. 589, 599 (1977). In its broadest sense, informational privacy might be defined as an individual's right to determine whether, when, how, to what extent, and for what purpose "personal" information about himself or herself may be obtained, used, or disclosed by others. *See* Alan F. Westin, *Privacy and Freedom* (New York: Atheneum, 1967), 7.

22. *See* Section 8-53 of the North Carolina General Statutes [hereinafter G.S.] through G.S. 8-53.13; Michael v. Foil, 100 N.C. 178, 6 S.E. 264 (1888); Jaffee v. Redmond, 518 U.S. 1 (1996). *See also* Dickson, *Confidentiality and Privacy in Social Work*, 32–50. Privileged information also may include information about a patient, client, or other person obtained by a doctor, attorney, or other person

speaking, laws protecting privileged communications generally prohibit their admission as evidence in legal proceedings without the consent of the person who made the communication. Some laws regarding privileged communications, however, are written or construed more broadly to protect the confidentiality of privileged communications in contexts other than legal proceedings.[23]

## THE LEGAL BASES OF CONFIDENTIALITY

Legal rights and obligations with respect to confidentiality, privilege, and informational privacy are based on many different types of law.

Courts, for example, have recognized

- a "common law" right to privacy that protects individuals from injuries resulting from the unreasonable public disclosure of personal information,[24] as well as
- a right to informational privacy under both the U.S. Constitution and North Carolina's Constitution that may limit the authority of government agencies to collect, use, and disclose personal information.[25]

Legal obligations regarding the use and disclosure of confidential information also are imposed by federal and state statutes and regulations and may be assumed voluntarily pursuant to legal contracts and agreements.

### Federal Confidentiality Laws

Dozens of federal statutes and regulations limit the disclosure of confidential information. The federal Privacy Act, for example, generally prohibits the disclosure of personal information from most record systems maintained by federal agencies unless the individual to whom the

---

in connection with a personal or professional relationship. *See* Sims v. Charlotte Liberty Mut. Ins. Co., 257 N.C. 32, 36, 125 S.E.2d 326, 330 (1962).

23. *See* Watts v. Cumberland County Hosp. System Inc., 75 N.C. App. 1, 10, 330 S.E.2d 242, 249 (1985).

24. *See* Hall v. Post, 323 N.C. at 268, 372 S.E.2d at 716; Woodruff v. Miller, 64 N.C. App. 364, 307 S.E.2d 176 (1983); Burgess v. Busby, 142 N.C. App. 393, 399, 544 S.E.2d 4, 7 (2001).

25. *See* Whalen v. Roe, 429 U.S. at 605; Treants Enters. v. Onslow County, 83 N.C. App. 345, 359, 350 S.E.2d 365, 374 (1986), *aff'd on other grounds,* 320 N.C. 776, 360 S.E.2d 783 (1987); ACT-UP Triangle v. Comm'n for Health Servs., 345 N.C. 699, 710–12, 483 S.E.2d 388, 394–96 (1997).

information pertains consents to disclosure of that information or disclosure is authorized by law.[26] The federal Privacy Act, however, does not apply to records maintained by state or county social services agencies.[27]

Other federal laws, though, *may* limit the authority of state and county social services agencies to obtain, use, or disclose confidential information.[28]

Federal regulations adopted pursuant to the Health Insurance Portability and Accountability Act (HIPAA), for example, limit, but do not competely prohibit, the disclosure of protected health information by most health care providers and health plans.[29] The federal Driver's Privacy Protection Act of 1994 limits the disclosure of personal information from the motor vehicle records maintained by state agencies.[30] And the Family Educational Rights and Privacy Act (FERPA) and FERPA regulations require that educational institutions that receive federal funding comply with federal requirements regarding the use and disclosure of student records.[31] Federal law also imposes significant restrictions with respect to the disclosure of information about persons who

---

26. 5 U.S.C. § 552a. The federal Freedom of Information Act allows federal agencies to refuse to release information from public records if disclosure of the information would constitute a clearly unwarranted invasion of personal privacy or the information is confidential or protected from disclosure under a federal law other than the federal Privacy Act. 5 U.S.C. § 552(b)(6). *See also* U.S. Dep't of Justice v. Reporters Committee for Freedom of the Press, 489 U.S. 749 (1989).

27. *See* St. Michael's Convalescent Hosp. v. California, 643 F.2d 1369, 1373 (9th Cir. 1981).

28. In some instances, these federal laws may create legal rights that may be enforced by individuals who have been harmed by the unlawful disclosure of confidential information. But in other instances, they do not. *See* Gonzaga Univ. v. Doe, 536 U.S. 273 (2002) (FERPA student records); Chapa v. Adams, 168 F.3d 1036 (7th Cir. 1999) (federal alcohol and substance abuse treatment records).

29. 45 C.F.R. §§ 160 and 164. The HIPAA medical privacy rule is discussed in more detail in Aimee N. Wall, "Health Privacy: The New Federal Framework," *Popular Government* 67(3) (Spring 2002): 44–52. The impact of the HIPAA privacy rule on county social services departments is discussed in more detail in a following section of this chapter and in Saxon, "The HIPAA Privacy Rule and County Social Services Agencies."

30. 18 U.S.C. §§ 2721 through 2725.

31. 20 U.S.C. § 1232g; 34 C.F.R. § 99. *See also* Laurie Mesibov, "Privacy and Public School Students," *Popular Government* 67(3) (Spring 2002): 36–43; Thomasin Hughes, "Releasing Student Information: What's Public and What's Not," *School Law Bulletin* 32(1) (Winter 2001): 12.

receive alcohol or substance abuse prevention or treatment services from federally assisted programs.[32]

In addition, the federal Computer Matching and Privacy Protection Act of 1988 restricts the use and redisclosure of personal information that state and county social services agencies receive from federal record systems for use in computerized data-matching programs.[33] And finally, provisions in the federal Social Security Act, the Child Abuse Prevention and Treatment Act, and other federal laws require state and county social services agencies to protect the confidentiality of information about individuals and families who receive child protective services, foster care and other child welfare services, food and nutrition assistance, Medicaid, and other types of federally funded public assistance and social services.[34]

In some instances, these federal confidentiality rules may preempt or "override" state law regarding the confidentiality or disclosure of information. In other instances, they may establish minimum requirements with respect to confidentiality that may be affected by state laws that are more lenient or more restrictive with respect to the acquisition, use, or disclosure of confidential information. And in some instances, federal confidentiality requirements that are imposed solely as conditions of receiving federal funding *may* not be sufficient to prevent the required disclosure of information pursuant to state law.[35]

32. 42 U.S.C. § 290dd-2; 42 C.F.R. §§ 2.1 through 2.67. The federal law and regulations regarding the confidentiality of information related to alcohol and substance abuse prevention and treatment services are discussed in detail in *Confidentiality and Communication: A Guide to the Federal Drug and Alcohol Confidentiality Law* (New York: Legal Action Center, 2000).

33. 5 U.S.C. §§ 552a(a)(8) through (12) and 552a(o)–(r).

34. *See* 42 U.S.C. § 5106a(b) (CAPTA); 42 U.S.C. § 671(a)(8) (foster care and adoption assistance); 45 C.F.R. § 1355.21(a) (child welfare services); 45 C.F.R. § 1355.30 (foster care and adoption assistance); 45 C.F.R. § 205.50 (foster care and adoption assistance); 7 U.S.C. § 2020(e)(8) (food and nutrition assistance); 7 C.F.R. § 272.1(c) (food and nutrition assistance); 42 U.S.C. § 1396a(a)(7) (Medicaid); 42 C.F.R. §§ 431.300 through 431.307 (Medicaid); 42 U.S.C. § 654(26) (child support enforcement); 45 C.F.R. § 307.13 (child support enforcement); 42 U.S.C. § 602(a)(1)(A)(iv) (TANF).

35. *See* Troutt Brothers Inc. v. Emison, 841 S.W. 2d 604 (Ark. 1992).

*State Confidentiality Laws*

North Carolina's General Assembly has enacted a number of statutes that may limit the collection, use, or disclosure of information by social services agencies.

State law, for example, limits the disclosure by state and local government agencies of information regarding

- individuals and families who apply for or receive public assistance or social services from county social services departments;[36]
- public employees, including employees of county social services departments;[37]
- children and families involved in juvenile court proceedings;[38]
- children and parents who receive adoption placement services or are involved in adoption proceedings;[39] and
- state and local taxpayers.[40]

State statutes and rules also protect the confidentiality of

- privileged communications to physicians, clergypersons, psychologists, school counselors, licensed marital and family therapists, licensed or certified clinical social workers, licensed counselors, optometrists, peer support group counselors, journalists, rape crisis centers, domestic violence programs, nurses, attorneys, and spouses;[41]
- financial records of customers of banks, credit unions, and other financial institutions;[42]
- persons who are HIV positive or have AIDS or other communicable diseases;[43] and
- patients of mental health facilities.[44]

---

36. *See* G.S. 108A-80. State statutes and rules regarding the disclosure of information from social services client records are discussed in more detail in the following sections of this chapter.

37. *See* G.S. 153A-98.

38. *See* G.S. 7B-2900 through G.S. 7B-2902; G.S. 7B-3000 through G.S. 7B-3001; G.S. 7B-3100 through G.S. 7B-3102.

39. *See* G.S. 48-9-102 through G.S. 48-9-105; G.S. 48-9-109; G.S. 48-3-205; G.S. 48-10-105.

40. *See* G.S. 105-259; G.S. 153A-148.1; G.S. 160A-208.1.

41. *See* G.S. 8-53.2 through G.S. 8-53.13; Scott v. Scott, 106 N.C. App. 606, 417 S.E.2d 818 (1992); G.S. 8-56 through G.S. 8-57.2.

42. *See* G.S. 53B-1 through G.S. 53B-10.

43. *See* G.S. 130A-143.

44. *See* G.S. 122C-52–56.

On the other hand, some state statutes limit informational privacy by requiring the release of otherwise confidential information to state or local government agencies. For example, state law generally requires individuals, businesses, professionals, and government agencies to disclose confidential information to county departments of social services in cases involving child abuse or neglect and child support enforcement.[45]

## Analyzing Problems Involving Confidentiality

The principle of confidentiality does not operate in a vacuum but in the day-to-day practice of social [services] agencies. Problems arise largely out of conflict between policy and practice, or out of a failure to decide what policy and practice should be.[46]

It is not always easy to determine what information is subject to protection and when information may be disclosed.[47]

While privacy and confidentiality often apply to the social worker's practice, one cannot assume that confidentiality laws will protect all communications and all records, or protect them in the same way. The legal privacy of communications and records may vary with the individuals involved, the setting where the communication takes place, where the record is maintained, and the content of the communication or record. * * * . . . different types of information—or even the same information communicated or recorded in different settings —have different types of privacy protections, ranging from near-total protection to no protection at all.[48]

45. *See* G.S. 7B-302(e); G.S. 110-139(d).
46. Dickson, *Confidentiality in Social Services to Individuals*, 8.
47. Theodore J. Stein, *The Role of Law in Social Work Practice and Administration* (New York: Columbia University Press, 2004), 106.
48. Dickson, *Confidentiality and Privacy in Social Work*, 6–7.

Finding the right answer to questions involving confidentiality, therefore, is often difficult, and, in some instances, there may not be a clear "black and white" answer to questions involving the use, protection, disclosure, or acquisition of confidential information.

Social services agencies, however, can use a three-step process to analyze problems involving confidentiality:

1. Define the problem, question, or issue.
2. Identify the applicable law or laws.
3. Apply the law or laws to the problem, question, or issue.

*Defining the Problem, Question, or Issue.* The first step of the process is crucial because the other two steps depend on clearly defining the problem, question, or issue. In this step, a social services agency should determine, first, whether the problem, question, or issue involves

- a social services agency's authority to *obtain* information from another agency or individual;
- the agency's authority to *use* confidential information in its possession for purposes other than that for which the information was obtained or generated;
- the agency's obligation to *protect* confidential information from unauthorized use or disclosure;
- the agency's authority or obligation to *disclose* confidential information to other agencies or individuals; or
- the right of an individual to *examine or obtain copies* of agency records that contain confidential information about that individual.

After determining the nature and context of the problem, question, or issue, the agency should ascertain the particular facts of the problem, question, or issue by asking and answering all or some of the following questions:

- What information is at issue?
- In what form (unrecorded, written, electronic) is the information maintained?
- Who has the information?
- Where is the information located?
- To whom does the information pertain?
- From what source was the information obtained?
- Who could consent to the use or disclosure of the information?

- Has consent been given?
- Can a valid consent be obtained?
- For what purpose was the information collected or obtained?
- Who is seeking the information?
- Why is the information being sought?
- For what purpose will the information be used?
- Will the information be redisclosed?

*Identifying the Applicable Law or Laws.* Identifying the applicable law or laws governing the collection, use, or disclosure of information in a given situation is virtually impossible without a thorough analysis of that situation. But having analyzed the situation or problem and having more clearly defined the question or issue, a social services agency should be able to identify the law or laws that apply to the situation, problem, question, or issue.

Identifying the law or laws that govern the collection, use, or disclosure of information in a particular situation, however, is much easier said than done. There are hundreds of laws governing the collection, use, protection, and disclosure of confidential information.[49] And determining whether a particular law applies usually requires a detailed legal analysis of

- the type, form, subject, and content of the information protected by the law;
- the class of persons or agencies that are subject to its requirements or restrictions with respect to the use, protection, or disclosure of confidential information;
- the class of persons whose interests or rights are protected by the law;
- the individual, governmental, and social interests or public policies that are protected or promoted by the law;
- the law's requirements with respect to protection of confidential information;
- the exceptions under which disclosure of confidential information is allowed or required; and

---

49. Many, but not all, of the federal and state statutes and regulations governing the disclosure of confidential information by or to state and county social services agencies are identified and summarized in Saxon, "An Annotated Index of Federal and State Confidentiality Laws."

# Figure 13.1 Disclosure of Confidential Information: An Analytical Framework

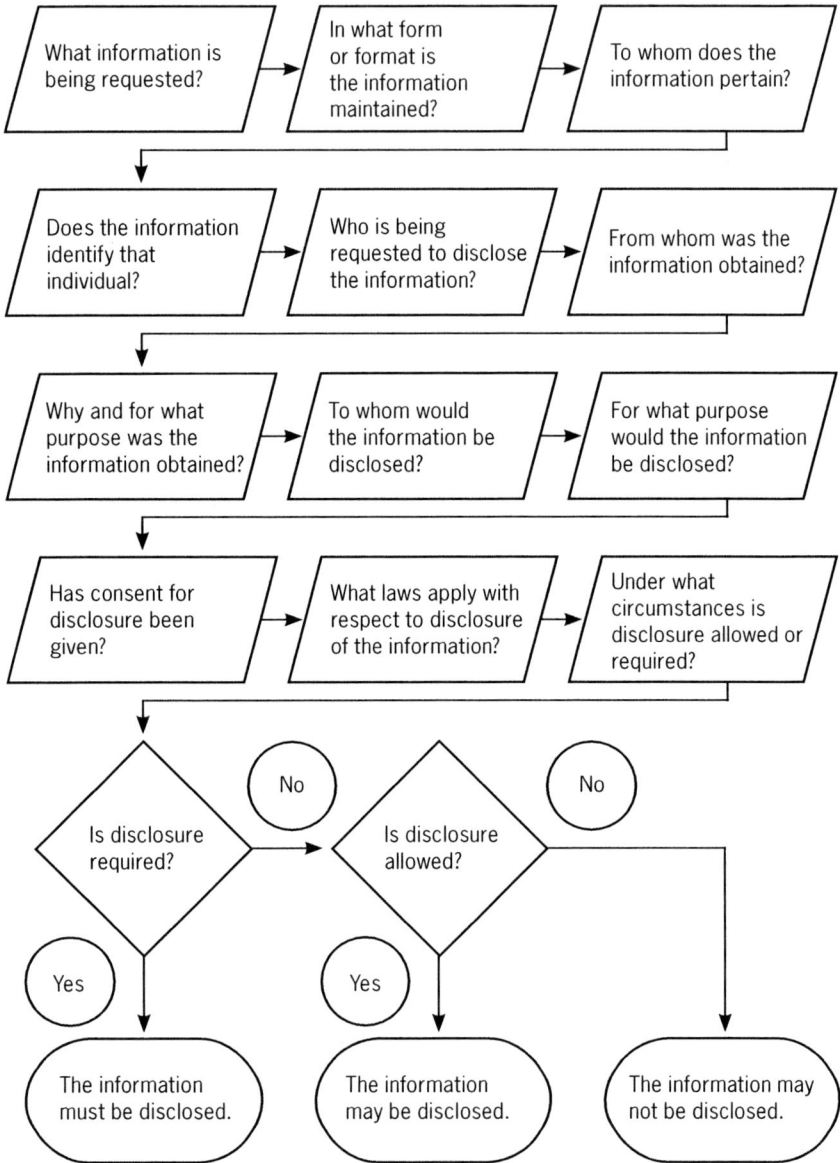

- the legal authority upon which the law's confidentiality requirements are based.

*Applying the Law or Laws to the Problem, Question, or Issue.* The third step of the process involves applying the applicable law or laws to the facts of the particular situation, problem, question, or issue.[50] Once again, though, this is easier said than done, and may require the assistance or advice of a lawyer.

If the applicable law prohibits disclosure of the information under the specific circumstances of the problem, issue, or situation, the information may not be disclosed.[51] If the applicable law requires disclosure of the information, the information must be disclosed. And if the applicable law allows disclosure of the information, the information may be disclosed.[52] See Figure 13.1.

## Confidentiality of Social Services Records

CONFIDENTIALITY OF INFORMATION REGARDING SOCIAL SERVICES CLIENTS

Issues regarding confidentiality often involve the use, sharing, or disclosure by state or county social services agencies of information regarding individuals or families who apply for or receive public assistance or social services.

### G.S. 108A-80

Section 108A-80 of the North Carolina General Statutes [hereinafter G.S.] is the primary, and most generally applicable, state statute governing the confidentiality of information regarding individuals and families who apply for or receive public assistance or social services from county social services departments.

---

50. In some instances, more than one legal rule may apply with respect to the collection, use, protection, or disclosure of the information in question. And in these cases, it will be necessary to determine, with the assistance of a lawyer if necessary, which law governs the use or disclosure of information in the particular situation.

51. If disclosure of confidential information is prohibited, a fourth step in the process may require identification and consideration of the legal remedies or sanctions that apply to unauthorized disclosure of the information.

52. If disclosure of confidential information is allowed, a fourth step in the process requires an individual or agency to determine whether the information should or should not be disclosed.

This statute makes it unlawful for any person to use, disclose, or obtain any information concerning persons who apply for or receive public assistance or social services that is directly or indirectly derived from the records, files, or communications of the state Department of Health and Human Services or a county department of social services or is acquired by these agencies in connection with their official duties except for purposes directly connected with the administration of social services programs or as otherwise allowed or required under other applicable federal or state laws or regulations.[53]

The state Social Services Commission and Department of Health and Human Services (DHHS) have adopted administrative rules under G.S. 108A-80 governing the confidentiality of information regarding social services clients.[54] These rules define "client information" as any information, including unrecorded information and information in the records, computer files, and computer databases of county social services departments, the state Division of Social Services, or the state Division of Medicaid Assistance, that

1. relates to a person or family who has applied for public assistance or social services, receives or has received public assistance or social services, or has been served by a county social services department, *and*
2. is received in connection with the performance of any function by a county social services department, the Division of Social Services, or the Division of Medical Assistance.[55]

The rules also require county departments of social services to ensure that all county social services employees and other persons who have access to client information receive training regarding the confidentiality of client information, to establish procedures to prevent accidental disclosure of client information from automated data processing sys-

---

53. Violation of G.S. 108A-80(a) is a Class 1 misdemeanor. G.S. 108A-80(c).

54. 10A N.C. ADMIN. CODE 69 .0101 through 69 .0605; 10A N.C. ADMIN. CODE 21A .0401 through 21A .0413.

55. The rules adopted by the Social Services Commission also address the confidentiality of information obtained by or disclosed to public or private agencies or individuals who provide services to the clients of a county social services department pursuant to contracts or agreements with department. 10A N.C. ADMIN. CODE 69 .0601 through 69 .0605.

tems, to provide a secure place for the storage of client records, and to ensure that only authorized persons have access to client information.[56]

*Disclosure of Information to the Client*

A social services client generally has the right, upon written or verbal request, to examine and copy, without charge, client information about himself or herself, to contest the accuracy, completeness, or relevancy of information in his or her record, and to request correction of incorrect information in his or her record.[57] A client, however, does not have the right to examine or copy confidential information regarding other persons, confidential information that was obtained from another agency when redisclosure is prohibited, or other confidential information when disclosure is prohibited by federal or state law.[58]

*Disclosure of Information with the Client's Consent*

A county social services department may disclose confidential client information with the client's consent.[59] The client's consent for the disclosure of information must be in writing, specify the information that may be disclosed, identify the agency, entity, or individual to whom the information may be disclosed, specify the time during which the consent is valid, and be signed and dated by the client, a person acting responsibly on behalf of the client in accordance with agency policy, the client's guardian if the client is an incapacitated adult, or an authorized

---

56. 10A N.C. ADMIN. CODE 69 .0203 and 69 .0204. Social services employees who disclose confidential client information in violation of the state confidentiality rule may be disciplined or fired. 10A N.C. ADMIN. CODE 69 .0205.

57. 10A N.C. ADMIN. CODE 69 .0301, 69 .0302, 69 .0305. The agency must allow the client to examine his or her record as promptly as feasible within five working days of the client's request. 10A N.C. ADMIN. CODE 69 .0302. A client's personal representative, including his or her attorney, may examine and copy all or part of the client's record with the client's written permission. 10A N.C. ADMIN. CODE 69 .0306. Although the rules do not define "personal representative," the term probably includes the parent, custodian, or guardian of a client if the client is a minor child, the guardian of an incapacitated adult who is a client, the next of kin of a deceased client or the administrator or executor of a deceased client's estate, and persons who are acting lawfully and responsibly on behalf of a client.

58. 10A N.C. ADMIN. CODE 69 .0301 and 69 .0303.

59. 10A N.C. ADMIN. CODE 69 .0401(c).

employee of the county social services department if the client is a minor child in the department's custody.[60]

*Disclosure of Information without the Client's Consent*
A number of federal and state laws allow or require a county social services department to disclose confidential information regarding social services clients.

G.S. 108A-80(b) provides that the listing of the names and addresses of persons who receive Work First Family Assistance or State–County Special Assistance and the amount of the assistance they receive is a public record that is open to public inspection in the county auditor's during regular business hours.[61]

Another state statute, G.S. 108A-11, allows county social services board members to examine any county DSS record regarding the provision of public assistance or social services.[62]

A county social services department must disclose confidential client information to the extent that disclosure is required by

- an applicable federal or state statute or regulation;[63] or
- a valid court order issued by a federal judge or a North Carolina judicial official.[64]

---

60. 10A N.C. ADMIN. CODE 69 .0402 and 69 .0403.

61. G.S. 108A-80(b). The information included on the list, however, may not be used for commercial or political purposes.

62. Social services board members may not use or disclose information from social services records except as otherwise allowed by law.

63. 10A N.C. ADMIN. CODE 69 .0504.

64. 10A N.C. ADMIN. CODE 69 .0505. *See also In re* Albemarle Mental Health Ctr., 42 N.C. App. 292, 256 S.E.2d 818 (1979); Ritter v. Kimball, 67 N.C. App. 333, 313 S.E.2d 1 (1984); State v. McGill, 141 N.C. App. 98, 539 S.E.2d 351 (2000); and Doe v. Swannanoa Valley Youth Dev. Ctr., 163 N.C. App. 136, 592 S.E.2d 715 (2004). If a court orders disclosure of confidential social services records, the agency should request the court to limit the amount of information disclosed and, if possible, to protect the information from redisclosure. *See* NASW Code of Ethics § 1.07(j). A county social services department is not required to disclose confidential information in response to a subpoena. Suggested procedures for responding to subpoenas requiring the disclosure of confidential information are discussed in John Rubin and Mark Botts, "Responding to Subpoenas: A Guide for Mental Health Facilities," *Popular Government* 64(4) (Summer 1999): 27–38, and in John Rubin and Aimee N. Wall, "Responding to Subpoenas for Health Department Records," *Health Law Bulletin* No. 82 (Chapel Hill: School of Government, The University of North Carolina at Chapel Hill, 2005).

The confidentiality rules adopted by the Social Services Commission allow county social services departments to disclose confidential information

- to other employees of the agency when necessary for referral, consultation, supervision, or determination of eligibility;[65]
- to other county social services departments when a client has moved and has requested assistance or services;[66]
- to the state Division of Social Services for the purpose of supervision or reporting;[67]
- for research studies if personally identifiable information will not be redisclosed;[68] and
- to federal, state, or county employees for the purpose of monitoring, auditing, evaluating, or facilitating the administration of other state and federal programs if there is a legitimate need for the information and there are adequate safeguards to protect the information from redisclosure.[69]

A county social services department, however, may not disclose confidential client information under these rules if another applicable federal or state law prohibits disclosure of the information.[70] And when client information is disclosed under these rules without the client's consent, the agency must notify the client of the disclosure, if possible, and document the disclosure in the client's file.[71]

When a county social services department is allowed or required to disclose confidential client information, it should disclose the least amount of information that is necessary to achieve the purpose of the disclosure.[72]

---

65. 10A N.C. ADMIN. CODE 69 .0501.
66. 10A N.C. ADMIN. CODE 69 .0501.
67. 10A N.C. ADMIN. CODE 69 .0501.
68. 10A N.C. ADMIN. CODE 69 .0502.
69. 10A N.C. ADMIN. CODE 69 .0503.
70. 10A N.C. ADMIN. CODE 69 .0201.
71. 10A N.C. ADMIN. CODE 69 .0506 and 69 .0507.
72. NASW Code of Ethics § 1.07(c).

**CONFIDENTIALITY OF CHILD PROTECTIVE SERVICES, JUVENILE, AND ADOPTION RECORDS**
A number of federal and state laws govern the confidentiality and disclosure of information regarding families and children who are involved in child protective services cases, juvenile proceedings, and adoptions.

G.S. 7B-302(a) provides that all information received by a county social services department in connection with its investigation of a report regarding abuse, neglect, or dependency of a juvenile must be held by the department "in the strictest confidence."[73] State law also protects the confidentiality of information in

- social services records of juveniles who are under a social services department's protective custody or under placement by a juvenile court;[74]
- the central registry of juvenile abuse, neglect, and dependency cases and child fatalities that is maintained by the state DHHS;[75]
- the list maintained by the state DHHS of individuals who have been determined to be responsible for the abuse or serious neglect of juveniles;[76] and
- adoption records maintained by social services agencies.[77]

State law, though, requires county social services departments to disclose certain information regarding child protective services cases to

- the person who reported the suspected abuse, neglect, or dependency;[78]
- law enforcement and government regulatory agencies;[79]
- a member of the public, upon request, when a person has been criminally charged with having caused a child fatality or near fatality or would have been so charged but for that person's death;[80]

---

73. *See also* 10A N.C. ADMIN. CODE 70A .0112 and 70A .0113.
74. G.S. 7B-2901(b).
75. G.S. 7B-311(a); 10A N.C. ADMIN. CODE 70A .0102.
76. G.S. 7B-311(b). DHHS may disclose information from the "responsible individuals" list to child caring institutions, child placing agencies, group home facilities, and other providers of foster care, child care, or adoption services that need to determine the fitness of individuals to care for or adopt children.
77. G.S. 48-9-102.
78. G.S. 7B-302(f), (g); 10A N.C. ADMIN. CODE 70A .0109.
79. G.S. 7B-307; 10A N.C. ADMIN. CODE 70A .0105, 70A .0107, and 70A .0113.
80. G.S. 7B-2902.

- local mental health facilities, local health departments, law enforcement agencies, public schools, and other designated agencies when disclosure of the information is necessary to protect an abused, neglected, dependent, delinquent, or undisciplined juvenile, to improve the juvenile's educational opportunities, or to protect others;[81]
- any federal, state, or local government entity or its agent that needs the information to protect a juvenile from abuse or neglect;[82]
- a community child protection team.[83]

## CONFIDENTIALITY OF OTHER SOCIAL SERVICES RECORDS

State law also protects the confidentiality of other information contained in the records of county social services departments or obtained by the county social services department in connection with the performance of its duties or functions, including

- some, but not all, of the information contained in the personnel files of county social services employees;[84]
- the identity of persons who report alleged child abuse, neglect, or dependency;
- the identity of persons who report alleged abuse, neglect, or exploitation of disabled adults;[85]
- information regarding the department's investigation of reports involving alleged abuse, neglect, or exploitation of disabled adults and the provision of adult protective services;[86]

---

81. G.S. 7B-3100; 28 N.C. ADMIN. CODE 01A .0301 and 01A .0302.
82. G.S. 7B-302(a).
83. 10A N.C. ADMIN. CODE 70A .0203.
84. G.S. 153A-98. The following information regarding county social services employees is a matter of public record: name; age; date of original employment or appointment to county service; current position title; current salary; date and amount of the most recent increase or decrease in salary; date of the most recent promotion, demotion, transfer, suspension, separation, or other change in position classification; and office to which the employee is currently assigned. G.S. 153A-98(b).
85. 10A N.C. ADMIN. CODE 71A .0802.
86. 10A N.C. ADMIN. CODE 71A .0803.

- the identity of persons who file complaints with the department under the Adult Care Home Residents Bill of Rights;[87]
- the identity of persons who provide information to the department in connection with the department's licensure inspection of an adult care home;[88]
- confidential or privileged information about adult care home residents obtained by the department in connection with the department's licensure inspection of an adult care home or investigation of complaints under the Adult Care Home Residents Bill of Rights;[89]
- criminal records checks of adoptive and foster care families;[90]
- information about children, custodians, and parents in child support enforcement cases;[91]
- Social Security numbers collected by the department;[92] and
- minutes of closed sessions of the county social services board.[93]

## Disclosure of Confidential Information to the County DSS

Issues regarding confidentiality arise when social services agencies collect or seek information from individuals or other agencies, as well as when social services agencies are asked to disclose information to others.

Federal and state laws expressly require state and county social services agencies to collect a great deal of personal or confidential information regarding social services clients. At the same time, though, it is generally accepted in social work practice that social services agencies should not collect personal information from or about a client unless the information is reasonably necessary to provide services to the client.[94] Similarly, when seeking information about a client from other agencies, a social services agency "must be responsible for know-

---

87. G.S. 131D-27.

88. G.S. 131D-2(b).

89. G.S. 131D-2(b); G.S. 131D-27.

90. G.S. 48-3-309(f); G.S. 131D-10.3A(g).

91. G.S. 110-129.1(a)(1); G.S. 129.2(i); G.S. 110-139(b); G.S. 110-139.1.

92. G.S. 132-1.10(b)(5). *See* Saxon, "Collection, Use, and Disclosure of Social Security Numbers."

93. G.S. 143-318.10(e).

94. NASW Code of Ethics, § 1.07(a).

ing enough about the function of the other agency to be able to request [only] information that is pertinent to the case situation."[95]

Federal law requires individuals who apply for Medicaid, food and nutrition services, and temporary assistance for needy families to provide their Social Security numbers to state or local social services agencies, and allows these agencies to request and use the Social Security numbers of clients in connection with the administration of other public assistance and social services programs.[96]

Rules adopted by the state Social Services Commission generally prohibit a county social services department from requesting the release of information regarding a social services client from other agencies or individuals without obtaining the client's signed consent, but also require clients to sign an authorization allowing the department to obtain from other agencies, entities, or individuals any information necessary to determine the client's eligibility for assistance or services.[97]

State and federal laws also require individuals, entities, and agencies to disclose confidential information to county social services departments.

North Carolina's Juvenile Code, for example, requires all individuals and institutions to report cases involving suspected child abuse, neglect, or dependency to the county social services department and provides that confidentiality and privilege are not grounds for failing to make such a report, even if the information upon which the report is based was acquired in a professional or confidential relationship.[98] And a number of state and federal laws expressly provide that otherwise confidential information may or must be disclosed to a county social services department to the extent that disclosure is necessary in order to report suspected child abuse, neglect, or dependency.[99]

---

95. Dickson, *Confidentiality in Social Services to Individuals*, 26, 27.

96. 42 U.S.C. § 1320b-7; 42 U.S.C. § 405(c)(2)(C)(i). *See also* G.S. 143-64.60 and G.S. 132-1.10(b)(1). The collection and use of Social Security numbers by state and county social services agencies is discussed in detail in Saxon, "Collection, Use, and Disclosure of Social Security Numbers."

97. 10A N.C. ADMIN. CODE 69 .0401(a) and 69 .0401(c). *See also* 10A N.C. ADMIN. CODE 69 .0404.

98. G.S. 7B 301(a) and G.S. 7B-310.

99. *See* G.S. 115C-400 (public schools); G.S. 122C-54(h) (mental health facilities); 42 C.F.R. § 2.12(c)(6) (alcohol and substance abuse treatment programs); 45 C.F.R. §§ 164.512(a)(1) and 164.512(b)(1)(ii) (HIPAA); 42 U.S.C. § 13031 and

Similarly, the Juvenile Code requires individuals and private and public agencies to disclose to the county department of social services, upon request, any information, including confidential information, that may be relevant to the department's investigation of reported child abuse, neglect, or dependency or to the provision of protective services to abused, neglected, or dependent juveniles unless the information is protected by the attorney-client privilege or disclosure of the information is prohibited by federal law or regulations.[100]

State law also provides that, notwithstanding any other provision of state law making information confidential, state and local government agencies, employers, banks, utility companies, and other specified entities must provide otherwise confidential information to state and county child support enforcement agencies for the purpose of locating absent parents and establishing, collecting, or enforcing their child support obligations.[101] And state law also requires that certain types of confidential information be disclosed to county departments of social services in connection with their provision of adult services.[102]

## Retention and Destruction of County Social Services Records

Although many of the records of county social services departments are exempt from the public disclosure requirement of the state Public Records Law (G.S. 132-6), they are "public records" as defined by G.S. 132-1(a) and, therefore, are subject to state law governing the custody, protection, retention, and destruction of public records.[103] Retention and destruction of records of county social services departments are governed by a schedule adopted by the Government Records Branch of the state Department of Cultural Resources.[104]

---

38 C.F.R. § 81.2 (physicians, teachers, child care workers, law enforcement officers, and other designated persons working in federal facilities or on federal lands); VHA Directive 2006-068 (U.S. Veterans Administration facilities).

100. G.S. 7B-302(e). *See also* G.S. 7B-3100 and 28 N.C. ADMIN. CODE 01A .0301 and 01A .0302.

101. G.S. 110-139. *See also* G.S. 20-7(b2)(2); G.S. 93-14(l); G.S. 110-129.1(a)(2).

102. *See* G.S. 108A-103(a); G.S. 131D-2(b); G.S. 131D-27.

103. *See* G.S. 132-2 through G.S. 132-5.1, G.S. 132-7 through G.S. 132-8.2, and G.S. 121-5. *See also* Lawrence, *Public Records Law for North Carolina Local Governments*, 47–52.

104. The 2006 edition of the schedule is available online at www.ah.dcr.state.nc .us/records/local/SocialServices/2006_SocialServicesRecRetention.pdf (last visited April 18, 2008).

# Chapter 14

# Legal Liability of Social Services Agencies, Officials, and Employees

State and county social services agencies, officials, and employees often are concerned about their potential legal liability.

> The expense and the trouble of lawsuits are unavoidable costs of doing [the] . . . government's business. [Eventually, a government agency, official, or employee will, in the course of the government's activities,] . . . cause damage to something or somebody. Indeed, even without any legitimate basis, a . . . government [agency] and its employees may still be made defendants to a . . . lawsuit. The challenge for [government agencies] . . . is therefore not the impossible task of eliminating lawsuits. Rather, the challenge is the difficult task of providing [public] services while minimizing the cost and disruption that lawsuits bring. The first step in accomplishing that task is learning the

basic legal principles that [govern] . . . the liability of
[government agencies] . . . and . . . public servants.[1]


## What Does "Liability" Mean?

In the law, the term "liability" generally refers to

- an obligation, sanction, or responsibility (for example, the
  obligation to pay damages to compensate a person for injury to his
  or her person or property)
- that is imposed pursuant to federal, state, or local law (including
  the federal and state constitutions; federal and state statutes,
  administrative rules, and regulations; local ordinances; and the
  common law)[2]
- by a court or quasi-judicial agency
- in a civil, criminal, or administrative proceeding or lawsuit
- on a person (including a local government official or employee)
  or other legal entity (including a local government or local
  government agency)
- in connection with that person's or entity's actions or omissions or
  the acts or omissions of persons acting on behalf of that person or
  entity.[3]

---

1. Anita R. Brown-Graham, "Civil Liability of the Local Government and
Its Officials and Employees," Article 12 in David M. Lawrence, ed., *County and
Municipal Government in North Carolina* (Chapel Hill: School of Government, The
University of North Carolina at Chapel Hill, 2007), 2, available at www.sog.unc.
edu/pubs/cmg/cmg12.pdf.

2. Liability also may be imposed with respect to legal obligations that are voluntarily assumed under a contract or other legal agreement.

3. The legal liability of North Carolina local governments and local government
officials and employees is discussed in detail in Anita R. Brown-Graham, *A
Practical Guide to the Liability of North Carolina Cities and Towns* (Chapel Hill:
Institute of Government, The University of North Carolina at Chapel Hill, 1999)
and Brown-Graham, "Civil Liability of the Local Government and Its Officials
and Employees." *See also* Thomas H. Thornburg, *An Introduction to Law for North
Carolinians*, 2d ed. (Chapel Hill: Institute of Government, The University of North
Carolina at Chapel Hill, 2000).

## ESTABLISHING LIABILITY THROUGH LEGAL PROCEEDINGS

The person or entity against whom liability is asserted in a legal proceeding generally is referred to as the defendant or respondent. In a
civil or administrative proceeding, the person who brings the proceeding and seeks to impose liability on the defendant generally is referred
to as the plaintiff or petitioner. Criminal proceedings against defen-
dants are brought by the state.

In order to bring a legal proceeding against a defendant, the plaintiff
must have standing, that is, legal authority to assert a particular legal
claim or to seek a particular legal remedy. Standing generally requires
that the plaintiff have been injured in some way by the defendant. In
addition, to impose liability on a defendant, a court must have jurisdiction, that is, legal authority to hear and decide the case.

A plaintiff who brings a lawsuit against a defendant has the burden
of proving the plaintiff's legal claim against the defendant. This means
that the plaintiff must present sufficient, legally admissible evidence to
establish a factual basis for each element of the plaintiff's legal claim.
In a civil lawsuit or administrative proceeding, the plaintiff's burden
generally is to prove facts to support his or her claim by a preponderance of the evidence. In a criminal proceeding, the state's burden is to
prove the elements of the offense beyond a reasonable doubt. A defendant may avoid liability by asserting a valid legal defense or claiming
legal immunity from liability.

Liability may be imposed in connection with several different types
of legal claims. Criminal liability, for example, results from a defendant's violation of federal or state criminal laws.[4] Civil liability may
result from a defendant's breach of a contract between the defendant

---

4. A defendant who is found criminally liable may be incarcerated in jail or
prison, placed on probation, or ordered to pay a fine. State and county social services officials and employees may be held criminally liable if they violate federal
or state criminal laws (for example, by embezzling public funds, misusing public
property, disclosing confidential information, or engaging in conflicts of interest)
in connection with their public duties. This chapter, however, does not focus on
the potential criminal liability of social services officials or employees.

and the plaintiff.[5] Civil liability also may result from a defendant's violation of civil statutes or rules.[6]

Civil liability also may be imposed in connection with a defendant's tortious conduct. A tort is a wrongful act or omission, other than a criminal act or breach of contract, that causes personal injury or damage to property and with respect to which the law provides a legal cause of action and a legal remedy.

> Tort law serves to protect a person's interest in his or her bodily security, tangible property, financial resources, or reputation. Unlike contract law, in which the appropriate standard of conduct is set by specific promises made between two parties, in tort law the defendant is being held to a standard of conduct (or duty) that is imposed by law. To succeed in the lawsuit, the plaintiff must demonstrate that the defendant violated that duty and that the violation caused an injury.
>
> Compensation is the primary concern of tort law. This area of law is premised on the belief that individuals who [have been harmed by the wrongful conduct of others] . . . should not be required to bear the loss; instead, the person whose wrongful act caused the harm must pay to restore the injured party to where [he or she] . . . was before the harm. Another purpose of tort law is to deter people from engaging in conduct likely to cause personal injury or property damage. Tort law assumes that people will be more careful in

---

5. If a defendant is found liable for breaching a contract, the court may enter a judgment against the defendant requiring him or her to compensate the plaintiff for the plaintiff's losses resulting from the breach. The state or a county may be held civilly liable if a state or county social services agency enters into a valid, legal contract and the agency or an official or employee of the agency breaches the contract. This chapter, however, does not focus on the contractual liability of state or county social services agencies.

6. The civil liability of state and county social services agencies, officials, and employees under one federal statute, 42 U.S.C. § 1983, is discussed in the penultimate section of this chapter.

conducting their day-to-day activities if they have to
pay for any harm that results.[7]

There are two broad categories of torts: (1) intentional torts and
(2) unintentional torts or negligence.

"Intentional torts are deliberate wrongful acts that cause personal
injury or property damage."[8] A defendant may be held liable for an
intentional tort if he or she "deliberately engaged in the wrongful act"
regardless of whether he or she "intended the consequences of the act
[or] . . . the particular damages caused."[9] The tort of battery, which the
law defines as the "intentional touching or striking of another person
without . . . that person's consent or a legally recognized authorization,"
is one example of an intentional tort.[10] Defamation (slander or libel) is
another.

By contrast, a defendant may be held civilly liable for negligence if

1. the defendant breaches his or her legal duty to exercise
   reasonable care in connection with his or her activities;
2. the defendant's failure to exercise reasonable care results in
   injury to another person or that person's property; *and*
3. the injury was a reasonably foreseeable result of the defendant's
   lack of care.[11]

One example of a negligent tort is an automobile accident that is caused
by a driver's inattention and results in injury to another driver or the
other driver's car.

If a defendant is found liable for an intentional tort or for
negligence, a judgment for monetary damages may be entered against
him or her. In most cases, the damages awarded in tort claims are
*compensatory damages* (damages that are awarded to compensate
the plaintiff for his or her physical injury, the damage to his or her
property, incurred medical expenses, lost future earnings, pain and

---

7. Brown-Graham, "Civil Liability of the Local Government and Its Officials
and Employees," 2.

8. *Id.* at 3.

9. *Id.*

10. *Id.*

11. *Id.* at 4. In North Carolina, a defendant may avoid liability for his or her
negligent acts or omissions by proving that the plaintiff's injuries were caused, in
part, by the plaintiff's contributory negligence.

suffering, or other losses). Courts sometimes award *punitive damages* against a defendant in order to "punish [the] defendant for especially culpable conduct and to deter such conduct in the future."[12] Punitive damages, however, "generally are not recoverable from a governmental body or agency," though they may be assessed against a "public employee or official in an 'individual-capacity' lawsuit."[13]

## Tort Liability of Social Services Agencies, Officials, and Employees

State and county social services agencies, officials, and employees may be sued, and sometimes held liable, for intentional torts or negligence. For example, they might be sued by

- the mother of a deceased child who alleges that her child died as a result of a social worker's failure to promptly and thoroughly investigate a report regarding the child's abuse or neglect by the child's father and failure to take action to protect the child from that abuse or neglect;[14]
- foster parents who allege that a foster child sexually abused their daughter and that the child's injuries resulted from a social worker's negligence in failing to inform the foster parents that the foster child had lived in an environment of sexual abuse and was likely to reenact that abuse on younger, more vulnerable children;[15]
- a child who was placed in a foster home by the county social services department and was injured by the foster parent's alleged negligence;[16]

---

12. Brown-Graham, *A Practical Guide to the Liability of North Carolina Cities and Counties*, 5-5, citing Jones v. McCaskill, 99 N.C. App. 764, 394 S.E.2d 254 (1990).

13. Brown-Graham, *A Practical Guide to the Liability of North Carolina Cities and Counties*, 5-6.

14. *See* Whitaker v. Clark, 109 N.C. App. 379, 427 S.E.2d 142 (1993); *see also* Gammons v. N.C. Dep't of Human Resources, 344 N.C. 51, 472 S.E.2d 722 (1996) and Coleman v. Cooper, 102 N.C. App. 650, 402 S.E.2d 577 (1991).

15. *See* Hobbs v. N.C. Dep't of Human Resources, 135 N.C. App. 412, 520 S.E.2d 595 (1999); *see also* Vaughn v. N.C. Dep't of Human Resources, 296 N.C. 683, 252 S.E.2d 792 (1979).

16. *See* Creel v. N.C. Dep't of Health and Human Servs., 152 N.C. App. 200, 566 S.E.2d 832 (2002).

- a parent who claims that he or she was falsely accused of child abuse or neglect by a county social services department;[17]
- the estate of a deceased, incompetent adult who allegedly died as a result of a social worker's failure to discharge his or her responsibilities as the adult's guardian;[18]
- a person who is injured by slipping on a wet floor at the county social services office;
- a social services employee who gets into an argument with another social services employee and is assaulted by the other employee at work;
- a client of a social services agency who claims that the agency unlawfully disclosed confidential information about the client; or
- an individual who is injured in a traffic accident involving an automobile driven by a social services employee during the course of the employee's official duties.

Although many of the legal rules that apply to tort lawsuits against private individuals, employers, and other legal entities also apply to tort lawsuits involving state and county agencies, officials, or employees, there are also a number of special legal rules that apply to the tort liability of state and county agencies, officials, and employees, including those associated with social services.

### TORT LIABILITY OF THE STATE AND STATE SOCIAL SERVICES AGENCIES

Sovereign immunity is a legal principle that protects the state of North Carolina and its agencies, including the state Department of Health and Human Services, from tort claims unless the state waives its immunity.[19] This means that even if a person has been injured by the negligence of a state employee in connection with that employee's official duties, the person cannot sue the state and the state cannot be held liable for the employee's negligence unless the state waives its sovereign immunity and allows itself to be sued and held liable.[20]

---

17. *See* Hare v. Butler, 99 N.C. App. 693, 394 S.E.2d 231 (1990).

18. *See* Meyer v. Walls, 347 N.C. 97, 489 S.E.2d 880 (1997).

19. *See* Zimmer v. N.C. Dep't of Transp., 87 N.C. App. 132, 134, 360 S.E.2d 115, 117 (1987).

20. The doctrine of sovereign immunity, however, does not protect a state employee from being sued and held liable for a tort committed in connection with the employee's official duties. *See* Wirth v. Bracey, 258 N.C. 505, 508, 128 S.E.2d 810, 813 (1963).

The state of North Carolina has *partially* waived its sovereign immunity with respect to certain tort claims. Under the State Tort Claims Act, a person who has been injured by the negligence of any state officer, employee, or agent acting within the scope of the officer's, employee's, or agent's scope of office, employment, agency, or authority may file a lawsuit against the state or the state department, institution, or agency under whose authority the officer, employee, or agent was acting.[21]

Lawsuits filed under the State Tort Claims Act are heard and decided by the North Carolina Industrial Commission.[22] If the Industrial Commission finds that the plaintiff's injuries were proximately caused by a state employee's negligence, that the plaintiff was not contributorily negligent, and that the state of North Carolina would be liable to the plaintiff if the state were a private person, the Industrial Commission may enter an order requiring the state to pay up to $500,000 in compensatory damages.[23]

The state Department of Health and Human Services (DHHS), therefore, may be held liable under the State Tort Claims Act for the negligence of DHHS officials or employees. Furthermore, DHHS may be held liable under the State Tort Claims Act for the negligence of a *county* social services director or employee if the county social services director or employee was acting as an "agent of the State" when the negligent act or omission occurred.[24]

### TORT LIABILITY OF THE COUNTY AND THE COUNTY SOCIAL SERVICES DEPARTMENT

As noted above, the State Tort Claims Act applies only to the state and to *state* government agencies. A county or county social services department may not be sued under the State Tort Claims Act for the negligence of a county social services employee even if the employee was

---

21. Section 143-291 of the North Carolina General Statutes [hereinafter G.S.]. The State Tort Claims Act does not apply to intentional torts committed by state officials, employees, or agents. *See* Frazier v. Murray, 135 N.C. App. 43, 48, 519 S.E.2d 525, 528 (1999).

22. North Carolina's superior courts do not have jurisdiction to hear and decide tort claims against the state under the State Tort Claims Act.

23. G.S. 143-291; G.S. 143-299.2.

24. Vaughn v. N.C. Dep't of Human Resources, 296 N.C. 683, 252 S.E.2d 792 (1979); Gammons v. N.C. Dep't of Human Resources, 344 N.C. 51, 472 S.E.2d 722 (1996).

acting as an "agent of the State" at the time the alleged tort occurred.[25] A county, however, may be sued in superior court for a county employee's tortious conduct.

*Respondeat Superior: County Liability for Torts Committed by County Employees*
The doctrine of *respondeat superior*, when applied to a county, means that a county (assuming it cannot claim governmental immunity, which is discussed below) is liable for the tortious conduct of its officials and employees if that conduct (1) occurs within the scope of the official's office or the employee's employment and in furtherance of the county's business, *or* (2) is ratified or approved by the county.[26] Although committing intentional torts is not within the scope of employment of county employees, a county may be held liable for an intentional tort committed by a county employee if the employee's act "was a means or method of doing that which he was employed to do."[27] The doctrine of *respondeat superior*, however, does not extend to tortious acts committed by someone who is an independent contractor, rather than an employee, of a county or county agency.[28]

If a person has been injured by the tortious conduct of a county social services official or employee, he or she may file a lawsuit against the county,[29] the county social services department,[30] one or more

---

25. Meyer v. Walls, 347 N.C. at 105, 489 S.E.2d at 884 (overruling *sub silento* Coleman v. Cooper, 102 N.C. App. 650, 403 S.E.2d 577 (1991)).

26. *See* Brown-Graham, *A Practical Guide to Liability for North Carolina Cities and Counties*, 3-3 through 3-4.

27. *See* Hogan v. Forsyth Country Club, 79 N.C. App. 483, 491, 340 S.E.2d 116, 122 (1986). The "mere fact that the act was unlawful and unauthorized will not preclude the employer's liability." Brown-Graham, *A Practical Guide to Liability for North Carolina Cities and Counties*, 3-5.

28. *See* Creel v. N.C. Dep't of Health and Human Servs., 152 N.C. App. at 202, 566 S.E.2d at 833. *See also* Brown-Graham, *A Practical Guide to Liability for North Carolina Cities and Counties*, 3-6 through 3-7.

29. North Carolina counties are political subdivisions of the state and corporate entities that have the legal capacity to "sue and be sued" in their own names and in their own right. G.S. 153A-11; O'Neal v. Wake County, 196 N.C. 184, 145 S.E.28 (1928); Johnson v. Marrow, 228 N.C. 58, 44 S.E.2d 468 (1947).

30. The county department of social services is an agency of the county government, not a separate or independent public, corporate, or legal entity that has the legal capacity to be sued in its own name. *See* Malloy v. Durham County Dep't of Social Servs., 58 N.C. App. 61, 66–68, 293 S.E.2d 285, 288–90 (1993); Meyer v. Walls, 347 N.C. at 104, 489 S.E.2d at 884; Craig v. Chatham County, 143 N.C.

social services officials or employees in their "official capacities,"[31] or
all or some combination of those. A lawsuit that names a county social
services official or employee in his or her "official capacity" is "in all
respects other than name an action against the [local government or
local government agency] . . . for which he or she works,"[32] and any
liability that is imposed against a county official or employee in his
or her official capacity is imposed against the county rather than the
official or employee personally.

### Governmental Immunity of Counties

A county may not be sued or held liable for the tortious act of a
county social services agency, official, or employee if the doctrine of
"governmental immunity" applies and the county has not waived its
governmental immunity.[33]

North Carolina's Supreme Court recognized the doctrine of
governmental immunity in 1889.[34] Under this doctrine, counties
are shielded from tort liability in connection with their performance
of governmental activities or functions, but not from liability with
respect to their proprietary activities or functions.[35] Applying the rules

---

App. 30, 31, 545 S.E.2d 455, 456 (2001). A lawsuit that names the county department of social services as a defendant, therefore, is, in essence, a lawsuit against
the county, not a lawsuit against the social services department per se.

31. The lawsuit also might name as a defendant one or more county social
services officials or employees in their "individual capacities." Lawsuits against
county social services officials or employees in their "individual capacity" are
discussed in the following section of this chapter.

32. Brown-Graham, *A Practical Guide to Liability for North Carolina Cities and
Counties*, 4-3, citing Whitaker v. Clark, 109 N.C. App. 379, 427 S.E.2d 142 (1993).
*See also* Hobbs v. N.C. Dep't of Human Resources, 135 N.C. at 420, 520 S.E.2d at
601.

33. A lawsuit against a county must specifically allege that the county is not
entitled to governmental immunity or has waived its governmental immunity
by obtaining liability insurance. *See* Whitaker v. Clark, 109 N.C. App. at 384, 427
S.E.2d at 145.

34. Moffitt v. City of Asheville, 103 N.C. 237, 9 S.E. 695 (1889). The governmental immunity of North Carolina counties and municipalities is similar to, but
different from, the state's sovereign immunity.

35. The tests for determining whether a function or activity is "governmental"
or "proprietary" are discussed in detail in Brown-Graham, *A Practical Guide to
Liability for North Carolina Cities and Counties*, 3-8 through 3-18 and 3-20 through
3-21. Governmental immunity applies with respect to *all* activities that are
reasonably related to the performance of a governmental function. For example,

that distinguish governmental and proprietary functions to specific activities performed by local governments and their employees is not always easy.[36] It seems clear, though, that most, if not all, of the activities performed by county social services agencies and employees in connection with the administration of public assistance and social services programs are governmental in nature and that governmental immunity, therefore, shields the county from liability in connection with allegedly tortious conduct by county social services employees who are engaged in the administration of those programs.[37]

A county, however, may waive its governmental immunity and, if it does, may be sued and held liable for torts committed by county social services employees in connection with their employment.

Under state law, a county waives its governmental immunity by obtaining liability insurance.[38] Governmental immunity, however, is waived only to the extent of the county's insurance coverage.[39] Thus, if

---

it would protect a county social services agency from liability with respect to a social worker's alleged negligence in driving a car while investigating a report of suspected child abuse or neglect as well as the social worker's alleged negligence in making a determination with respect to whether a child has been abused or neglected and needs protection. *See* Lewis v. Hunter, 212 N.C. 504, 193 S.E. 814 (1937).

36. *See* Millar v. Town of Wilson, 222 N.C. 340, 341, 23 S.E.2d 42, 44 (1942) and Koontz v. City of Winston-Salem, 280 N.C. 513, 528, 186 S.E.2d 897, 907 (1972).

37. *See* Hare v. Butler, 99 N.C. App. at 698, 394 S.E.2d at 235; Whitaker v. Clark, 109 N.C. App. at 381, 427 S.E.2d at 143.

38. G.S. 153A-435. "There are three basic ways that a local government can waive its governmental immunity through insurance coverage. First, insurance includes liability coverage provided by companies licensed to [issue] . . . [liability] insurance [policies] in [North Carolina] . . . . Second, participation in a local government risk pool [as defined in G.S. 58-23-1 through G.S. 58-23-45] is considered to be the equivalent of purchasing insurance. Third, a local government may ["self insure" by] explicitly [setting aside money] . . . to pay claims against it." Brown-Graham, "Civil Liability of the Local Government and Its Officials and Employees," 9. Many, if not most, North Carolina counties have purchased liability insurance, participate in a local government risk pool, or have established a "self insurance" fund. Some of the reasons that counties may decide to waive their governmental immunity through the purchase of liability insurance are discussed in Brown-Graham, "Civil Liability of the Local Government and Its Officials and Employees," 8–9.

39. If a county obtains liability insurance, the county has the authority to determine what torts it will choose to cover or exclude under its insurance, the maximum amount of claims that will be covered through the insurance, and any

a plaintiff's damages exceed the amount of the county's insurance coverage, the plaintiff "may not recover damages for injuries in excess of the policy amount . . . ."[40] And similarly, if a county's insurance policy has a deductible or does not cover claims below a certain amount, the county "retains governmental immunity for damages that fall within the amount of the deductible" or below the coverage threshold.[41]

### The Public Duty Defense

A defendant may not be held liable for negligence unless he or she has breached a legal duty of care that he or she owed to the plaintiff. The public duty defense allows some government agencies to avoid liability for negligence because their legal duties of care are owed to the general public rather than to any particular person who may have been injured as a result of their breach of those duties.

> The public duty doctrine holds that certain . . . government activities do not create liability to individual members of the public. Under the public duty doctrine, there are circumstances in which [government agencies and employees have] . . . no legal duty to protect an individual citizen from harm caused by a third person. Although the government may undertake a duty to protect the public at large, that duty does not extend to any specific individual.[42]

In a 1999 decision, the North Carolina Court of Appeals held that the county could raise the public duty doctrine as a defense in a case involving the alleged negligence of a county social services department in connection with an investigation of reported child abuse or neglect, but that the "special relationship" and "special duty" exceptions to the

---

deductible. A county does not waive its governmental immunity by purchasing a liability insurance policy that explicitly and unambiguously covers only those "wrongful acts for which the defense of governmental immunity is clearly not applicable." *See* Patrick v. Wake County Dep't of Human Servs., ___ N.C. App. ___, 655 S.E.2d 920 (2008).

40. Brown-Graham, *A Practical Guide to Liability for North Carolina Cities and Counties*, 3-19.

41. *Id.* at 3-22.

42. Brown-Graham, "Civil Liability of the Local Government and Its Officials and Employees," 10.

public duty doctrine might apply.[43] But in a different case decided a year later, the North Carolina Supreme Court held that, in lawsuits against *local* governments, the public duty defense applies only to "law enforcement departments when they are exercising their general duty to protect the public."[44] Counties, therefore, may not use the public duty doctrine as a defense in lawsuits involving the alleged negligence of county social services employees.

### PERSONAL TORT LIABILITY OF COUNTY SOCIAL SERVICES DIRECTORS AND EMPLOYEES

A person who has been injured by the tortious conduct of a social services director or employee who was engaging in official duties may sue the director or employee in the director's or employee's "individual capacity."[45] A lawsuit that is filed against a social services director or employee in his or her individual capacity seeks to hold the director or employee *personally* liable for the damages the plaintiff has suffered.[46]

It is not always easy to determine, however, whether a public official or employee is being sued in his or her official capacity, in his or her individual capacity, or in both capacities.

> The crucial question for determining whether a [public official or employee] . . . is sued in an individual or official capacity is the nature of the relief sought, not the nature of the act or omission alleged. If the plaintiff seeks an injunction requiring the defendant to take an action involving the exercise of a government power, the defendant is [sued] . . . in an official capacity. If money damages are sought, the court must ascertain whether the complaint indicates that the damages are sought from the government or from the pocket of the

43. Hobbs v. N.C. Dep't of Human Resources, 135 N.C. App. at 418–19, 520 S.E.2d at 600–01 (1999).

44. Lovelace v. City of Shelby, 351 N.C. 458, 461, 526 S.E.2d 652, 654 (2000).

45. *See* Meyer v. Walls, 347 N.C. at 110, 489 S.E.2d at 887. *Cf.* McCarn v. Beach, 128 N.C. App. 435, 496 S.E.2d 402 (1998). A county social services director or employee also may be sued in his or her official capacity or in his or her official *and* individual capacities. Lawsuits against county social services officials and employees in their official capacities are, in essence, lawsuits against the county and are discussed in the preceding sections of this chapter.

46. *See* Hare v. Butler, 99 N.C. App. at 700, 394 S.E.2d at 236; Meyer v. Walls, 347 N.C. at 110, 489 S.E.2d at 887.

individual defendant. If the former, it is an official-
capacity claim; if the latter, it is an individual-capacity
claim; and if it is both, then the claims proceed in both
capacities.[47]

In ascertaining the capacity in which the plaintiff
seeks to sue [a public official or employee] . . . the court
will typically look first to the caption of the complaint
[which should indicate the capacity or capacities in
which the defendant is being sued]. If the [caption
doesn't clearly indicate the capacity in which the defendant is being sued] . . . the court will look to the allegations of the complaint and then to the course of the
proceedings. Absent some clear indication in the allegations or the procedural history of the case, the court
will not presume that the plaintiff sought to impose
personal liability on the defendant. Instead the pre-
sumption will operate in favor of finding only official-
capacity liability.[48]

## Public Official Immunity

Local government officials and employees are not entitled to governmental immunity when they are sued in their individual, rather than
official, capacities.[49]

Public officials, however, are protected by a limited immunity when
they are sued in their individual capacities for alleged negligence.[50] This
public official immunity protects a public official from liability for his
or her alleged negligence in "the exercise of a discretionary act while
engaged in a governmental activity, unless the officer acted with malice,

---

47. Meyer v. Walls, 347 N.C. at 110, 489 S.E.2d at 887.

48. Brown-Graham, *A Practical Guide to Liability for North Carolina Cities and Counties*, 4-5.

49. *Id.* at 4-7. *Cf.* Cherry v. Harris, 110 N.C. App. 478, 480, 429 S.E.2d 771, 772 (1993).

50. This immunity does not apply when a public official is sued for an intentional tort. A public official or employee, however, may assert a separate, limited
immunity if he or she is sued for the intentional tort of defamation in connection
with conduct that was not malicious. *See* Brown-Graham, "Civil Liability of the
Local Government and Its Officials and Employees," 4.

for corrupt reasons, or outside the scope of his or her official duties."[51] A discretionary act is one that requires personal deliberation, decision, and judgment, contrasted with a ministerial act that is "absolute, certain, and imperative, and involve[s] merely the execution of a specific duty arising from fixed and designated facts."[52]

Unlike public officials, public employees are not entitled to public official immunity.[53] North Carolina's courts generally have employed a four-factor test to determine whether a government defendant is a public official or a public employee:

1. whether the defendant's position was created by statute (if it was, the defendant is more likely to be considered a public official rather than a public employee);
2. whether the defendant's position required the defendant to take an oath of office (if it did, the defendant is more likely to be considered a public official rather than a public employee);
3. whether the defendant performs legally imposed public duties (if he or she does, he or she is more likely to be considered a public official rather than a public employee);
4. whether the defendant exercises a certain amount of discretion in performing his or her job (if he or she does, he or she is more likely to be considered a public official rather than a public employee).[54]

It is clear that the county social services director is a public official.[55] Before 1999, a number of appellate court decisions held that assistant social services directors, social services supervisors, social workers, and other county social services staff were public employees, not public

---

51. Brown-Graham, *A Practical Guide to Liability for North Carolina Cities and Counties*, 4-8, citing Wiggins v. City of Monroe, 73 N.C. App. 44, 49, 326 S.E.2d 39, 43 (1985).

52. Brown-Graham, *A Practical Guide to Liability for North Carolina Cities and Counties*, 4-8, citing Hare v. Butler, 99 N.C. App. at 700, 394 S.E.2d at 236.

53. Brown-Graham, *A Practical Guide to Liability for North Carolina Cities and Counties*, 4-10. *See also* Meyer v. Walls, 347 N.C. at 112, 489 S.E.2d at 888.

54. Piggott v. City of Wilmington, 50 N.C. App. 401, 403–04, 273 S.E.2d 752, 754 (1981). Public employees, by contrast, generally act at the direction of others and their duties are "more administrative or ministerial than discretionary in nature." Brown-Graham, *A Practical Guide to Liability for North Carolina Cities and Counties*, 4-10.

55. Hare v. Butler, 99 N.C. App. at 700, 394 S.E.2d at 236.

officials, and therefore were not entitled to public official immunity.[56] In 1999, however, the North Carolina Court of Appeals decided that when a county social services employee is performing a discretionary activity pursuant to a delegation of legal authority from the county social services director, the employee acts as a public official, not as a public employee, and is therefore entitled to public official immunity.[57]

### Personal Tort Liability of County Social Services Board Members

County social services board members are public officials and, therefore, are entitled to public official immunity to the same extent and under the same circumstances as the county social services director. In addition, county social services board members may be immune from tort liability with respect to any quasi-legislative or quasi-judicial functions of the social services board.[58]

### Personal Tort Liability of Social Services Volunteers

The federal Volunteer Protection Act (VPA) of 1997 protects volunteers from liability for injuries caused by their negligent acts or omissions while working with state or county social services agencies.[59] The VPA, however, does not protect volunteers from liability for criminal, intentional, or reckless conduct; for gross negligence; activities that are not within the scope of their volunteer duties; injuries caused by their operation of vehicles for which the state requires a license or insurance; injuries caused while they are under the influence of alcohol or drugs; or misconduct that violates federal or state civil rights laws.

---

56. Hare v. Butler, 99 N.C. App. at 700, 394 S.E.2d at 236; Coleman v. Cooper, 89 N.C. App. 188, 197, 366 S.E.2d 2, 8 (1988); Meyer v. Walls, 347 N.C. at 114, 489 S.E.2d at 889.

57. Hobbs v. N.C. Dep't of Human Resources, 135 N.C. App. at 421–23, 520 S.E.2d at 602–03. *See also* Dalenko v. Wake County Dep't of Human Services, 157 N.C. App. 49, 55–56, 578 S.E.2d 599, 603 (2003).

58. *See* Vereen v. Holden, 121 N.C. App. 779, 468 S.E.2d 471 (1996); Fugual Springs v. Rowland, 234 N.C. 299, 79 S.E.2d 774 (1954).

59. 42 U.S.C. §§ 14501 through 14505. *See also* G.S. 1-539.10.

## Liability of Social Services Agencies and Employees under Federal Law

State and county social services agencies are subject to a number of federal laws, including but not limited to the due process provisions of the U.S. Constitution; the nondiscrimination requirements of Title VI of the Civil Rights Act of 1964; the prohibitions on employment discrimination in Title VII of the 1964 Civil Rights Act, the Age Discrimination in Employment Act of 1967, and the Rehabilitation Act of 1973; the compensation requirements of the Fair Labor Standards Act and the Equal Pay Act; and the requirements of the Americans with Disabilities Act of 1990 and the Family and Medical Leave Act. In some instances, these or other federal statutes authorize a person to sue a social services agency or employee for injunctive relief or monetary damages based on the agency's or employee's alleged violation of federal law.

### Liability Under 42 U.S.C. § 1983

Another federal statute, 42 U.S.C. § 1983, authorizes a person to sue and recover damages from a local government or local government employee if the government's or employee's official conduct violates the person's legal rights under the U.S. Constitution or a federal statute.[60]

Liability under Section 1983 is distinct from liability under North Carolina's tort law. Section 1983, therefore, may allow for a finding of liability in some cases in which there is none under state law and, in other cases, an official action may result in liability under both state law and Section 1983.

Although some of the Section 1983 lawsuits filed against state or county social services agencies involve alleged violations of a person's constitutional rights, most claim that a social services agency has violated a person's legal rights under a federal statute.[61]

---

60. The liability of local governments and local government employees under this statute ("Section 1983") is discussed in detail in chapters 6, 7, 8, and 10 of Brown-Graham, *A Practical Guide to Liability for North Carolina Cities and Counties,* and in Brown-Graham, "Civil Liability of the Local Government and Its Officials and Employees," 14–18.

61. *See* Maine v. Thiboutot, 448 U.S. 1 (1980). Section 1983, however, may not be used in cases in which the federal statute in question does not create a legal right that is enforceable by the plaintiff or if the statute provides an exclusive remedy for its own enforcement. Pennhurst State School and Hosp. v. Halderman, 451 U.S. 1 (1981); Middlesex County Sewerage Auth. v. National Sea Clammers Ass'n, 453 U.S. 1 (1981).

State and county social services agencies were sued frequently under Section 1983 during the 1960s, 1970s, and 1980s by persons who had applied for or were receiving public assistance or social services and alleged that the agencies had violated the plaintiffs' legal rights by failing to comply with the requirements of the federal Social Security Act or other federal social services statutes.[62] Recent decisions of the U.S. Supreme Court, however, have limited somewhat the ability of social services clients and others to bring Section 1983 lawsuits against state and county social services agencies for alleged violations of federal social services statutes.[63]

State and county social services agencies, officials, and employees may be sued for prospective injunctive relief under Section 1983. The state of North Carolina and state social services agencies, however, are not liable for monetary damages in lawsuits brought under Section 1983 unless the state has waived its sovereign immunity or Congress has abrogated the state's immunity from suit.[64] By contrast, county social services agencies (or, more precisely, the counties of which social services departments are a part) may be held liable for monetary damages in Section 1983 lawsuits.[65]

---

62. *See* King v. Smith, 392 U.S. 309 (1968); Shapiro v. Thompson, 394 U.S. 618 (1969); Rosado v. Wyman, 397 U.S. 397 (1970); Lewis v. Martin, 397 U.S. 552 (1970); Wyman v. James, 400 U.S. 309 (1971); Townsend v. Swank, 404 U.S. 282 (1971); Jefferson v. Hackney, 406 U.S. 525 (1972); Carleson v. Remillard, 406 U.S. 598 (1972); New York State Dep't of Social Servs. v. Dublino, 413 U.S. 405 (1973); U.S. Dep't of Agric. v. Moreno, 413 U.S. 528 (1973); Maine v. Thiboutot, 448 U.S. 1 (1980). Legal aid attorneys have filed a number of Section 1983 lawsuits against North Carolina social services agencies. *See* Carter v. Morrow, 526 F. Supp. 1225 (W.D.N.C. 1981) (denial of child support enforcement services); Alexander v. Hill, 549 F. Supp. 1355 (W.D.N.C. 1982) (failure to process Medicaid applications in a timely manner); Morris v. Morrow, 783 F.2d 454 (4th Cir. 1986) (Medicaid eligibility rules); Wilson v. Lyng, 662 F. Supp. 1391 (1987) (food stamp eligibility rules); Warren v. N.C. Dep't of Human Resources, 65 F.3d 385 (4th Cir. 1995) (food stamp eligibility rules).

63. *See* Deshaney v. Winnebago County Dep't of Social Servs., 489 U.S. 189 (1989); Suter v. Artist M., 503 U.S. 347 (1992) (child welfare services); Blessing v. Freestone, 520 U.S. 329 (1997) (child support enforcement services).

64. *See* Anita R. Brown-Graham, "When You Can't Sue the State: State Sovereign Immunity," *Popular Government* 65(4) (Summer 2000): 2–14.

65. *See* Monell v. New York City Dep't of Social Servs., 436 U.S. 658 (1978). Local governments are not liable for punitive damages in Section 1983 lawsuits. City of Newport v. Fact Concerts Inc., 453 U.S. 247 (1981).

The doctrine of governmental immunity does not protect a county from liability under Section 1983. Instead, a county may be held liable for monetary damages under Section 1983 if

1. the county or a county agency, acting through its public officials, officially adopts an ordinance, policy, rule, or decision that violates a person's federal constitutional or statutory rights, *or*
2. a person's federal constitutional or statutory rights are violated by the persistent and widespread practices or customs of the county's officials or employees that are so permanent and well-settled that they have the force and effect of law.[66]

The doctrine of *respondeat superior* does not apply in Section 1983 lawsuits.[67] A county social services employee's violation of a person's federal civil rights, therefore, will not necessarily make the county liable for monetary damages under Section 1983.[68]

State and county social services officials and employees may be held liable for monetary damages under Section 1983 when they are sued in their individual capacities. They are entitled, however, to a qualified immunity that protects them from personal liability unless their conduct "violates clearly established statutory or constitutional rights about which a reasonable person in similar circumstances would have known."[69]

State and county social services agencies and employees also may be liable for paying a plaintiff's attorneys fees in a Section 1983 lawsuit.[70]

---

66. Monell v. New York City Dep't of Social Servs., 436 U.S. at 690–92.

67. *See* Bryan County Board of County Comm'rs v. Brown, 520 U.S. 397 (1997).

68. The improper hiring, inadequate training, or inadequate supervision of county social services employees, however, may constitute a county policy or custom if it exhibits a "deliberate indifference" by county policy-makers or administrators to the federal constitutional or statutory rights of individuals. *See* Brown-Graham, *A Practical Guide to Liability for North Carolina Cities and Counties*, 6-17 through 6-19.

69. Brown-Graham, "Civil Liability of the Local Government and Its Officials and Employees," 18, citing Wood v. Strickland, 420 U.S. 308 (1975) and Anderson v. Creighton, 483 U.S. 635 (1987). Punitive damages may be awarded against a county social services employee if he or she is held personally liable under Section 1983 and the court finds that his or her conduct was reckless or deliberately indifferent to the plaintiff's legal rights. Smith v. Wade, 461 U.S. 30 (1983).

70. Brown-Graham, *A Practical Guide to Liability for North Carolina Cities and Counties*, 10-5 through 10-6.

## Protecting County Social Services Agencies, Officials, and Employees from Civil Liability

### Obtaining Liability Insurance for Counties and County Officials and Employees

State law authorizes "counties . . . to purchase insurance to protect themselves and any of their officers, agents, or employees from civil liability for damages."[71] The board of county commissioners "has absolute discretion in deciding which liabilities and which . . . [county officials and employees], if any, will be covered by this insurance" and in deciding whether it will cover claims under federal, as well as state, law and cover claims against officials and employees in their individual, as well as official, capacities.[72]

### Defending Lawsuits against County Officials and Employees

Counties are "authorized, but not required, to provide for the defense of any civil or criminal action brought against current or former . . . [county social services officials or employees] in state or federal court on account of alleged acts or omissions committed in the scope and course of their employment" or office.[73] The county may defend the official or employee through the county attorney, the attorney who represents the county social services department, an attorney retained by the county, or, if the county has purchased liability insurance that requires the insurer to defend lawsuits brought against county officials or employees, an attorney retained by the county's liability insurance company.

### Paying Judgments against County Officials and Employees

State law authorizes, but does not require, counties to pay all or part of any settlement or judgment entered in a lawsuit that is brought against a county official or employee in the official's or employee's individual capacity for an act committed within the scope of the official's office or employee's employment.[74]

---

71. Brown-Graham, "Civil Liability of the Local Government and Its Officials and Employees," 18. *See* G.S. 160A-485. As discussed above, a county's purchase of liability insurance constitutes a waiver of its governmental immunity.

72. Brown-Graham, "Civil Liability of the Local Government and Its Officials and Employees," 18.

73. *Id.* at 19. *See* G.S. 153A-97.

74. G.S. 160A-167.

> No statutory limit is placed on the amount of money
> that a local government may appropriate to pay a
> settlement or judgment [against a local government
> employee]. However, funds may not be appropriated to
> pay . . . [the] settlement or judgment if the . . . [official
> or employee] acted or failed to act because of fraud,
> corruption, or malice.[75]

In addition, a county may not pay a settlement or judgment against a county official or employee unless, before the settlement is reached or the judgment is entered, the county has adopted a set of uniform standards under which settlements or judgments against county officials and employees will be paid and the official or employee gives the county notice of the claim.[76]

---

75. Brown-Graham, "Civil Liability of the Local Government and Its Officials and Employees," 19. *See* G.S. 160A-167.
   76. G.S. 160A-167.